P9-EKJ-237

THE RUHLE HANDBOOK

ROADS

AND

TRAILS

OF WATERTON-GLACIER
INTERNATIONAL PEACE PARK

About the Editor

Rebecca (Becky) Williams is a Biology graduate of Iowa State University and has been a Glacier National Park Ranger-Naturalist since 1967. She and husband Larry have hiked nearly every trail described in this guide. In past years she has volunteered some fall and winter time to the park's bald eagle research project. Becky and Larry reside in Bozeman, Montana.

Copyright © 1986 by Glacier Natural History Association

All rights reserved, including the right to reproduce this book or any part thereof, in any form, except for inclusion of brief quotations in a review.

Library of Congress Catalog Card Number: 85-80516

ISBN 0-916792-03-X

Edited by Rebecca (Becky) Williams

Front cover photo, Chief Mt. by B. Riley McClelland.
Back cover photo, Beargrass along Grinnell Glacier Trail with the Garden Wall and Glaciers in the background. Photo by Marilyn Casteel.

Publishing Consultant:
Falcon Press Publishing Co., Inc.
Helena and Billings, Montana

FALCON PRESS PUBLISHING CO. INC.

Preface

In 1929, Howard H. Hays, President of the Glacier Park Transport Co., requested the author to compile annually a "Driver's Manual" with information on the park. The National Park Service found the manual useful in training their personnel and park visitors sought access to the information as well. In 1946, Newton B. Drury, then Director of the National Park Service, suggested publication of the material for general use. The result was "The Guide to Glacier National Park," long out-of-date. This subsequent attempt to increase enjoyment of Waterton-Glacier through better understanding is a product of the field for use in the field. At the invitation of Superintendent Herbert Knight, I gave talks and conducted guided trips afield in Waterton in 1929 and 1930, possibly the first naturalist services given in a Canadian National Park. In 1968-71, the author traversed every major and secondary trail in the two parks to collect and re-check data for current, first-hand information.

This book is the result of encouragement and cooperation given by the National Park Service and the staffs of Waterton and Glacier National Parks. The parks granted use of scientific, library, and photographic facilities. They gave logistic support and supplied data on distances, regulations and campsites, incorporated here without change; The Smithsonian Institution of Washington, D.C. permitted the author free access to its busy personnel, vast study collections and library.

In the two parks and elsewhere, it has been my great fortune to spend days, even years in the field with recognized authorities: Bailey Willis, Francois E. Matthes, W.C. Alden, David White, the Fentons, and others in geology, E.P. Meinecke in forest pathology and environment, Julian Huxley in biology, Ira N. Gabrielson and Joseph Grinnell in zoology, Roger Tory Peterson in ornithology, Ralph W. Chaney in paleobotany, and Clark Wissler in anthropology. These experts have been consulted for accuracy, while giving valuable assistance and stimulating company. Time on the trails was shared with Mel Ruder, editor of the singular "Hungry Horse News," Columbia Falls, Montana, known as the family newspaper and chronicle of the park region. His photographs in this book reveal why Mel was named a Pulitzer Prize winner in his particular class.

I am particularly grateful to Fred M. Packard, my congenial co-partner international specialist in the National Park Service. Fred and Mrs. Jean Packard repeatedly reviewed and gave valuable advice in refining the manuscript. My hard-working publisher has supplemented my task with his aggressive interest and helpful criticism. He, too, loves the region with a passion. Assistance with preceding guides pervades this work, but is not acknowledged anew. However great my desire, it is impossible in limited space to acknowledge individually the abundant help given me in this task. To the collective many, my sincere thanks.

George C. Ruhle, January 1976

NOTE: In July, 1983, on the recommendation of Glacier Park Chief Naturalist Clyde Lockwood, Dr. Ruhle authorized long-term seasonal naturalist Becky Williams to revise and update the 1976 handbook for publication in 1986.

Canoeing on Bowman Lake. B. Riley McCelland photo.

Mountain Goat. John Tyers photo.

Foreword To The 1986 Edition

By Russell E. Dickenson

Only a few serving in the National Park Service today have longer periods of active service than myself, but "Doc" Ruhle is one. It is a rare privilege to know an individual willing to try the untried. George Ruhle helped "write the book" on nature education and naturalist activities in several western national parks starting over 50 years ago. An accomplished, energetic mountaineer and hiker, Doc combined these activities with a love of the land, and a desire to share his knowledge and enthusiasm with generations of park visitors. Such is the essence of the National Park Service stewardship. In today's world-class National Park System, we provide visitor services, maintenance and protection in 335 outstanding natural, historical and recreational areas. This 79 million acre legacy for the future, authorized by the Congress of the United States as meeting the highest standards of national significance, will always depend on solid, continuing public understanding for its support.

I am convinced that the interpretation of these park values—wildlife, geology, plants, history, mountains, canyons, lakes and streams—provides the real basis for the widespread public support of national parks.

Dr. George Ruhle has spent a lifetime nationally and internationally aiding this effort, and I commend this new version of the handbook to anyone wanting to gain better understanding of Glacier National Park.

Editor's Note

For the past two decades my husband Larry and I have faithfully packed along one edition or another of Dr. George Ruhle's *Guide to Roads and Trails* on all our outings in Waterton-Glacier Park. Several years ago when Dr. Ruhle declined to attempt yet another revision himself, it was with both excitement and trepidation that I accepted the challenging assignment. I have tried not to alter Dr. Ruhle's inimitable style nor his overall outline, but rather have concentrated on updating the general road, trail and interpretive information. Separate sections of the previous editions on geology and ecology have been completely deleted; those topics are covered extensively in other, more specialized publications (see Additional Reading).

I would like to thank Clyde Lockwood, Glacier Park's Chief Park Interpreter and Secretary of the Glacier Natural History Association, for his advice on structuring the 1986 edition. Duane Barrus, Chief Park Interpreter of Waterton Lakes National Park, very graciously provided contemporary material on Waterton's roads and trails. Glacier Park Trails Supervisor Jack Potter was extremely helpful in pinpointing details of Glacier's extensive trails system to make this revision more accurate and current.

Several fine photos by Mel Ruder are retained from the 1972 edition. Glacier Park and Glacier Natural History Association files provided other pictures, including those by T.J. Hileman and Danny On. Finally, I want to express my grateful and enthusiastic appreciation to the following additional photographers, all dedicated park devotees, for their contributions, photos displaying some of the splendor of Waterton-Glacier: Kathy Ahlenslager, Marilyn Casteel, Clyde Lockwood, Ursula Mattson of the Glacier Institute, B. Riley McClelland, John Tyers and Larry D. Williams.

Becky Williams, March 1986

Hikers on Logan Pass Boardwalk. Ursula Mattson - Glacier Institute photo.

Contents

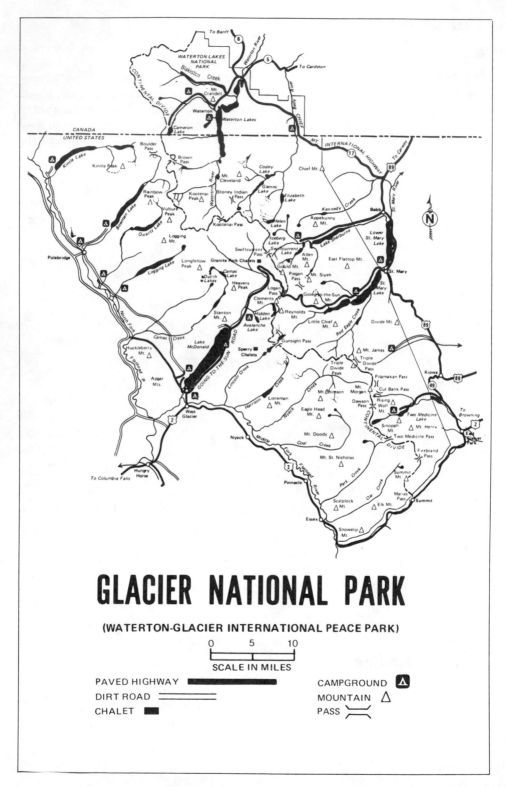

GLACIER NATIONAL PARK

(WATERTON-GLACIER INTERNATIONAL PEACE PARK)

0   5   10

SCALE IN MILES

PAVED HIGHWAY

DIRT ROAD

CHALET

CAMPGROUND

MOUNTAIN

PASS

Introduction

John Muir described the Waterton-Glacier region as "the best care-killing scenery on the continent." He earnestly counseled, "Wander here a whole summer, if you can...big days will go by uncounted...The time will not be taken from the sum of your life." Your experience in this blessed land may well become the richest in your treasure-house of memory as you move from the giddy everyday world into the pristine purity of nature.

Some of the most sparkling wilderness of the Rocky Mountains is held within these 2000 square miles. It is a land of precipitous peaks, pointed spires, sharp knife-edges and deep valleys whose lowland is wrapped in verdant forests. Several score glaciers glisten in the shadow of mighty cliffs. From the lofty summits, streams glide to the distant Pacific, Hudson Bay and the Gulf of Mexico.

Here plants meet from far-separated provenience: the Pacific Coast, the Arctic slopes, the broad Midcontinent, the dry Southwest. Their ancestors lived in warm, humid zones, frozen tundra, expansive grasslands, snug valleys, high mountains, hot deserts and cold bogs. Today the abundance of plant life provides protection, homes and food for abundant, varied birds and mammals.

Waterton-Glacier has prime significance in geology. Here oldest sedimentary rocks retain in clarity characteristics impressed in the ancient time of deposition. Here is the archetype of thrust faults with fault line sharp and distinct, although separating strata whose ages differ by almost a billion years. Here, as fossils, are the earliest distinguishable forms of life: one-celled organisms which had acquired the habit of association in distinctive, readily apparent colonies. Here landscape features are revealed as if in a diagram.

The region marks the confluence of tribes of plains, plateau, mountain, forest and subarctic Indians. It is a part of the Old Frontier with history of Indian, trapper, trader, explorer, pioneer, lumberjack and railroad builder. Its color of the Old West is tinted with hues of present day. Now it beckons all young in spirit who seek high adventure and unspoiled nature.

Waterton-Glacier International Peace Park was conceived in 1932 to commemorate the goodwill between Canada and the United States. In the late 1970's Waterton and Glacier were recognized as part of the international network of Biosphere Reserves. A dedicatory plaque states, "This network of protected samples of the world's major ecosystem types is devoted to conservation of nature and scientific research in the service of man. It provides a standard against which can be measured the effects of man's impact on his environment." Glacier has also been nominated as a World Heritage Site.

Looking down McDonald Valley from Highline Trail. Marilyn Casteel photo.

ROADS

IN WATERTON-GLACIER
INTERNATIONAL PEACE PARK

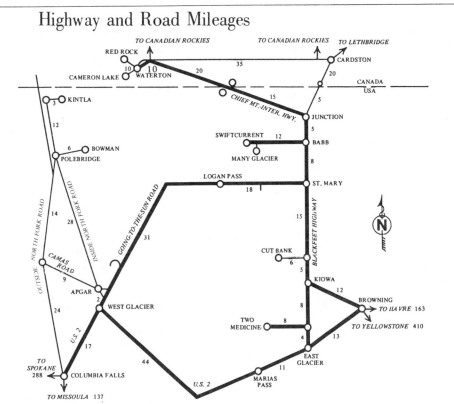

Highway and Road Mileages

Highway and Road Mileages Running descriptions on the following pages of Going-to-the-Sun Road, U.S. Highway 2, Blackfeet Highway and Chief Mountain International Highway are offered in one direction, with mileages for forward movement shown for each point of interest on the left side of each feature name. Mileages shown on the right are for the same trip made in reverse direction. Other highways, used less frequently, or (because they are not through routes) used initially in a single direction, are logged only one way, i.e. forward. Odometers vary from car to car and under varying conditions of tire inflation, so that indicated mileages may not agree with individual motorists' readings. Initial letters adjacent to mileages: L for left, R for right, A for ahead, B for views to the rear of the direction of travel. Both elevations above sea level and trail numbers are shown in parentheses, but there should be no ambiguity. Sections of principal roads and highways are shown on the fold-out map.

Going-to-the-Sun Road

West Glacier to St. Mary, Montana, 50.8 miles.

Going-to-the Sun Road traces the shores of glacier-carved lakes, winds through solemn forests carpeted with ferns, passes beneath trickling waterfalls, half-tunnels frowning cliffs and climbs gently but steadily above timberline to meadows on Logan Pass. It clings to the Garden Wall out of which it is hewn, with a protective guardrail along it for miles. When opened for traffic each June, it runs through canyons of snow a dozen feet deep and cascades of sparkling crystals shower its sides. The name for this road was suggested by the author to the Secretary of the Interior in 1931 to replace the earlier "Logan Pass Road." The name seems poetic and appropriate: legendary Going-to-the-Sun Mt. thrusts its magnificent uplift into the blue above the road modestly skirting its base. Sections of this route are included in the fold-out map.

MILES FROM WEST GLACIER		MILES FROM ST. MARY
0.0	**U.S.Highway 2**	**50.8**

The southwest terminus of the road is at the park boundary on the Middle Fork Flathead River opposite West Glacier (3215), Montana, and the official mailing address of Glacier National Park, zip 59936. West Glacier is on a Chicago-Seattle main line of Burlington Northern Railroad and on U.S. Highway 2. The rustic railroad station, however, retains the historic name of the village, Belton. Visitors arriving by rail here or at East Glacier Park, 55 miles east, begin their park experience in Glacier Park Incorporated buses painted with the vermilion of mountain ash berries in autumn. Motorists arrive via U.S. Highway 2 which skirts the southern boundary of the park.

The pleasant village, set among cottonwoods and native conifers, has a post office, motels, cottages, cafes, snack bars, tap room, service stations, art and curio shops, laundromat and an inviting 18-hole golf course on a river terrace. Local information may be obtained at West Glacier Mercantile Company near the river bridge or at Glacier Highland Services opposite the railroad depot on U.S. 2. Reservations for Sperry and Granite Park Chalets are made at Belton Chalets, also opposite the depot.

0.2	**Park Boundary**	**50.7**

The Middle Fork Flathead River, fringed by great cottonwoods throughout most of its course, rises in the Flathead Range south of the park and on the Continental Divide some 30 miles southeast of Marias Pass. It joins the North and South Forks of the river a dozen miles below West Glacier to form the Flathead River which then flows through Flathead Lake and empties into the Clark Fork Columbia River near Dixon, Montana. The north bank of the Middle Fork forms the south boundary of the park for 40 miles above its confluence with the North Fork. The North Fork is the west boundary of the park as far as the Canadian line.

0.5R	**Park Headquarters**	**L 50.3**

Entrance to the administrative center of Glacier National Park. In a picturesque setting at the base of BELTON HILLS (6339), the spread of offices, residences of park employees, warehouses and workshops is neatly screened from view.

0.6L	Apgar Fire Lookout	R 50.2

The lookout (5236) is visible on the southeast crest of APGAR MTS. (6613 and 6651), a long ridge trending northwest and terminating in Huckleberry Mt.

0.8	West Entrance	49.9

Visitors must stop to purchase or display an entry permit. The ranger in forest green uniform greets you and distributes park maps with information on rules, regulations and warnings on fire, water and bear safety. You may be reminded that pets must be confined or kept on leash and not allowed on trails. The ranger will also direct you to the Information Center at Apgar (1.8 miles ahead on a side loop road) to register for any special entry permits and for details on weather, campgrounds, accommodations and hiking trails.

1.1 L	Service Lane	R 49.6

Service lane to park and concessioner corrals, maintenance facilities and site of the old North Fork Ranger Station. This is the start of the route to Apgar Fire Lookout.

For access to the lookout, turn left on this lane. At the first junction, 0.4 mile, turn right, then left again almost immediately, down an unimproved lane to Quarter Circle Bridge over Lower McDonald Creek, 1.0 mile. Beyond this point the road is narrow, not maintained, and subject to occasional washouts; you may choose to leave your vehicle at the parking area near the approach to the bridge.

For the next mile the road curves with the bank of the Middle Fork to a faint service lane (signed) branching off to the right. (The main lane continues another 3 miles to the unmanned North Fork Ranger Station, near the confluence of the Middle Fork and the North Fork.) In 0.5 mile this side lane becomes trail 42 and climbs 1850 feet in 2.8 miles by two long switchbacks to the lookout on the crest. The lookout is unmanned, serving mainly as a repeater station for the intrapark radio network.

Saddlehorses may be rented at the concessioner corral, on the right beyond the first junction of the service lane off Going-to-the-Sun Road. Rides are conducted daily from approximately mid-June through Labor Day.

For two miles Going-to-the-Sun Road crosses a flat on which a luxuriant red cedar-hemlock forest flourished when the park was established. Pioneers voiced admiration for its somber beauty while, at the same time, extracting much valuable timber from it. In August, 1929 the relict stand, still magnificent, was destroyed by fire started through carelessness on private land near Halfmoon, two miles west of Columbia Falls. Only the enclave at park headquarters was saved by heroic effort. The present cover, crowded yet vigorous, is dominated by lodgepole pine and larch whose monotony of conifer growth is relieved by the shimmery green of cottonwoods and aspens also acting as pioneer species. Old larches top everything; they survived the holocaust because of thick bark, especially that near the base of the trees.

The red cedar-hemlock forests of lower McDonald Valley represent the northeasternmost extension of a Pacific Coast climatic peninsula. Plant species thrive here whose main distribution centers are on the west coast, but whose range is narrowly restricted in northwestern Montana and Idaho. Most tree species of Waterton-Glacier are growing in this community. This is the richest floral zone in the region.

The flat between Belton Hills and Apgar Mts. is covered by a thin veneer of silty loam, underlain by sand and gravel, composing, in part at least, the natural dam which impounds Lake McDonald. A great fault trending southeast from upper McGee Creek crosses the valley at the foot of the lake and extends along the northeast slope of South Fork Flathead Valley beyond Spotted Bear at the head of Hungry Horse Reservoir. This fault separates the older strata of Belton Hills from the younger rocks of Apgar Mts.

2.0	Road T-Junction	48.8

Going-to-the-Sun Road turns right, facing the Belton Hills. The turn to the left, however, offers an attractive alternative. This road, after a right turn at 0.3 mile, leads to Apgar and a superb view of Lake McDonald (3154). It goes through a forest past Apgar Campground, largest in the park, to rejoin Going-to-the-Sun Road within 1.5 miles. From Apgar junction, the left leg continues ahead across Lower McDonald Creek to private homes along the lakeshore, to Fish Creek Campground, 2.5 miles, and the narrow, unimproved Inside North Fork Road up Glacier's west side, and to Camas Creek Park Entrance, 10.0 miles.

Apgar settlement, predating the park, is attractive and convenient for park visitors. It has comfortable motels, restaurant, general store and arts and crafts shops. The National Park Service provides an information center with exhibits, boat ramp, picnic area and a large amphitheater for church and naturalist services. The village was named for Milo B. Apgar, its first settler, who built cabins and provided overnight accommodations for visitors in the 1890's. The surrounding area was quickly patented into private ownership. Everything was rustic, primitive; a mighty forest wrapped all in its shade. But the great fire of 1929 wrought a big change in patterns of use and appearance of the land. Local charm vanished along with friendly woodland shelter. Later, the National Park Service purchased many of the private inholdings to provide campgrounds and other facilities and better lake access for the public.

2.8 L	Junction	R 47.9

The loop from Apgar joins Going-to-the-Sun Road. Apgar Campground, picnic area and sylvan amphitheater are located in the grove a short distance to the left.

LAKE McDONALD, the largest in the park, is about 10 miles long, one to one and a half miles wide, and 472 feet deep. Its basin seems to have been gouged into relatively soft rocks. The lake is deepest near its head; the bottom, apparently as uniform as the sides, drops sharply to a depth of 400 feet, which is maintained for three-quarters of the length of the lake. McDonald Valley was scoured by glacial activity which created a trough of typical U-shaped cross section with smooth contours on the sides.

McDonald, unlike St. Mary Lake, does not extend into the mountains at its head. STANTON MT. (7750), with MT. VAUGHT (8850) behind it, is on the left. The GARDEN WALL closes the upper end of the valley. Both HOWE RIDGE on the northwest and SNYDER RIDGE on the southeast have relatively gentle slopes and smooth crests although they rise 2000 feet above lake level. Howe Ridge and Apgar Mts. across the lake shine resplendently at twilight, tinted with the flare of sunset, especially in autumn when larches, cottonwoods and birches add their golden hues.

The earliest name, Lac de Peches, for Lake McDonald appeared on remarkably good maps prepared for the Belgian explorer, Father de Smet, in 1846; the first English maps in the 70's labeled it Terry's Lake.

Huckleberry Mt. (6593), the northwest peak of Apgar Mts., has a fire lookout on its summit which is acccessible by trail 35 from Camas Road. Another lookout on the southwest shoulder of Mt. Brown is clearly visible ahead on road tangents below Lake McDonald Lodge. This lookout is described in the chapter on trails.

The road runs along the southeast shore of Lake McDonald in a dense forest of red cedar, hemlock, larch and white pine, highlighted here and there by the gleaming white bark of paper birches and the shimmery green of cottonwoods swaying with the breezes. Showy flowers are few, although twinflower (*Linnaea borealis*) trails in abundance along the forest floor. A misty haze of loose panicles of lacy foamflower hangs over a billowy cushion of oak ferns, and solitary chalices of queencup are scattered at random. For the poetic soul seeking quiet and solitude, soft banks of moss drape duff, rocks and prostrate logs; beard lichens sway in rhythm with branches, bending in gentle winds; and wolf lichen adorns lifeless boles and limbs with chartreuse-green artistry.

6.3 A	Mt. Wilbur	B 44.7

The most distant mountain peak visible up the valley is MT. WILBUR (9321) which peers over the left end of the Garden Wall. It is a prominent feature at Many Glacier. Mountains on the east side of the valley seen from here are, L to R, CANNON (8952), BROWN (8565), EDWARDS (9072) and LINCOLN PEAK (7440). Observation stations or pullouts are located along park roads at favorable sites.

9.8 R	Lincoln Lake Trail	L 41.2

Trail 47 climbs in forest for 1.7 miles to Snyder Ridge Trail (45) and the broad summit of the ridge (4925) a mile beyond. Thence it drops 700 feet by short switchbacks to Lincoln Creek Trail (68), 4.4 miles from Sun Road. The Middle Fork of the Flathead is six miles downstream. LINCOLN LAKE (4598) is 3.6 miles upstream, a total of 8.0 miles from Going-to-the-Sun Road. This beautiful lakelet is exquisitely cupped in an elongate cirque with sheer cliffs a half-mile high on three of its sides. Lake Ellen Wilson is in the cirque above. BEAVER CHIEF FALLS, 1334 feet high, has perhaps the greatest sheer drop in the park as it tumbles down an awesome overhang above the inlet. The lake and falls are usually admired from Gunsight Pass Trail (52), above on the left, after crossing Lincoln Pass from Sperry Chalets. This viewpoint is 7.5 miles from Lake McDonald Lodge.

10.2 L   Sprague Creek Campground   R 40.5

Campsites for automobiles but not trailers. Each campsite has a rustic table and fireplace. Sanitary facilities are nearby. Naturalist programs are presented in the auditorium of Lake McDonald Lodge, a mile above.

11.1   Snyder Creek   39.8

The parking strip for LAKE McDONALD LODGE is 200 yards beyond. Here also is the head of a major trail system: 52 to Sperry Chalets, Lake Ellen Wilson, Sun Point and connecting with 51 to Sperry Glacier; 50 to Snyder Lake; 49 to Mt. Brown; 56 to Avalanche Campground and Lake Trail and connecting with 259 and 59 as the circuit to Sacred Dancing Cascade and 9 to Trout and Arrow Lakes. See chapter on trails.

Lake McDonald Lodge is at the far end of the strip. Rustic, alpine style structure; meals, lodging, gift and curio shop, cocktail lounge, auditorium, ranger naturalist programs, launch cruises, boat rentals and horseback trips. To its right is a coffee shop, soda fountain and general store with a rural branch post office (Lake McDonald R Br, West Glacier, Montana 59921). The store carries groceries, outdoor clothing and equipment, fishing tackle, souvenirs and miscellaneous articles. Horse corrals are located a short distance across Going-to-the-Sun Road from the store. The gas station is the last for the next 30 miles.

Since its establishment, Glacier National Park has contained land in continuous private ownership, 134 private parties presently owning tracts within it. This property is concentrated at the head and foot of Lake McDonald and along the two forks of the Flathead River. Landowners in the park enjoy the same rights and merit the same consideration and respect as property owners in other places. Trespass should be avoided. Private land can be brought into federal ownership by exchange, gift or purchase, and much has been acquired.

12.5 R   North Lake McDonald Road   L 38.3.

Route to the bridge over UPPER McDONALD CREEK and trails up the west bank of the creek to McDonald Falls, 0.4 mile, and to LAKE McDONALD RANGER STATION on the lakeshore, 0.8 mile. The road continues as a dirt lane 1.5 miles to the foot of trail 9 to Trout and Arrow Lakes; to private homes and the head of trail 43, 2.7 miles, which goes down the northwest lakeshore past a small backcountry campground to Fish Creek Campground, 7.2 miles farther, and to Apgar, 8.6 miles from the end of North Lake McDonald Road. The horse trail crossing Going-to-the-Sun Road to trails 59 and 9 is 0.1 mile south of this point.

12.8 L   McDonald Falls   R 38.0

Upper McDonald Creek, which has cut a narrow canyon in grayish-green Prichard Formation, foams as it plunges over a rocky ledge. For the next nine miles the road keeps close company with the sparkling stream.

Beautiful as it is, over the years this stretch of Upper McDonald Creek has been the site of numerous drownings which result when unwary visitors venture too close to the rushing torrent and lose their footing on the algal-slickened rocks. Along this and other fast-flowing streams, especially during periods of high runoff, please be cautious, and watch your children.

13.0   Wooded Trail   37.8

Horse Trail 57 from Lake McDonald Lodge dips sharply down the bank on the right, passes under the road and crosses the creek on a rustic bridge as an alternative part of the Sacred Dancing Cascade circuit. Just 0.2 mile farther, foot trail 259 drops to the road from Avalanche Trail (56) and Johns Lake.

13.3	**Sacred Dancing Cascade**	37.6

The ancient name for Lake McDonald was Sacred Dancing Lake, given by the Kutenais who came to its shores in summertime to perform their ceremonial rites. For years the author strove without success to have the traditional name restored to lake and stream. Former Chief Park Naturalist Francis Elmore finally was able to perpetuate it for this bit of singing water. STANTON MT. is across the valley.

13.9	**Moose Habitat**	37.0

Beaver have dammed the watercourses; their structures are visible from the road. The resultant ponds and backwater have formed attractive habitat for wildlife, including moose (see roadside sign at mile 14.0) which come here at times to provide a thrill for the visitor. The road runs close to the base of the perpendicular walls of Mt. Brown. Across the creek several beautiful waterfalls plunge over ledges in deep forest on Mt. Vaught.

14.5 R	**Pullout**	L 36.4

A short path leads to a group of big red cedars.

14.7	**Upper McDonald Creek Viewing Platform**	36.2

16.6 R	**Avalanche Campground**	L 34.1

The spacious campground is located on a shady flat under giant red cedar and cottonwood trees. Campfire programs and religious services are held in the sylvan amphitheater. Extensive picnic grounds are provided on McDonald Creek. AVALANCHE CREEK, which flows along the upper edge of the camp and picnic grounds, has cut a deep gorge in bright red Grinnell argillite, 0.3 mile above the bridge. This gem of a canyon, accessible through the campground, has been formed by the fusion of potholes, scoured by pebbles swirled round and round by rushing water, a process common in the region. It is well worth the few moments needed to visit this feature.

Trail 60 continues 2.0 miles up the creek to Avalanche Lake, a popular destination. The self-guiding TRAIL OF THE CEDARS (256), 0.3 mile long, is across the creek from the campground and can be entered from either end of the campground, mile 16.7, or from a bridge below the gorge; a boardwalk provides handicapped access. Cathedral quiet and loftiness go with those who take the Trail of the Cedars.

From Lake McDonald to Avalanche Creek the bedrock along the route has been greenish Appekunny argillite; for the next four miles reddish Grinnell argillite appears, in places interfingered by gray-green members of Appekunny lithology and adorned by the golden tapestry of crustose lichens or padded with deep green mosses and liverworts. Throughout its course McDonald Creek has hollowed out many potholes in its bed, like those seen in cross section in Avalanche Gorge.

17.4 A	**Red Rock Point**	B 33.4

At times, mountain goats wander on the low ledges above the road, especially on cool days early and late in the season. Early morning or late afternoon and evening are the most likely hours to see them. Mountain goats and bighorn sheep also live along the Garden Wall, and both appear at times at Logan Pass.

The floor of McDonald Valley is good habitat for wildlife. Whitetail and mule deer are common. Elk are sometimes seen above Avalanche Campground or heard bugling during the fall rut. Moose love the bottomlands. Especially early in the season, black and grizzly bears may be spotted feeding on new, succulent vegetation near the roadways or on winter-killed carcasses of elk, deer and goats. Marmots and ground squirrels are numerous at higher elevation. At night porcupines may be seen shuffling along the pavement, and the bright eyes of pack rats reflect the gleam of headlights as they scamper in front of one's car.

19.5 A   Mt. Gould   B 31.3

Mt. Gould (9553), the GARDEN WALL and the harsh, straight line of the road scratched across its length. Gould looms 6000 feet above the road at this point.

The awesome cliffs of Mt. Cannon rise on the right. Its treeless swaths, overgrown by pliant alders, are swept by repeated avalanches in winter and spring. The term "avalanche chutes" is used for these paths made by the unstable snow masses which collect in pockets and are set into motion by overbalance, tremors or acute noise. Avalanches have been clocked as high as 157 miles per hour, with the air blast snapping trees far ahead of the course of crashing snow.

21.2   Logan Creek   29.6

Water flows here from Oberlin Falls and Logan Pass. The creek and pass were named after Major William Logan, in 1910 Glacier's first superintendent. A patrol cabin is upstream on the left bank. Others are scattered around the park for use by park rangers on winter patrol.

Along Logan Creek and other fast-flowing streams you may be lucky to spot the handsome but shy harlequin duck. The male is strikingly marked with white, chestnut and slate blue-gray; females and young are dark brown, with white head spots. These ducks rest on gravel bars or bob like corks on the creek's turbulence, diving for food. By July the males have left Glacier for the Pacific coast, but females and young may linger until fall.

22.0   Ascent To Logan Pass   28.0

The road starts a relentless 10-mile 6% grade to Logan Pass. On ascending, a look back yields an exciting view of MT. CANNON and BIRD WOMAN FALLS. The immediate mile was burned in the lightning-caused forest fire of 1967.

22.8 L   Packers Roost Spur   R 28.0

A lane, 0.7 mile long, drops to Packers Roost on the floor of the valley. From this point Flattop Mt. Trail (63) climbs to FIFTY MOUNTAIN and connects with trails to Granite Park, Many Glacier and Waterton Lake.

23.7 R   Algal Colony   L 27.1

The biostrome or algal reef which is exposed here was recently buried beneath detritus washed down in a storm. The cover of debris was removed by park crews and parking space provided on the outer side of the road below the feature.

Rosettes, six or more inches in diameter, weave a fancy pattern in the rock wall. They are the fossilized remains of one-celled algae, identified as *Conophyton* which thrived when the region was beneath a sea and which built great reefs extending over vast areas. Reef limestone is largely built up in coherent form from the start without any process of cementation. Because it is very hard, it erodes slowly and stands out as cliffs and ledges, persistent and discernible even at a distance. It forms the cover of rocky flats such as those at Logan Pass. Imprints showing rosettes are caused by weathering and are plenteous, but a clear cross section like this exhibit is not found elsewhere along the road. The Helena (Siyeh) Formation bearing the rosettes was laid down in Proterozoic (Dawn of Life) time. One-celled organisms began to associate in colonies but without differentiation of functions which is the next step in evolution. Aside from such primitive colonies as these, which appear today as traceries, evidence of other life in Proterozoic rocks is sparse. A relative of these primordial plants persists as a living species today.

24.0   Road Tunnel   26.8

Two windows frame stunning views of HEAVENS PEAK (8987). Parking space is provided outside below the tunnel but stopping inside is dangerous and not permitted.

| 24.7 | The Loop | 26.1 |

This sharp turn in the road commands imposing LIVINGSTON RANGE, including the summit of LONGFELLOW PEAK (8904). The Garden Wall, up which the road ascends, is a part of the LEWIS RANGE, the eastern of the two parallel ranges within Glacier National Park. The Loop reverses the direction of the road from northwest to southeast. Parking spaces above and below the turn are connected by a stone staircase. A roadside plaque discusses recent fires. A sign on the curve (L) indicates a 0.6-mile connection with trail 62 to Granite Park Chalets, a hike of 4.0 miles.

The mantle of glacial material above The Loop was scraped away during road construction, exposing greenish argillite ledges with edges rounded and faces smoothed, striated and polished by glacial action. Outcrops from Logan Creek to Logan Pass belong to the Helena (Siyeh) Formation.

In 1936 a lightning fire started below Heavens Peak, swept across McDonald Valley past The Loop, jumped over Swiftcurrent Pass and could not be brought under control until it reached Swiftcurrent Lake. In all, 7,642 acres were burned. Fire as a natural ecological force continues periodically to exert its presence in Glacier.

| 25.3 | Crystal Point | 25.5 |

Named for the large, square, shiny, brass-yellow crystals of pyrite, or fool's gold (iron sulfide) which is visible in the pinkish quartz vein inclined toward the road, here half-tunneled out of the cliff. During the initial stages of construction the workers were lowered over the face in belays secured to trees above. For years afterwards bits of telltale rope remained dangling as mute reminders of early hazards.

| 26.1 L | Algal Colony | R 24.7 |

An extraordinary cross section of a fossil colony, related to the rosettes at mile 23.7 yet strikingly different, is etched on the vertical rock face.

Several kinds of algae thrived in Algonkian seas. They differed in shape, mode of growth and occurrence, depending on depth, temperature, clarity of water and similar factors. Some formed extensive reefs while others grew in isolated clusters on a sea bottom with the result that clay, sand or lime might have been incorporated. Each colony was composed of billions of plants. The fossils are thin shells of lime which have been deposited in the jelly-like masses of the cells. The smaller aggregates in this specimen are layered like an onion and grew to several inches in diameter; they then massed into a great ball several feet in diameter, a development readily seen on examination. As the main mass grew larger, soft underlying beds, also fossil-making, were depressed to form a huge concavity. When growth stopped subsequent beds were arched over the top, as is readily apparent in this specimen and in photographs of it. Elsewhere in the region comparable structures have been quarried from the bedrock by erosive forces and appear in the landscape as huge, isolated spherical boulders.

| 26.9 R | Road Camp | L 24.8 |

Site of former Garden Wall Camp Nine. A water faucet is located near the end of the guard-rail, a boon to motorists troubled with vapor lock. Views of the Livingston Range to the west become increasingly better as the road ascends to Logan Pass. From Heavens Peak north principal mountains are: LONGFELLOW PEAK (8904) peering over the shoulder of Heavens Peak; ANACONDA (8279); GEDUHN (8375); TRAPPER (7702); VULTURE (9638) with Vulture Glacier and Two Ocean Glacier glistening on its flanks; yellow, barren, pyramidal RAINBOW PEAK (9891) and Rainbow Glacier; and MT. CARTER (9843).

| 28.3 R | Roadside Exhibit | L 22.5 |

This exhibit tells the story of McDonald Valley. There is a space for stopping for a good view of the U-shaped trough of the valley and the lower road, 2500 feet below. Chiseled out of the sheer cliff ahead, the Highline Trail (121) between Logan Pass and Granite Park appears as a faint buff streak one-third of the distance up HAYSTACK BUTTE (7486). This knobby protuberance on the Garden Wall, quite imposing here, is dwarfed by the towering mass of Mt. Gould when viewed from the valley floor. The dark band halfway up the slope is a diorite sill of igneous rock. It appears on the opposite site of the Garden Wall as the prominent band above Grinnell Glacier.

| 29.5 L | Weeping Wall | R 21.3 |

Named for the rills which shower over the face of the long, dark cliff in early season.

| 29.7 | Natural Amphitheater | 21.0 |

The road curves around the amphitheater between Haystack Butte and BISHOPS CAP (9127). So much snow accumulates in the col every winter that it is a major task to clear the roadway by June 15. When snow plows have finished their job, they leave a gorge deeper in early season than the height of a car, so travelers from warmer climes may perhaps get the first thrill of something they have seen previously only at a distance and known only from a photograph or an imperfect description in words. Any child can here enjoy the fun of snow well through summer. A marmot colony occupies the rocky slide nearby. Bighorns graze the grassy pastures above.

The dark greenish diorite sill mentioned at mile 28.3 is visible above the road on the cliff ahead. This basaltic rock, while still molten, was intruded between layers of Helena (Siyeh) limestone. To the right it frays out into fingers. The main mass of the sill passes under Logan Pass and can be traced with the eye along the face of Mt. Oberlin, dipping towards Logan Creek. Snow persists on the talus which masks much of this part. The band reappears east of the pass and is seen at the base of the cliff at mile 32.8, against which a deep snowdrift lodges most of the summer. From Logan Pass it can be followed eastward to a lofty location high on Pollock Mt. and again as it encircles the summits of Going-to-the-Sun Mt. and Matahpi Peak. To the southeast on the opposite side of the valley, it appears near the top of the cliff below Hanging Gardens. It is prominent near the summits of Citadel, Little Chief and Mahtotopa Mts.

| 30.4 A | Triple Arches | A 20.2 |

The road span ahead is called Triple Arches, for obvious reasons.

| 32.0 L | Subalpine Meadow | R 18.8 |

Glacier lilies spread a carpet of gold over the lush ground cover in early season. Heather, globe flowers and fragrant heliotrope keep them company. As their glory fades, scarlet monkeyflowers, fringed parnassias and deep-blue gentians hasten to replenish the ranks.

The transition from robust, upright trees at lower elevations to stunted, twisted dwarfs is pronounced. Tough and resilient individuals crowd closely into low mats for mutual protection amidst the vicissitudes of their world, a picture of misery seeking company. Ecologists use the apt term *krummholz* (from the German *krumm*, crooked, plus *holz*, grove or thicket) for these misshapen assemblages. Snow compaction, slides and open exposure to fierce winds armed with fragments of ice and rock have caused deformation and damage, have scuffed the bark and stripped the needles. Most leaders bear brown needles from winter kill or are dead. Those protruding above a shielding snow base succumb to the severity of the Arctic clime with its sudden, violent changes of light and temperature. In the mellow glow of a perfect summer day, it is hard to envision the fury of a winter storm on the mountain. Most of the trees are subalpine firs, with random whitebark pines. Fir has the advantage in that once started it reproduces by vegetative means.

Botanist James R. Habeck of the University of Montana investigated Logan Pass ecology. He concluded that a more continuous mat once covered the pass, and that the present pattern of krummholz has resulted from fires whose evidence has been removed by snowslides. Fires have always had important influence on vegetative cover at higher elevations in Waterton-Glacier Park.

Northwest from Logan Pass: on left, Oberlin; (1) Flattop; (2) Cathedral Peak; (3) Kipp; (4) Cleveland; (5) Swiftcurrent; (6) Haystack Butte; (7) Garden Wall; (8) Gould.

32.6   **Logan Pass**   18.2

Logan Pass (6680) is located on the Continental Divide separating major drainages of North America, here those of the Pacific and Hudson Bay. A visitor center with exhibits and viewfinders is situated by the parking area. Two popular trails start on Logan Pass: Hidden Lake Trail (120) and Highline Trail (121) for Granite Park Chalets. See chapter on trails. Naturalists are on hand to give information and conduct daily walks afield.

Damage from idle strolling on the insubstantial terrain by great hordes is too apparent everywhere. In an attempt to alleviate the situation the National Park Service built 3700 feet of boardwalk over trail 120 from the visitor center. Wood planking was chosen over asphalt and similar materials which are more out of place in the natural scene. Boards blend well as they weather, allow circulation of air under them and do not alter natural drainage patterns and are not permanent. It is a worthy experiment. Someday, other means may be tried for a more satisfactory solution. For the sake of fragile beauty, please refrain from straying off the board-walk.

Views are superb on all sides. REYNOLDS MT. (9125) dominates the scene to the south with CLEMENTS MT. (8760) and MT. OBERLIN (8180) to its right. Beyond the valley of Logan Creek, up which the road has climbed, the matchless summits of the Livingston Range extend past Vulture and Rainbow Peaks to KINTLA PEAK (10,101), third highest in the park and 25 miles air line from Logan Pass.

Nearby to the north, POLLOCK MT. (9190) is the highest point of the southern end of the Garden Wall. In 1895 W. C. Pollock, W. M. Clements and G. B. Grinnell made up a commission to purchase the Blackfeet territory between the Continental Divide and the present reservation boundary to open it for mineral prospecting. This territory is now the eastern half of Glacier Park.

Mt. Gould and Haystack Butte are above the road behind Pollock. SWIFTCURRENT MT. (8436), beyond the far end of the Garden Wall, can be recognized by the fire lookout which protrudes above its summit. A sharp eye can discern Granite Park Chalets at the base of the uniform left shoulder of the peak. Mountains behind Swiftcurrent are surmounted by MT. CLEVELAND (10,466), highest in the park.

PIEGAN MT. (9220), pronounced peagan, is above the road to the right of the Garden Wall. Several streams fed by melt water from Piegan Glacier on the opposite side of the mountain gush from high on its rocky flank. The water seeps through the mass, following the dip of the strata which is 6 degrees to the southwest.

GOING-TO-THE-SUN MT. (9642) across the mouth of Siyeh Canyon is the paramount feature between the pass and St. Mary. To the southeast the southern rampart of St. Mary Lake rises dominantly above the deep waters.

The old Kutenai name for Logan Pass, "Big Feet Was Killed," stems from some long-forgotten incident involving caribou, whose wide-spreading hooves adapt the animal for life in the snow and marshes. These great wanderers of the northland no longer haunt Glacier Park, but do live in similar habitat to the west. Ever since that name was used, the pass has been associated with wildlife, stirring interest and admiration.

In an exciting game of "now-you-see-us, now-you-don't," mountain goats, the natural complements of high cliffs and crags, appear and disappear as they move about indistinct rocks and ledges. Bighorns prefer grassier inclines on the Garden Wall and Piegan Basin. Black bear seldom venture to the higher elevations around Logan Pass, but grizzlies seasonally frequent the area to dig for edible bulbs and abundant small mammals. Common favorites for bear to eat and visitors to photograph are the fat marmots, related to groundhogs. They are identified by grayish head and shoulders and brownish hindquarters. Marmots display nose-pointed-on-high vigilance, wary confidence, shuffling gait and emit an ear-piercing whistle when alarmed. They obligingly pose for everyone who has a pinch of patience and modicum of calm. Their cousin ground squirrel squeaks loudly for a share of attention. Please refrain from feeding any park animal.

The world of birds on Logan Pass is full of excitement. The observant searcher, upon hearing a hen clucking softly to her chicks, becomes aware of the presence of ptarmigan. Or a fortunate stroller may stumble across an attentive mother with her fluffy family blending neatly into the background. Even happier is the discovery of a brooding bird on her nest beneath a fir bough or amid the purple heather. If approach is quiet and steady she will not become ruffled but will pose quite calmly for close up photographs.

In early season the brushland resounds with the melody of white-crowned sparrows and fox sparrows, here as in lower valleys. Water pipits curtsy on rock shelves as one passes, or are lifted high, kite-like, in the wind, lilting ethereal flightsong as they rise. Clark's nutcrackers, rosy finches and solitaires are associated with high places, but bird visitors from lower elevations—robins, mountain bluebirds, Swainson's and hermit thrushes, violet-green swallows and siskins—may appear on the scene or even still-hunt the walker, gladdening his day on Logan Pass.

The HANGING GARDENS, celebrated for floral beauty, extend from Logan Pass to HEAVY RUNNER MT. (8016). They suggest the ancient landscape which existed before the present one. Apparently they were once the floor of a previous cirque or trough, the remnants of whose walls stand today as Reynolds, Clements and the Rimrock.

Reynolds Mt., which presents its broadest face to the pass, is representative of what geologists term a horn, as in "Matterhorn,"—a sharp, irregular pinnacle resulting from a mountain mass whose sides have been eroded by three or more glaciers.

The rocks around the pass are of the Helena (Siyeh) formation. Massive reefs of fossilized algae can be seen around the visitor center and along Hidden Lake Trail. Their concentric structure is obvious. The filigree pattern of engravings and wavy lines on their discolored yellow surfaces results from a process called differential weathering. The limestone contains magnesite, which, being more soluble, weathers more rapidly and creates the intricate design.

Because of the dichotomy between preservation and use, Logan Pass presents a perplexing dilemma for the conscientious administrator. Popularity, overuse and apathy as to the results have robbed it of much of the intimate charm it once possessed. Evidence of human erosion is plentiful. Natural flower gardens are being trampled and paved; weeds replace dainty alpines; wildlife is disturbed; what thin soil was once present is being washed away.

What can administration do to grapple with this problem? How can it graciously control excessive crowds and discreetly channel the movements of visitors to minimize aftereffects? How can it muffle the din of traffic and alleviate atmospheric pollution caused by the exhaust from thousands of motors? What must be done to destroy or remove the tons of human wastes which continue to accumulate? These are but a few of many problems which must be solved if a visit is to be the supreme alpine experience which park objectives profess it should be. Logan Pass, like any sensitive area, like a national park itself, simply cannot mean everything to everybody.

A five-year project to rehabilitate the denuded landscape around the pass was recently concluded. By use of protective matting over areas reseeded with native plants, park resource management specialists hope that the natural vegetation will eventually be re-established. Ultimate success of these efforts depends upon visitors' continued cooperation in confining their activities to designated walkways.

Opportunity is ample for pleasant pursuits without serious injury to this fragile site: merely relaxing and escaping from everyday pressures, breathing deeply the invigorating air away from centers of concentration, observing and studying life and geology, taking photographs, hiking and staying on trails, rock-scaling for experienced climbers who make certain to sign the register. For such simple enjoyments, Logan Pass should still be tops!

32.8 L	**Big Drift**	R 18.1

In some years snow piles to a depth of 80 feet and some usually remains all summer.

33.4	**Lunch Creek**	17.4

The road crosses Lunch Creek, swinging around a flower-carpeted cirque with the tabular summit of Pollack Mt. in back. Piegan Basin lies between this mountain and Piegan Mt. on the right.

33.8	**Tunnel**	17.0

The short tunnel bores through a spur of Helena (Siyeh) limestone on Piegan Mt. A sparkling waterfall tumbles to the road on the lower side.

35.5	**Siyeh Bend**	15.5

There is a parking area at this point. Bleak MT. SIYEH (10,014) is at the head of the valley on the right; Going-to-the-Sun Mt. is across Siyeh Valley. MATAHPI PEAK (9365) is between these two mountains. SIYEH PASS (7750) is northeast of Matahpi Peak. The Siyeh Bend Cutoff Trail (115) starts above the road and climbs the brushy slope above the road for 1.2 miles to join Piegan Pass Trail (113) as it traverses from Sun Point to Many Glacier. This trail can be seen as it sweeps in a rising arc to PIEGAN PASS (7570) at the head of the valley to the left. CATARACT MOUNTAIN (8180) is the low summit behind the pass and the trail.

35.7 R	**Blackfoot Glacier**	A 15.5

The best view from the road of the upper shelf of BLACKFOOT GLACIER resting against snow-girdled BLACKFOOT MT. (9574). This is obtained after rounding the big bend in either direction. Now and then in late season, elk are seen along the road as it swings around Going-to-the-Sun Mt. CITADEL MT. (9030) with a typical hanging valley cut into its flank is across St. Mary Valley. The prominence on its left is called DUSTY STAR MT. (8573), a name once suggested for the whole mass to avoid confusion with Citadel Peaks at the head of Waterton Lake. "Dusty Star" is Blackfeet for "puffball." In Indian lore puffballs pop up where meteors strike the ground. They are often represented on the bases of tipis by black circles along with mountains, symbolized by black triangles.

The forest here is far different from that in McDonald Valley. The luxuriance of the west side forest is lacking. Englemann spruce and lodgepole pine, rarely attaining 100 feet in height, are the dominant trees in the community.

37.3 R	**Jackson Glacier**	L 13.4

Pullout and roadside exhibit for Jackson Glacier, lying between MT. JACKSON (10,052) and Blackfoot Mt. This was once a part of a greater Blackfoot Glacier, which in the past century lay astride the Continental Divide, fused with Pumpelly and Harrison Glaciers on the Pacific slope. Other formerly larger ice masses in the park—Kintla, Agassiz and Grinnell, for example—have split into smaller glaciers through ablation. Piegan Pass Trail (113) between Sun Point and Many Glacier crosses the road beyond the lower end of the parking area.

38.1 R	**Gunsight Pass View**	L 12.7

View of GUNSIGHT PASS (6946) and GUNSIGHT MT. (9258). Gunsight Lake lies in the pocket below the pass. Gunsight Pass Trail (52) to Sperry Chalets and Lake McDonald can be seen faintly as it climbs the rocky face of Mt. Jackson to the pass.

The head of St. Mary Lake and VIRGINIA FALLS are visible across the valley. St. Mary Cutoff Trail (261) drops from here to connect with Gunsight Pass, Piegan Pass and St. Mary Lake Trails (52, 113, 109) 0.3 mile below.

39.7   **Red Argillite**   **11.0**

The road has been cut through Grinnell argillite. This formation gives RED EAGLE MT. (8881) across St. Mary Lake and GOAT MT. (8826) their ruddy summits. Almost-a-Dog Mt. (8922) is seen between Citadel and Little Chief.

40.0   **Sunrift Gorge**   **10.5**

Limited parking space is provided to the right on both sides of the variegated native stone bridge, well worth a closer look. The gorge, 75 feet above the road, is incised along vertical fractures at right angles to a normal course. A trailside exhibit explains the phenomenon. Siyeh Pass Trail (117) passes here for Siyeh Pass, 5.6 miles; a circuit around Going-to-the-Sun Mt. 14.5 miles; and over Piegan Pass to Many Glacier, 17.7 miles.

BARING FALLS, 0.3 mile downstream, is a favorite haunt of ouzels or dippers—birds which fly through its spray for access to their mossy nests behind the falls. The creek plunges over a ledge of Grinnell argillite, a short distance above the lakeshore and on trail 113 up St. Mary Valley. The sturdy trees along lower Baring Creek bed are cottonwoods.

40.6 R   **Sun Point**   **L 10.0**

The paved spur drops to a large parking area for Going-to-the-Sun Point, generally referred to as SUN POINT. An exhibit, viewfinders, start of a self-guiding trail, pit toilets and picnic tables are located here. The site of Going-to-the-Sun Chalets, now razed, is on the purple promontory above the lake. Some of the best photographic shots can be taken here.

41.2 L   **Lost Lake**   **R 9.6**

A charming lake, almost hidden in a wooded pocket, is seldom noticed by the too-hurried passerby. The forest along the road is obviously in a losing struggle for existence. Many trees are dead or dying; many have been blown over by wind. The site is obviously unfavorable for vigorous growth. In a dense, slowly developing stand, individual trees can extract maximum strength from sun and soil while providing mutual support and protection. However, when the right of-way was cleared a vast canyon was opened down which chill, drying winds howl, and in which the normal growth pattern was suddenly and permanently disrupted.

42.2 R   **St. Mary Lake**   **L 8.6**

Bow-shaped ST. MARY LAKE (4484), 10 miles long, varies in width from a quarter of a mile to a mile and is 292 feet deep. Road cuts expose Appekunny argillite, the second oldest formation in Glacier Park.

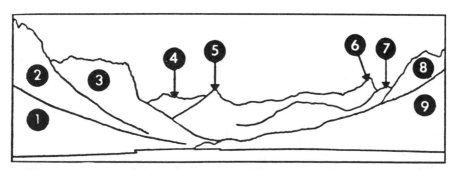

St. Mary Lake at Narrows: (1) Mahtotopa; (2) Little Chief; (3) Citadel; (4) Gunsight; (5) Fusillade; (6) Reynolds; (7) Heavy Runner; (8) Going-to-the-Sun; (9) Goat.

43.8 R   **Wild Goose Island**   **L 7.0**

A favorite for photographers. The small rocky island in the lake has been a nesting site for Canada geese, hence its name, WILD GOOSE ISLAND. The mountains across the lake, L to R, are RED EAGLE; MAHTOTOPA (8672); LITTLE CHIEF (9541), rising 500 feet above the lake and CITADEL.

44.1   **The Narrows**   **6.6**

The narrow neck of St. Mary Lake results from the resistance of Altyn limestone, the oldest outcropping formation on Glacier's east side, which forms the face of the Lewis Thrust Fault, the most distinctive geological feature in the area. The rock is pale bluish gray when freshly fractured but soon turns buff on weathering.

44.4 R   **Boat Dock**   **L 6.4**

Lane leading to a public boat-launching ramp and dock where launches are boarded for lake cruises and boats can be rented.

44.5 L   **Rising Sun Campground**   **R 6.3**

Accommodations for automobiles and trailers. Going-to-the-Sun Road crosses ROSE CREEK. A ranger is stationed here.

44.7 L   **Rising Sun Motor Inn**   **R 6.0**

Here is a motel, coffee shop, campstore and service station. Rose Creek Trail (112) to Otokomi Lake (6482), 5.0 miles distant, starts by the creek above the campground and follows the trace of the Lewis Thrust Fault for more than two miles. The pale buff cliff on the left is Altyn limestone. The dark Cretaceous rocks along the foot of the trail are crammed with fossils, mostly oyster shells. The contact between resistant ancient rocks above and soft, undisturbed, underlying Cretaceous rocks is remarkably distinct. At a site beside the trail, the contact was once as thin as a knife-blade, but the spot was buried under slide rock and detritus from the 1964 flood.

44.7 R   **Picnic Ground**   **L 5.1**

Opposite the access road to the coffee shop area, a lane leads to a picnic ground near the lakeshore.

46.5 R   **Triple Divide Peak**   **L 4.3**

This unique peak (8020), visible up Red Eagle Valley, is identified on the roadside exhibit placed at the edge of the parking space. This is the only point on a major road at which this modest-looking but singular mountain is clearly visible. The summit is merely the high point of a ridge extending southeast from NORRIS MT. (8882), the pyramid seen to the right of Triple Divide. It marks the meeting place of the three largest drainages in North America: Atlantic, Pacific and Hudson Bay. Water draining from this peak flows into the Missouri-Mississippi, Flathead-Columbia and Saskatchewan-Nelson river systems.

The stunted, contorted broadleaf trees are quaking aspens, whose leaves are never at rest. Groves of these natives to Eurasia and North America are characteristic of plains across Canada and far beyond Edmonton, Alberta. Lower forested slopes on the east side of the mountains are subjected to repeated fires, often creating grasslands.

47.2 LL   **Singleshot Mt.**   **R 3.6**

Singleshot Mt. (7926) culminates on the right with NAPI ROCK (7487), an isolated pinnacle around which the Blackfeet wove stories. Napi or Old Man was a capricious cultural trickster appearing in legends of Indians from coast to coast, especially those of Algonkian stock, to which the Blackfeet belong.

The conspicuous bands forming the upper strata are quartzite. Near the summit of CURLY BEAR MT. (8099) across the valley, a prominent light-colored quartzite band contains a readily discernible thrust fault. This appears roughly like a reversed letter Z beneath the left profile of the mountain. Cretaceous rocks beneath the overgrown slope north of the lower lake are slippery when wet. This has caused much slumping and has given the grassy surface a hummocky aspect.

49.9 L   **St. Mary Campground**   **R 0.9**

Located at the northeast end of the lake, this campground is convenient, but not as scenically inviting as some of the others because the site is exposed and the trees are scraggly. Campsites are equipped with fireplaces and tables. Water hydrants, garbage cans and flush toilets are near at hand.

50.1   **St. Mary River**   **0.7**

Connects St. Mary Lake with LOWER ST. MARY LAKE (4471).

50.4   **Entrance Station**   **0.4**

During the park season rangers are stationed here to check or issue entrance permits and to give information. They answer questions about roads, campgrounds, accommodations and similar matters of importance to the visitor. St. Mary VISITOR CENTER, to the northeast, has ample parking space in the rear. An information desk, free exhibits, auditorium and restrooms are inside. The naturalist on duty conducts informal shows, walks and evening programs.

50.6 R   **St. Mary Utility Area**   **L 0.2**

Looking back, mountain peaks visible (L to R) are DIVIDE (8665), WHITE CALF (8893), CURLY BEAR, JAMES (9375), KAKITOS (7841), NORRIS and SPLIT (8792). STIMSON (10,142), 20 miles away, peers over the right shoulder of Split Mt. On the south shore of St. Mary Lake are RED EAGLE, MAHTOTOPA, LITTLE CHIEF and CITADEL. OTOKOMI (7935), SINGLESHOT and EAST FLATTOP (8356) are on the right, north of the lake.

A paved road leads to a park utility area, employees' residences, the site of St. Mary Chalets, now razed, and the restored 1913 Ranger Station. From the 1913 Ranger Station the Red Eagle Trail (107) leads to Red Eagle Lake, 7.7 miles, and continues as a part of the Inside Trail to Cut Bank, Two Medicine and East Glacier. Red Eagle Trail also connects with scenic St. Mary Trail (109) which follows the southeast shore to join trails at the lakehead.

Before the construction of the road on the north shore of St. Mary Lake, a passenger launch shuttled between St. Mary and Going-to-the-Sun Chalets, with a stop at Red Eagle Landing to pick up or discharge passengers for Red Eagle Camp. This attraction was popular because of the activity on the boat docks, the shrill boathorn, the dashing spray, the roll of the boat among the usual whitecaps on the lake, which is also used for swimming, despite the fact that it is very cold. For years just before World War II, Winold Reiss, celebrated portrait artist of the Blackfeet, used the chalets as an art school.

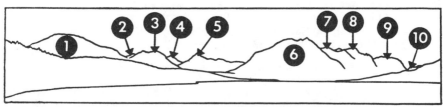

From Foot of St. Mary Lake: (1) Curly Bear; (2) James; (3) Kakitos; (4) Norris; (5) Split; (6) Red Eagle; (7) Mahtotopa; (8) Little Chief; (9) Citadel; (10) Gunsight.

Park boundary at this point.

50.8   Road Junction: Village of St. Mary

U.S. 89, Blackfeet Highway, leads north to Many Glacier, Waterton Lakes National Park, Calgary and Canadian points, and leads south to East Glacier Park, to U.S. Highway 2 and to points east and west. Description of this highway is provided elsewhere in this chapter.

Passers-by on U.S. 89 are urged to take Going-to-the-Sun Road to Logan Pass, 18.2 miles, and to The Loop, 7.9 miles farther.

Camas Road

Going-to-the-Sun Road near Apgar to Camas Entrance, 10.1 miles.

This newest road in Glacier National Park was opened in 1965. With the exception of the small segment of Chief Mountain International Highway cutting across the northeastern tip, it is the only new route in the park since the completion of Going-to-the-Sun Road in 1932. It offers an improved short route to the Outside North Fork Road and Polebridge and makes unnecessary a reconstruction of a parallel road within the park, which would create conspicuous highway scars and invade a wilderness much needed for the welfare of park wildlife. Camas Road coincides with the Inside North Fork Road for the first 1.4 miles. Roadside exhibits interpret geological and ecological features along the route. Thousands of pines killed by mountain pine beetles are scattered throughout the forest along this and other Park roads.

0.0   Road Intersection

Consult description of Going-to-the-Sun Road for approaches to this point. Camas and Inside North Fork Roads go west, pass the road to Apgar at 0.3 mile and cross Lower McDonald Creek at 0.5 mile. The old road to Fish Creek turned right after crossing the bridge; it now has a dead end and serves private homes.

1.4   Road Junction

Camas Road continues straight ahead. Inside North Fork Road to Fish Creek Campground turns right.

Looking back over the weedy lodgepole pines, the majestic panorama of peaks above Lake McDonald is spread over the top of HOWE RIDGE: L to R are MT. VAUGHT (8850), the GARDEN WALL, MT. GOULD (9553), MT. CANNON (8952), MT. SIYEH (10,014), EDWARDS MT. (9072), GUNSIGHT MT. (9258), MT. JACKSON (10,052), WALTON MT. (8926) and MT. STIMSON (10,142).

3.4   Fern Creek

The road crosses a slight rise and drops down to Fern Creek in a forest of western larch, white pine, spruce, fir and various shrubs: maple, alder, willows, thimbleberries, huckleberries and elder. Climbing another gentle crest at mile 5.4, the road brings the first view of the great peaks in the northwest sector of the park.

5.5 R   McGee Meadow Overlook

This boggy meadow is a good place in which to see wildlife, especially in early and late hours of the day. Mountains (R to L) are: Jackson, Gunsight, Edwards, Brown (8565), Cannon, Stanton (7750), Heavens (8987), Rogers Peak (7320) and Vulture Peak (9638) with its glistening glaciers due north from here. An upper bit of SPERRY GLACIER is visible between Gunsight and Edwards Mt.

6.0 L   Huckleberry Lookout Trail

Huckleberry Lookout Trail (35) climbs briskly to 6000 feet, then follows below the crest of Apgar Mts. to the lookout on Huckleberry Mt. (6613), 6.0 miles. The trail is wearisome, but distant views are rewarding. Hikers must carry their own drinking water on this trip for none is available at the lookout.

8.4 R   Camas Creek Overlook

KINTLA PEAK (10,101), 22 miles north, looks like a long ridge near the left end of the mountain wall. RAINBOW PEAK (9891) has a pointed, yellow summit. Vulture Peak can be identified by its glacier. MT. GEDUHN (8375) is to the northeast with ANACONDA PEAK (8279) huddling close to the right; it can be recognized from many angles by the long, 100-foot-tall rectangular block on its southern crest, locally dubbed PAUL BUNYAN'S CABIN. Paul Bunyan was a fictitious giant lumberjack of northwest lumber camps who, with his blue ox, logged off all the northland and performed amazing feats, most of them ecologically abominable today. Rogers Peak is on the left and yellow Heavens Peak is at the head of the Camas Valley. Green Mt. Vaught and pointed Stanton Mt. follow on the right. Mt. Brown above Lake McDonald Lodge is next right, while lofty Mt. Jackson straddles the road down which we have come. Bold Mt. Stimson is in the distance (R).

10.0 A   Glacier View Mt.

(6097) on the left and DEMERS RIDGE (6235) on the right are in Flathead National Forest across North Fork Valley. WINONA RIDGE (5403) is to the right beyond them. The scars on Huckleberry Mt. resulted from a 1967 fire.

10.1 R   Camas Creek Entrance Station

11.1   Huckleberry Mt. Nature Trail

This 0.9 mile self-guided trail loops through the site of a 1967 lightning-caused forest fire. There the visitor can observe both the natural regrowth of vegetation after fire and some effects of man's fire suppression efforts on that recovery.

11.0 L   Flathead River Overlook

Flathead River Overlook of the mountains on both sides of the river. In succession (L to R) park peaks include the mountains of the Kintla Group, Rainbow, MT. CARTER (9843) and Vulture. Geduhn, Anaconda and WOLF GUN MT. (8000) at the head of Logging Valley are to the left of Longfellow Peak.

11.3   Bridge Over The Flathead River (North Fork)

The river meanders in a broad trough which extends for 30 miles southeast from the International Border. It is confined between the highly dissected Livingston Range in the park and similar ranges of hard, upturned Belt Series rocks in the national forest.

The great glacier which moved down North Fork Valley in the Ice Age appears to have continued in a straight course to merge with McDonald Glacier in that valley. It overrode but did not cut through Howe Ridge, which was an obstacle in its course. A glacier flows uphill if pressure backing it is sufficient to force it over obstructions.

It has been conjectured by some that parallel Snyder, Howe and the truncated ridges on the northeast side of North Fork Valley represent erosional remnants of an ancient, possibly continuous peneplain on Tertiary rocks. As these are now covered with forests and drift, confirming evidence is small.

Below the bridge, the river suddenly changes character as it swings abruptly west and plunges into a wild, narrow gorge below Apgar Mts. It is possible that this course was determined by a structural feature, such as a minor fault. The Outside North Fork Road goes 24 miles downstream to the town of Columbia Falls. To the right, it follows the river 14 miles to Polebridge to connect with the Inside North Fork Road.

Inside North Fork Road.

Going-to-the-Sun Road near Apgar to Kintla Lake, 43.0 miles.

The Inside North Fork Road is a narrow, unimproved road that winds up the North Fork Flathead River. Entrepreneurs, spurred by dreams of mineral wealth, built it in 1901 as the first road to penetrate deeply into the park region. Along the way the impressive peaks of the Livingston Range march in procession with the traveler, but they are often masked from view by bordering forest. The Outside North Fork Road affords better views, as it is on the opposite side of the valley and higher above the river; combined with Camas Road it offers a faster alternative route to Polebridge. Seasonally both roads can be very dusty, with heavy logging truck traffic on the Outside Road.

North Fork Valley is a broad trough over 30 miles long and up to four miles wide. The mountains of the park are older than the Whitefish Range in the national forest, but rocks exposed along the river are stratigraphically much higher than those of either of these mountain systems. Many regard the depression as a graben bounded by high-angle normal faults, but positive evidence is lacking. Glaciation has played a major role in the history of the valley. At maximum stages ice probably filled the valley completely to depths of almost a mile and overrode entirely the lower Whitefish and Galton Ranges to the west. The Inside Road passes over alluvium and associated deposits of Tertiary Age, covered here and there with Pleistocene material, chiefly glacial.

Tiny tracts of Transition Zone life along the road have distinctive facets of interest not to be found elsewhere in the park. Ponderosa pine groves and sagebrush flats are the most notable. In early spring, grassy bogs are buried under the bloom of kalmia or mountain laurel, a dainty undershrub; and fields flaunt solid covers of creamy glacier lilies, more pallid than their bright yellow kin at Iceberg Lake or Logan Pass.

The valley is excellent range for deer and elk; moose find living to their liking in ponds and swamps; grizzlies roam the shrubby hillsides and open places. This matchless habitat is essential for assured survival of its singular plant and animal communities, but in the mid-fifties its integrity was seriously threatened by proposals to build a high dam on the Flathead below the mouth of Camas Creek.

Currently, resource exploitation activities in the North Fork Valley outside Glacier Park include expanded logging operations and seismic exploration for oil and gas, plus drilling of some test wells. During seismic activity, thunder-like rumblings from distant dynamite blasts may be heard by visitors in otherwise seemingly remote areas, even well inside the Park.

Another resource development that undoubtedly will ultimately affect the North Fork plant, animal and human communities is the proposed Cabin Creek open pit coal mine, immediately across the International Boundary in extreme southeastern British Columbia.

Local, state, federal and international discussions continue on possible ways to minimize adverse impacts of such developments in previously nearly pristine habitats, and upon vulnerable park lands, waters and air.

0.0   Road Intersection

Going-to-the-Sun Road, Inside North Fork Road, and Camas Road meet at this point. The Inside North Fork and Camas routes go west.

0.3 R   Road to Apgar

Visitor facilities, campground and foot of Lake McDonald. See description of Going-to-the-Sun Road.

0.5   Lower McDonald Creek

Lower McDonald Creek, the outlet of Lake McDonald. (See Salmon and Eagles, page 131.)

1.4   Road Junction

Inside North Fork Road turns right. Camas Road continues ahead to Camas Entrance Station, 10.0 miles, and the junction with the Outside North Fork Road, 11 miles.

2.4 R   Fish Creek Picnic Area

2.5R   Fish Creek Ranger Station, Campground and Amphitheater

A large, pleasant campground is located on Fish Creek on a level terrace above Lake McDonald. MT. JACKSON (10,052) has been added to the magnificent panorama of mountains seen from the foot of the lake. It has a relief of almost 7000 feet.

The blacktop surfacing ends, and the road becomes primitive. It winds up Fish Creek through a forest burned in 1926; but here and there, as at Fish Creek crossing, mile 4.5, the old cover escaped the blaze. The red cedars are members of the humid Pacific Coast flora mentioned at mile 1.1 in the log of Going-to-the-Sun Road. The road climbs steep McGee Hill to McGee Meadow (3915), lying between Howe Ridge (R) and Apgar Mts. A fire lookout is visible on the crest of HUCKLEBERRY MT. (6593), the northwest peak of Apgar Mts.

' 2.8 R   Lake McDonald Trail (43) to North Lake McDonald Road   6.7 miles.

6.3   McGee Meadow

The road crosses McGee Meadow and enters a spruce forest at its upper end.

7.3   R Howe Lake Trail

Howe Lake Trail (38) goes to marshy HOWE LAKE (4106), 2.0 miles, in which fish and beaver find themselves at home. Moose, met occasionally on this trail as well as on the road, should be treated with greatest respect. At 1.7 miles beyond Howe Lake, trail 38 meets the Howe Ridge Trail (37). From this junction it is 3.2 miles on trail 37 back to the Inside North Fork Road or 6.4 miles to the junction with the West Lakes Trail (9), 2.3 miles from North Lake McDonald Road.

9.3   Camas Creek

The glaucous aspen along our route grow so straight and robust that they do not seem kin to the low, deformed specimens found on the high plains. Across the creek, CAMAS CREEK TRAIL (39) goes 13.9 miles upstream along a chain of six lakes in a deep valley. These are more readily accessible by West Lakes Trail (9) from North Lake McDonald Road.

This is prime grizzly habitat. Grizzlies should be permitted to have some territory in which they can range undisturbed by man, so precautions must be taken to prevent incidents such as the well-known fatal encounter which occurred at the foot of Trout Lake in 1967. Visitors are encouraged to make daytime use of the Camas Valley. All lakes in the valley are restricted to fly fishing.

In the course of authorized scientific studies, a northern bog lemming was captured on July 30, 1949, in a trap three miles east of the road bridge, the only record of this species in Montana. No additional specimens were collected. Who knows how many other forms of life, vegetable and animal, await discovery in pristine national parks? Bog lemmings are creatures of bleak, circumpolar tundra from Labrador to Alaska and in the Old World. They are cuddly rodents, four or five inches long, with stumpy tails, short ears, furry feet and tawny coats varied with black and sometimes red. They are well known for their unstoppable mass migrations, some of which end in the ocean.

12.3 R   Dutch Creek

Dutch Creek Trail (34) left for primitive access is infrequently maintained. Dutch Lake lies 12.3 miles upstream. Homesteading was attempted along the North Fork a quarter of a century before the establishment of the park. Because farming, ranching, logging and tourism yielded small returns for efforts expended, only the most rugged souls have clung to their claims. The lane goes downstream to private homes.

15.0   Anaconda Creek

After crossing another small meadow and the southwest tip of Dutch Ridge, Anaconda Creek is reached. Beaver activity is apparent both above and below the road. Anaconda Creek Trail (33) goes 5.4 miles upstream to the North Fork of Anaconda Creek, but is a low use trail and infrequently maintained.

15.9   Ponderosa Pines

Ponderosa pines in a magnificent grove. In recent years this area has been the site for several research fires to measure the effects of fire and monitor fire behavior. As stated in a National Park Service News Release in 1983:

The knowledge to be gained from this research will help park managers to understand the natural role of fire in maintaining the complex Glacier ecosystem. . . . It is the policy of the National Park Service to maintain natural ecosystems in natural areas and not to manage in favor of any single component of the system. Fire is a very powerful force in nature and is as necessary to a natural system as is sunshine and rain.

A natural occurrence such as the killing of trees by insects or fire is not always sightly to the park visitor; however, this activity is very important to the health of the overall park ecosystem. The dead trees become homes for many species of mammals and birds. The openings created allow grass and shrubs to grow which are valuable food for wildlife. Gradually the dead trees decompose and their nutrients and energy are released to be utilized by other plants, animals and eventually a new revitalized forest. The diversity created by these natural cycles is what makes the parks so fascinating and attractive to the park visitor.

20.0   Logging Creek and Ranger Station

Logging Creek Campground is on the right. Logging Lake Trail (20) follows the north bank 4.4 miles to LOGGING LAKE (3810), six miles long, and lying outside the high mountains. ANACONDA PEAK (8659) and MT. GEDUHN (8375) are prominent above its head. The trail continues along the north shore of Logging Lake for some 8.4 miles to GRACE LAKE (3920). Both lakes can be good fishing. Glacial Logging Valley heads in a compound cirque on TRAPPER PEAK (7702), the triple divide for North Fork, Middle Fork and Waterton drainages.

21.7 L   North Fork Flathead

Note that the soft, gravelly clay beds of the 70-foot east bluff of the river are Tertiary sediments deposited in quiet, shallow lakes which were impounded, it is believed, in times of mountain building. The mountains of the Whitefish Range across the river rise gently to remarkably uniform crests at an elevation of about 7000 feet. They probably represent erosional remnants of a peneplain.

22.5 R   Quartz Creek Campground

Quartz Creek Campground on Quartz Creek. 0.3 mile farther on, Quartz Creek Trail (17) proceeds 6.9 miles upstream to the foot of Lower Quartz Lake, then another 3.1 miles past its east shore and Middle Quartz Lake to the foot of QUARTZ LAKE (4416), four miles long and 254 feet deep. A ford of Quartz Creek below Lower Quartz Lake may be difficult to negotiate safely during high water. More convenient routes to Quartz Lakes are described below under Bowman Lake Campground.

In a rockbound basin two miles beyond Quartz Lake (no trail), CERULEAN LAKE (4650) receives the melt waters of RAINBOW GLACIER on the west (L). On the opposite, southeast side of the basin, VULTURE PEAK (9638) is fronted by kaleidoscopic CARNELIAN CLIFF and is capped with TWO OCEAN GLACIER straddling the Continental Divide. A quartz vein on Vulture Peak at the extreme headwaters of Quartz Creek contains a little copper ore, the discovery of which in 1876 stimulated prospecting.

23.1 L   Mud Lake

Mud Lake (3492), a shallow, willow-bordered pond with beaver huts, is a good place to look for moose, loons and marsh birds, shrub-loving songsters and numerous bright blue damselflies.

24.7   Lone Pine Prairie

Lone Pine Prairie (3592). Dignified aspen are gradually crowding the edges of the open field.

28.1 L   Polebridge Ranger Station

Polebridge Ranger Station, utility sheds and bridge across the North Fork are below the road. The alternative route to Polebridge via the Outside Road joins the Inside Road as mentioned in the log of Camas Road. A general store, saloon, hostel and post office are located in the settlement of Polebridge, a mile downstream across the bridge.

28.3 R   Bowman Creek Campground

Bowman Creek Campground (3556) on the north bank of Bowman Creek has no source of treated water, hence no fees are collected. A tenth of a mile beyond, a narrow tortuous lane climbs the right bank by a horseshoe curve, and continues for six miles to BOWMAN LAKE CAMPGROUND, PICNIC AREA and the foot of Bowman Lake (4030), 256 feet deep. Grouped around its head is a striking panorama of stately mountains among which the sinuous lake, seven miles long, penetrates for half its length.

Princely RAINBOW PEAK (9891) dominates as it towers 5800 feet into the blue. The jagged summit of MT. PEABODY (9216) is to the north. NUMA (Kitunahan for "thunder") RIDGE, terminating in NUMA PEAK (9003) on the northwest and CERULEAN RIDGE on the east enclose the sides of the lake.

Bowman Lake Trail (15) follows the north shore to Upper Bowman Campground, 7.1 miles and continues 6.7 miles up Bowman Creek to BROWN PASS (6255), where it joins Boulder Pass Trail (6) and descends by Olson Creek to Waterton Lake (Goat Haunt), 8.5 miles farther.

0.7 mile on the Bowman Lake Trail from the foot of the lake is the Numa Ridge Lookout Trail (14). From this junction to the seasonally-manned lookout is 4.9 forested miles. Hikers should carry their own water.

Fishing in Bowman Lake is better done by boat than from shore, with a 10 horsepower limit on motors. Several trails described below lead to backcountry lakes with very good fishing potential. Because of lower elevation, these lakes are generally accessible to fishermen earlier in the season than many of those on Glacier's east side.

From the Bowman Lake Campground, it is 3.6 miles on West Lakes Trail (9) to its junction with the Akokala Lake Trail (12), then another 2.2 miles to Akokala Lake, lying in forest on the north side on Numa Ridge.

At the southeast end of Bowman Lake past a locked patrol cabin, a 0.4 mile segment of West Lakes Trail (9) leads to the junction with the Quartz Lake Trail (16). From this junction it is 5.8 well-graded miles over Cerulean Ridge to Quartz Lake via trail 16 or 3.1 somewhat steeper miles across the ridge on trail 9 to the foot of Lower Quartz Lake and the junction with Quartz Creek Trail (17).

28.7   Akokala Creek

30.2 L   River Campground

River Campground has seven pleasant sites which are seldom full. Since there is no source of treated water, no fees are collected here. Information on alternative park access to the river can be obtained at the Polebridge Ranger Station, (406) 888-5416.

30.7 L   Big Prairie

Four miles long and a mile wide, Big Prairie is a sagebrush flat completely surrounded by lodgepole pines and aspens. Quarter Circle MC Ranch, formerly a large private enterprise but now government-owned, is on the left at 31.8 miles. This North Fork region was a favorite with early homesteaders, and reminders of their activities are plentiful. As opportunity presents, the National Park Service is acquiring title to private lands in the park to convert them for visitor enjoyment.

As previously observed in reference to research fires in the park, one major goal of park resource management is to maintain the integrity of Glacier's natural biotic communities. Therefore, efforts are made whenever possible to reduce or eliminate "exotic" (that is, non-native) plants and animals. Problems with exotics establishing themselves in place of natives tend to be especially acute where there have been past ecological disturbances, such as road cuts or former homesteads. In recent years research has been conducted on established Big Prairie populations of the noxious weed leafy spurge to test possible control techniques, such as frequent mowing or burning. Studies continue in an effort to identify an environmentally acceptable and effective method of control.

A mile north of the Quarter Circle MC Ranch, Akokala Creek Trail (11), little used, goes 6.6 miles to West Lakes Trail (9) and connects with Akokala Lake Trail (12) to Akokala Lake, 2.7 miles beyond. A shorter route to the lake is described above, under Bowman Lake Campground.

35.6   Round Prairie

Round Prairie supports the densest growth of big sage in the park. The open grasslands along the road are important range for wildlife and offer a fine opportunity to study natural communities in order to learn how life responds to environment. Grasslands result from and are maintained by repeated fires, and natural fires are a big factor in the ecology of the northwest. Most are caused by lightning in dry electric storms of late summer when little or no rain falls.

The bluff on the sharp river bend exposes stratified Tertiary deposits of gray sandy clay and sandstone which contain thin interbedded layers of lignite.

36.7   Ford Creek

Ford Creek is crossed.

38.4 L   Oil Well Site

The site of Kintla oil well, which was sunk in a period of oil fever, 1902-1904. It is 0.2 mile west on the riverbank.

40.3   Kintla Creek

Kintla Creek, draining Kintla Lake, has cut 200 feet into the terrace at the site of the bridge. The road climbs to the top of the terrace. A dense growth of uniformly aged lodgepoles, locally called "dog hair," covers old burns.

40.5 L   Kishenehn Creek

A barricaded lane goes four miles upstream to KISHENEHN CREEK and Kishenehn Ranger Station, now unmanned. It is 4.5 miles by Kishenehn Creek Trail (1) from the station to the International Boundary. At 1.4 miles, trail 1 is met from the south by Kintla Trail (2), a tiresome route over Starvation Creek and Ridge to the center of north Kintla lakeshore, 6.0 miles farther, where it meets the major BOULDER PASS TRAIL (6) which goes across Boulder Pass to Waterton Lake, 28.0 miles. Make local inquiry before attempting travel over these trails.

43.0   Kintla Campground

Kintla Campground at the foot of KINTLA LAKE (4008). This lake lies between Starvation and Parke Ridges, which some geologists believe are remnants of an old peneplain that was dissected by the great glaciers of the Ice Age and now lies buried beneath accumulations of drift. If so, this peneplain may possibly be correlated with the Flaxville Peneplain east of the Rockies. The upper end of the lake is pinched between jagged PARKE PEAK (9038) and elongate BOUNDARY MOUNTAINS on the border and topped by LONG KNIFE PEAK (9784). Long Knife is a wide-spread Indian name for "white man," traceable way back to early Virginia times.

Fishing in Kintla Lake is spotty. Motorboats are limited to 10 horsepower or less.

Boulder Pass Trail (6) starts at the upper end of the auto campground and follows the north shore to a campground at the head of the lake, 6.5 miles. Above Upper Kintla Lake, trail 6 is one of the most spectacular trails of the Glacier area.

U. S. Highway 2
West Glacier to East Glacier Park, Montana, 55.4 miles.

This route is also followed by the Burlington Northern Railroad. Amtrak rail passengers will find this material helpful in identifying and understanding features as they travel for 60 miles along the boundary of Glacier National Park.

Above West Glacier, U.S. Highway 2 ascends John F. Stevens Canyon, the name given to the lower valley of Middle Fork Flathead River and that of its tributary, Bear Creek, from their confluence to MARIAS PASS (5216). Past the summit the highway descends in a mountain re-entrant to the Great Plains. Except for the seasonal Going-to-the-Sun Road, this is the only highway crossing the Rockies from Crowsnest Pass on Alberta Highway 3 at the Alberta, B.C. border to Rogers Pass (5609) on Montana State Highway 200 between Great Falls and Missoula, an air distance of 200 miles.

Scenic and notable features abound throughout the length of U.S. 2, which differs noticeably in topography and vegetative cover from the route over Logan Pass. The two roads complement each other well to provide, with the connecting link of Blackfeet Highway, an exciting 140-mile circuit. Reputable guest ranches and ample facilities for lodging, food, gasoline and supplies are on U.S. 2.

MILES FROM WEST GLACIER		MILES FROM EAST GLACIER PARK
0.0	Park Boundary	55.4

Leaving Glacier National Park, bridge over the MIDDLE FORK of the FLATHEAD RIVER.

0.2	Railroad Underpass	55.2

Junction with U.S. 2 coming from Kalispell (32 miles) and the Pacific Coast.

0.6 R	Belton Chalets	L 54.9

Rustic and attractive, these chalets were built by Great Northern Railway when the park was created. Old Belton village, now mostly razed, was located across the tracks. Entrance to the park was by a bridge, one-half mile upstream.

1.0 L	Flathead Gorge	R 49.5

For the next five miles the Flathead River winds through a deeply incised gorge between the BELTON HILLS (6339) in the park and OUSEL PEAK (7157) in the adjoining Flathead National Forest. The stream has established a winding pattern on a former soft flood plain. On encountering hard bedrock, it continued cutting downward in the pattern established, thus creating a meandering stream in a young valley. Such a feature is termed "entrenched meanders." From the mouth of Lincoln Creek to the mouth of Bear Creek an advanced or later stage of development is seen as the river wanders freely over a modern flood plain.

Belton Hills were swept by the great 1929 fire, but the open, south-facing slopes now provide good winter-range for wildlife.

2.5	Geologic Sequence	48.5

Large roadcuts in the rock expose well-bedded limestone with a dip of 45 degrees NE. An argillaceous member is also present. The road follows limestone for several miles, progression being from older to younger rock. Greenish argillite appears at 5.6 miles; then a quartzitic member, 5.8 miles; red argillite, 6.5 miles; and more limestone, 6.9 miles, all dipping at the same angle. These correspond with members of a variable, incompletely studied asssemblage of Beltian rocks known as the Missoula Group, younger than the Helena (Siyeh) Formation and widely spread in the region. The group, once regarded as absent from the park, embraces members of red, brown and gray-green shades, dominantly argillites with intercalated beds of limestone and quartzite. Park units formerly classed as Shepard and Kintla Formations as well as local members of the Spokane Formation are now usually correlated within the Missoula Group.

4.6   **Kootenai Creek**   **50.8**

The forests on PYRAMID PEAK (7399) to the right were burned in 1929. The first of many stunning views of the park peaks is on the left.

5.5   **Ousel Creek**   **49.2**

At its mouth LINCOLN CREEK, across the Flathead River, has cut through a broad gravel terrace. MT. BROWN (8565) at the head of Lake McDonald, can be seen up the narrow canyon of the creek. Lincoln Creek Trail (68) follows the stream to Lincoln Lake (4698), 9.4 miles. At 5.8 miles it is joined by Lincoln Lake Trail (47), coming from Going-to-the-Sun Road, 4.4 miles farther. As there are no bridges over the Middle Fork from West Glacier to Walton, a distance of over 30 miles, access to trails in the park is made either by fording the river or via South Boundary Trail (67), starting at park headquarters or Walton Ranger Station. Check at the Walton Ranger Station (406) 888-5628 for conditions of trails and river fords.

6.5 L   **Harrison Creek Trail**   **R 48.7**

Across the Flathead River Harrison Creek Trail (69) goes 2.9 miles up Harrison Valley to HARRISON LAKE (3693), 2.5 miles long. The established trail ends 2.0 miles above the lake. HARRISON CREEK has recently shifted several times on the gravel bar across its mouth. The creek receives the melt waters of impressive Harrison Glacier on Mt. Jackson and drains Harrison Lake. STANTON MT. (7750), MT. VAUGHT (8850) and HEAVENS PEAK (8987) project over the ridges to the northwest. MT. JACKSON (10,052) and BLACKFOOT MT. (9574) are seen up Harrison Valley. Blackfoot Mt. is a quarter-mile south of the Continental Divide but 1000 feet higher than it. A century ago when park glaciers were much larger than those of today, Blackfoot Glacier, then two square miles in area, spread like a blanket over the divide, and Blackfoot Mt. rose as a nunatak above its surface.

7.2 L   **Moccasin Creek**   **R 48.2**

GUNSIGHT MT. (9258) appears as a sharp spire to the left of Jackson. EDWARDS MT. (9072) is still farther to the left. The trail from Sperry Chalets to Sperry Glacier passes over COMEAU PASS (8000) between these two mountains. The broad hump of WALTON MT. (8926) is in front of Jackson. The mountain just across the river is LONEMAN MT. (7181). It has a fire lookout on the summit, accessible by trails 67 and 70 from Nyack Ford of the Middle Fork, 6.3 miles.

The road crosses a four-mile level stretch; from the lower end the awesome spire of ST. NICHOLAS (9376) is seen. The most striking peak in the vicinity, it is of special interest to the author since he climbed it during a storm on September 1, 1939, with constant climbing companion, glacier guide Leo Seethaler. Returning from the climb they learned that Germany had invaded Poland to start World War II. Some years before, Mr. Seethaler, who had been a guide in the Dolomites and Tyrolean Alps, came to work for the Glacier Park Hotel Co. Renowned for his skills as a guide on Grinnell and Sperry Glaciers, he was widely regarded as the greatest among many excellent climbers in park history.

10.5 A   **Nyack Mt.**   **45.0**

The broad summit in Flathead National Forest on the right is NYACK MT. (7750). The higher, sharper peak to the right of Nyack Mt. is MT. PENROSE (7875), named for Dr. Charles B. Penrose of Philadelphia who was seriously mauled by an enraged grizzly bear after he had shot her cub on GREAT BEAR MT. (7668), two miles west. Though every foot of the way had to be cleared, he was carried on a make-shift litter down what was later named Rescue Creek and rushed by train to a hospital. The story of the incident and his miraculous recovery was told in the National Geographic Magazine of February, 1908.

11.5 L   **Nyack (Red Eagle)**   **R 43.4**

Nyack Valley, across the Flathead River from this settlement, is the most imposing along the route. From the lowest elevation at the mouth (3350), MT. STIMSON (10,142) rises sheer above Nyack Creek. THREESUNS (8205) is in front of Stimson, and the wooded summits of THREETOPS (6790) are just across the river. MT. PINCHOT (9310) is to the right of Stimson. The craggy, claw-shaped pinnacle ahead is MT. DOODY (8640).

NYACK CREEK TRAIL (73) goes up forested, hook-shaped Nyack Valley. It may be reached by turning off U.S. 2 on a lane into the settlement, crossing the railroad tracks and fording the river above a horsehoe bend to the site of old Nyack ranger station and South Boundary Trail (67). The foot of Nyack Trail is across Nyack Creek, 0.7 mile downstream. The trail follows above the west bank around the base of Loneman Mt. to a locked patrol cabin (3650), 6.5 miles above the trail junction. In ascending farther, good views open up: especially of the three spires of Threesuns Mt.; the mighty wall of Mt. Stimson; Mt. Thompson (8527) and PUMPELLY GLACIER, which is on Blackfoot Mt. to the left up Thompson Creek; and, as Nyack Creek bends eastward, the sharp ridge of RAZOREDGE MT. (8560) looming above Pacific Creek. Quiet pools alternate with cascades in the stream, but in some places a gorge has been cut into the bedrock. 6.2 miles above the patrol cabin, historic, spectacular Red Eagle Pass Trail, now abandoned, climbed on the left to Red Eagle Pass (6640), thence dropping to Red Eagle Lake and St. Mary. Locked Upper Nyack Patrol Cabin (4455) is located 1.9 miles farther, a short distance below falls in Pacific Creek.

At 16.8 miles from the old Nyack Ranger Station, Nyack Creek Trail connects with Cut Bank Pass Trail (80) which embarks on a strenuous climb over Cut Bank Pass (7900), 21.8 miles to connect with Pitamakan Pass Trail (102) for Two Medicine, 29.5 miles, or for Cut Bank Campground, 32.2 miles from Nyack Ranger Station.

The foot of Cut Bank Pass Trail is steep and like the floor of Nyack Valley is in heavy timber. It climbs rapidly to an open, exposed alpine cirque with boggy flower gardens. The trail swings south and climbs the precipitous headwall by many switchbacks to the ridge connecting McCLINTOCK PEAK (8285) on the Continental Divide and TINKHAM MT. (8442), formerly Camels Hump, which is the culmination of a spur trending west. A good topographic map is essential for direction. As distant views grow increasingly magnificent, awesome Razoredge Mt. and the wall of the Divide are to the north and east. Pumpelly and Harrison Glaciers and the rugged companions of Mt. Jackson are in the west. Approaches to Cut Bank Pass on both west and east sides are over steep, slippery, treacherous scree.

2.2 miles above its junction with Cut Bank Pass Trail (80), Nyack Creek Trail (73) continues as SURPRISE PASS TRAIL (74) coming from the southwest.

From its northern end on Nyack Creek, Surprise Pass Trail ascends a tributary which like Avalanche Creek above Avalanche Campground has incised a narrow gorge in highly colored argillite. As the defile widens, brushland and meadow replace forest; the trail crosses from the east to west banks only to recross again a half-mile farther upstream. Passage is difficult and novices may have difficulty keeping on the trail. The valley is quite broad and Surprise Pass (5760) is wooded, so that transit would be unnoticed were it not for the location sign on the summit. The pass lies between MTS. PHILLIPS (9494) and PINCHOT, 2.5 miles above Nyack Creek trail junction. The southern end of the trail is 0.7 mile farther at another T-junction on COAL CREEK.

The left hand member is COAL CREEK TRAIL (75). The right hand member, MARTHAS BASIN TRAIL (76), climbs rapidly up the forested stream to a fork at 0.9 mile in the double cirque called MARTHAS BASIN. The left limb proceeds ahead 0.5 mile farther to BUFFALO WOMAN LAKE (6090) nestled beneath a small waterfall under highly colored cliffs of EAGLEHEAD MT. (9140) and PERIL PEAK (8645). The right limb rises 0.7 mile to BEAVER WOMAN LAKE (5870) in a rocky, shrubby niche on Mt. Pinchot.

Below Surprise Pass, Coal Creek and trail 75 sweep boldly from southeast to due west, confined in a narrow canyon beneath beetling crags of CAPER PEAK (8310) and BATTLEMENT MT. (8830) on the left, CLOUDCROFT PEAKS (8690) and Mt. Doody on the right. The many-pinnacled ridge of Battlement Mt. terminates in "The Frightful Cliffs" of St. Nicholas, awesomely rising a mile above the valley floor.

Locked Coal Creek Patrol Cabin (3850) is passed at 11.6 miles from Surprise Pass. As Coal Creek enters a gorge cut 200 feet deep into a river terrace for more than a mile above its mouth, Coal Creek Trail leaves it and turns abruptly south. Thin beds of impure, low-grade coal outcrop in places along the stream but have attracted little attention. Sites of old timber operations, fortunately small, occur in the bottomland. These were never cleaned up nor has their mess been obliterated with time.

South Boundary Trail (67) is met again at 15.0 miles from Surprise Pass and followed 0.3 mile west to a spur which drops 0.4 mile beneath big cottonwoods to the Coal Creek Ford in a broad rippling stretch of the Middle Fork Flathead River. It then climbs 150 feet up the opposite bank to the top of the terrace on which the railroad and U.S. 2 are located 0.3 mile away. The trail circuit around Mt. Stimson from Nyack village via Nyack Creek, Surprise Pass and Coal Creek trails and back to U.S. 2 is under 38 miles.

Instead of using the Coal Creek Ford across the Middle Fork, the hiker can continue on the South Boundary Trail back to the Nyack Ford for a complete trail circuit.

12.0	Railroad Overpass	43.5

Rescue Creek is crossed at mile 12.3. The road runs at river grade for the next three miles. A second viaduct is at mile 14.8, with Mt. Doody ahead on the left.

15.2 R	Crystal Creek	L 40.2

On the far side of the bridge, a serpentine forest lane climbs a mile to the site of former GARRY LOOKOUT TOWER in the national forest. The forest along the roadside burned in 1984.

15.5 L	Coal Creek	R 40.0

The mouth of Coal Creek is across the Middle Fork. For access to the ford and the foot of Coal Creek Trail (75) described above, cross the tracks at mile 16.5 to a lane on the other side. Follow it to the left to the ford, a half mile away. See mile 11.5.

Mt. St. Nicholas and Battlement Mt. from Highway 2. Mel Ruder photo.

17.3 R   Stanton Creek   L 38.2

A pleasant trail into the national forest's Great Bear Wilderness follows the northwest bank of the creek to STANTON LAKE, a mile above, set in a subalpine basin beneath GRANT GLACIER on MT. GRANT (8590) and STANTON GLACIER on GREAT NORTHERN MT. (8705), highest in the Flathead Range.

20.1   Tunnel Creek   35.4

Much of the forest along the highway is pure lodgepole, indicating that fires have burned through the valley in the past. DOUBLE MT. (6003) is across the Flathead River. St. Nicholas, visible in its broadest profile, is up the valley of MUIR CREEK. Great Northern Mt. and its associated glaciers can be seen from the highway by looking back to the southwest on the road curve at mile 20.8.

21.0   Pinnacle Hamlet   34.0

21.9   Paola Creek   32.5

25.0   Dickey Creek   30.4

The big valley across the Flathead River is that of PARK CREEK.

PARK CREEK TRAIL (85) goes upstream 11.4 miles to connect with Two Medicine Pass Trail (87) for Two Medicine. Access to Park Creek Trail can be made by following South Boundary Trail (67) for 3.2 miles from Walton Ranger Station at mile 27.7.

Notable views of peaks along wooded Park Creek Trail include CHURCH BUTTE (8808) named for its tall spire; STATUARY MT. (8250) for its many statuesque pinnacles; and VIGIL PEAK (8593) after a mountain goat that kept close surveillance over topographer R. T. Evans as he mapped this region early in this century. MT. ROCKWELL (9272) prominent in the Two Medicine area, makes its first appearance from an open tract farther upstream.

At Upper Park Creek Patrol Cabin and campground (4800), 14.6 miles from Walton, LAKE ISABEL TRAIL (86) goes 2.3 miles to LAKE ISABEL (5715), a destination popular with fishermen who usually start at Two Medicine. Park Creek Trail ends officially at Upper Park Creek Cabin, but TWO MEDICINE PASS TRAIL (87) starts here and goes over TWO MEDICINE PASS (7440) to Two Medicine, 11.8 miles beyond.

27.1 R   Essex   L 28.4

Spur to Essex depot above on the terrace. Hotel, dining service and post office are available. ESSEX CREEK is crossed at mile 27.2.

27.7   Flathead River   27.7

Bridge over the Middle Fork Flathead River, rebuilt after the 1964 flood. The north bank of the river is the boundary of Glacier National Park. WALTON RANGER STATION (3760) and picnic area are located under sturdy larches which have survived the many fires along the river.

South Boundary Trail (67) starts at the ranger station for its long stretch of 31 miles to park headquarters at West Glacier. The trail is not maintained between Park Creek and Coal Creek, but a detour can be made around this washed-out section by following the Fielding-Coal Creek Trail (82) between Park and Coal Creeks.

Trail 67 serves locally as access to Ole Creek Trail (89), 1.1 miles, and Scalplock Lookout Trail (91), 1.3 miles. The latter climbs to the fire lookout on SCALPLOCK MT. (6919), 4.5 miles from Walton. The mountain was named from a thin line of trees that have escaped fires and stand on the crest below the summit.

OLE CREEK TRAIL ascends Ole Creek beneath Scalplock Mt., then passes along the bases of SHEEP MT. (8569), BRAVE DOG MT. (8446) and BARRIER BUTTES (7402), while RUNNING RABBIT MT. (7674), MT. SHIELDS (7131), ELK MT. (7835), LITTLE DOG MT. (8610) and SKELETON MT. (7480) appear in sequence across the valley. At 7.2 miles from Walton, trail 89 crosses FIELDING-COAL CREEK Trail (82) which connects Coal Creek, 2.1 miles above Coal Creek Patrol Cabin, with Fielding Patrol Cabin on the horseshoe bend of the railroad above road mile 38.6, a trail length of 16.7 miles. At 16.6 miles from Walton, trail 89 reaches OLE LAKE (5535) and bends right above DEBRIS CREEK, which it crosses 0.4 mile farther.

A quarter-mile above the trail crossing at an elevation of 5800 feet, Debris Creek has cut clear through the Lewis Thrust Fault block, exposing a small area of underlying Cretaceous strata. Such an erosional break through a thrust fault mass, exposing rock upon which it rests, is called a "fenster," from the German word for window. This is the only place in the park where such a singular geological feature can be seen. Some believe that Debris Creek received its name from the resultant jumble of rubble, but this is not so. Topographers of the region named the creek after debris left by hot forest fires early in the century. These fires also yielded names: Firebrand Pass, from an ember carried by winds to ignite more forest across the pass; Skeleton Mt. from the skeletal masts of burned trees; Jackstraw Lake from a tangle of prostrate trunks, and Soldier Mt. (7320) for soldiers drafted to fight the fire.

19.5 miles from Walton, Ole Creek Trail (89) officially ends on FIREBRAND PASS (6951), but the trail continues as FIREBRAND PASS TRAIL (90), dropping in 4.8 miles past the site of the former Lubec Ranger Station, burned in 1980, to Highway 2 at False Summit, mile 49.1.

For the next half-mile above Walton Ranger Station, the forest along the Middle Fork is verdant with spruce, fir, white pine, larch, cottonwood and aspen. This is the last remnant along the route to resemble the lush forests of the Pacific slope. The road is built along Running Rabbit Mt., which, like Mt. Shields and Snowslip Mt. (7290), bears the scars of repeated fires. However, the resulting open slopes make good winter range, so that wildlife is frequently seen from both automobiles and trains. The Middle Fork cuts through broad terraces appearing across the river below Mt. Cameahwait (7879). Maintenance of this section of the railroad is troublesome and very expensive. For this reason, it is the subject of continuous, exhaustive study.

29.4 R	Goat Lick Exhibit	L 26.1

The grayish clay at the river's edge contains minerals which attract mountain goats to this exceptionally low site (3800) opposite the mouth of Sheep Creek. As many as 70 animals have been counted as they briskly lick the rocks. The best time to see them is either early or late in the day, mostly spring and early summer.

A convenient parking area with short trail to a viewpoint of the lick allows observers to avoid traffic congestion and hazards of the main road above. In February 1979, the highway bridge here was swept away by an avalanche to lie for several years as a pile of twisted debris near the river far below. The bridge and road near here were rebuilt in 1981 with underpasses for the goats incorporated in the design. During winters when conditions are ripe, avalanches temporarily close both the railroad and the highway.

31.1	Park Boundary	24.3

Leaving Glacier National Park, the road swerves from southeast to northeast and ascends BEAR CREEK. Middle Fork Canyon continues southeast for another 20 miles.

33.2 L	Snowslip Mt.	R 19.3

The top of Snowslip Mt. on the left is Helena (Siyeh) limestone with the diorite member visible at 36.4 miles. The numerous snowsheds over the railroad indicate the instability of the snowpack above. The rumble of a passing train can start an avalanche that shoots over the roofs of the sheds into the canyon.

36.0 R	Silver Stairs	L 19.5

The shimmery creek ripples daintily over thin ledges of rock.

36.3 R	Campground	L 19.2

Devil Creek is a Forest Service campground. The creek drains a basin behind DEVILS

HUMP (7667) on the right. Ahead is pyramidal LITTLE DOG MT. with BLACKTAIL HILLS (6092) to the left.

The dark, soft, shaly beds of Blacktail Hills are of Cretaceous or earlier age. Fire-scarred ELK MT. (7835) is across AUTUMN CREEK to the left of Blacktail Hills. The fault line of the Lewis Thrust Fault is at the eastern base of Elk Mt. and is buried under valley fill as it crosses under the highway somewhere near Fielding (see below). The Autumn Creek Trail (93) which lies in Glacier Park above the road and railroad tracks is a popular crosscountry ski route, but gets light use from hikers. Skiers start the trail from the Summit end, just off Marias Pass, mile 44.1.

The formation of the mountains south of the park are of Paleozoic Age, being much younger than those of park ranges, but much older than underlying rocks upon which they too have been overthrust. Similar Paleozoic strata probably lay above the Algonkian formations exposed in the park; these have been completely worn away because the upward thrust in the park area is higher by many thousands of feet than that south of U.S. 2.

38.2 L   McCarthysville Flats   R 17.3

The camp of McCarthysville flourished near this site in railroad construction days when lawlessness was rife. It bore the reputation as the wildest, wickedest town in Montana.

38.6 R   Fielding   R 16.8

Across the valley on the left, the railroad makes a famous horseshoe curve while climbing arduously in broad Fielding Valley. The access road to the Ole Creek Trail (89) and Elk Mt. turns left (north) about 0.2 mile east of the Bear Creek Bridge. Hikers should park by the gravel pit, then walk up the dirt road, taking the first right fork. The trailhead lies across the railroad tracks. Three-tenths mile up trail 89, just beyond a locked patrol cabin, the Elk Mt. Trail (92) branches right, climbing steeply in 2.5 miles to the site of a former lookout. With its southern exposure, Trail 92 often offers early season access and excellent views of Mt. St. Nicholas and to the south, the Great Bear Wilderness.

42.3 R   Skyland Creek   L 13.1

The highway makes its final curving ascent to the Continental Divide.

Above mile 43.0 the rocks in roadcuts on the right are fissile, black Jurassic shale interbedded with sandy limestone. LITTLE DOG MT. is the northwest guardian of Marias Pass and appears from this place over the forest on the left. "Little Dog" was the name of the Blackfeet chieftain who accurately described the location of Marias Pass to Governor Isaac I. Stevens of Washington Territory in 1855, thus starting a 34-year search for it.

The name was formerly applied to the present BRAVE DOG MT., a peak across Ole Creek Valley four miles west and not visible from Summit. Present Little Dog Mt. was unnamed at the time. The author suggested these changes to the National Board of Geographic Names as being more suitable commemoration of significant history. The Brave Dogs are a distinguished society of the Blackfeet, who maintained discipline and order during vital buffalo drives. Equidistant with Little Dog Mt. from the pass, FLATTOP MT. (6640), in the national forest, is the less impressive southwest anchor. Higher, greenish SUMMIT MT. (8770) appears as a twin behind and to the right of Little Dog Mt.

44.1   Marias Pass   11.3

Locally pronounced Ma-rye-us, with accent on middle syllable. At the head of Marias River, the pass (5216) was named by Meriwether Lewis for his cousin, Miss Maria Wood. Upon approaching it from the west the road skirts the Blacktail Hills in a constricting canyon and climbs briskly by bold curves to the broad, flat pass on the Continental Divide.

A tall granite obelisk on the summit, commemorating the leadership of Teddy Roosevelt in forest conservation, rises squarely in the middle of the road. A plaque nearby on the south side of the road recognizes William Morrison, a trapper and prospector who donated the title to this land, his home for many years, so that it might be used as a memorial to TR.

A heroic statue of John Franklin Stevens in winter garb stands near the obelisk. Engineer Stevens explored the pass on a bitter December day in 1889 and found it feasible for a railroad. Coonsa Creek to the east was named for his Flathead guide, left at this place as Stevens pushed onward alone. In 1905 Stevens was selected by President Roosevelt to be Chief Engineer of the Panama Canal. The successful completion of the canal is the result mainly of this brilliant appointment. North of the tracks is the Summit (94) trailhead. In 1.0 mile it joins the Autumn Creek Trail which then covers 4.2 miles to its terminus at Autumn Creek (refer to mile 36.3).

Ice Age glaciers on Marias Pass apparently moved northeast from a center far southwest of today's Continental Divide to merge with Two Medicine Glacier. THREE BEARS LAKE (5282) on the divide a half-mile northwest of the pass, drains into Summit Creek, tributary to Two Medicine River. The big basin above appears from the drainage pattern to have contributed at one time to the lake; it now holds the headwaters of Bear Creek, which with its steeper gradient and greater erosive power, has stolen the upper tributaries of Summit Creek. Among the colorful terms for the diversion of flow from one stream to another through headward growth are "piracy," "stream robbery," "stream capture" and "beheading."

For some dozen miles the passage straddling the summit is officially designated as THEODORE ROOSEVELT PASS. The Continental Divide forms the boundary between Lewis and Clark National Forest and Flathead National Forest. A Forest Service campground is on the right at mile 44.2.

| 49.1 | False Summit | 6.4 |

At highway mile post number 203 the road crosses False Summit (5084) , the low divide between Summit and Railroad Creeks. The barricaded lane on the left ascends a half mile past the site of the former Lubec Ranger Station to the foot of Firebrand Pass Trail (90). Within a mile this trail meets AUTUMN CREEK TRAIL (93) to East Glacier Park (8.1 miles from the junction) and with OLE CREEK TRAIL (89) on Firebrand Pass, 4.4 miles from Lubec. Refer to mile 27.7.

| 49.2 R | The Old Squaw | L 6.9 |

A towering pinnacle of green argillite broke off from the northeast summit of SQUAW MT. (7353) to slide 500 feet down the talus, a half-mile from the summit mass. It is clearly visible on the right skyline of the mountain.

The trace of the Lewis Thrust Fault line is distinct at the base of the cliffs to the northwest (sharp left). Dark patches of Cretaceous shales show through the talus beneath. Altyn limestone is very thin or missing altogether in this section; but a long, pale, sharp-pointed sliver of Altyn has been thrust like a dagger into darker Appekunny argillite in the wall northeast of Summit Mt. The black outcrops and roadcuts expose crumbly Cretaceous shale. Much of the country east of the Continental Divide is treeless, in large part owing to repeated fires.

| 49.3 L | Lubec Lake | R 6.0 |

Inhabited by beaver. Many waterfowl nest in the vicinity, and sharp-tailed grouse appear on the road at times. After crossing an old lake bed, the road and creek have cut through a series of tilted ledges of hard, brownish Cretaceous sandstone.

| 52.7 | Blackfeet Reservation | 2.8 |

Leaving Lewis and Clark National Forest and entering Blackfeet Indian Reservation, the road crosses a willowy marsh and rounds a low shoulder, revealing the wide expanse of plains covered with ground moraine of Two Medicine Glacier. The rim of the deep canyon of Two Medicine River is a dark dent in the middle ground ahead.

| 54.2 R | Heart Butte Road | L 1.3 |

A dirt road follows the mountain base through Indian country to Heart Butte community, 25 miles away. Railroad Creek has cut deeply into Cretaceous strata and plunges over a ledge as DAWSON FALLS, only a quarter-mile off the road but not visible from it. The waterfall is accessible from the Heart Butte road.

55.3   **Midvale Creek**   **0.1**

The mountains to the left from Summit Mt. northeast are CALF ROBE (7948), RED CROW (7891), SQUAW and BISON (7833). Firebrand Pass is between Calf Robe and Red Crow Mts.

Calf Robe, a Blackfeet, is the character in a tale which some ethnologists aver is an example of the beginning of a neo-myth. Some time in the 1870's Calf Robe was so seriously injured on a marauding raid far to the south, that his companions were forced to abandon him, placing him beside a brook, leaving plenty of food and making him as comfortable as possible until death.

Awakening from a state of delirium, he was horrified to see a grizzly leering above him. In stoic calm he closed his eyes tightly in silent prayer that dispatch should come quickly and painlessly. In suspense, the agony he was suffering was for the moment blocked out as a soft breeze cooled his fever and the little stream chanted his requiem. Miraculously he felt the soft fur and soothing warmth of the animal's body being drawn close to him. The bear licked his wounds, each stroke of the tongue alleviating pain.

After a time the beast disappeared, only to return, dragging warm, freshly-killed meat to his ward. Under such care Calf Robe gradually recovered and wounds healed. One day the grizzly repeatedly withdrew a short distance, only to come back, lie down and gently nuzzle his patient, indicating as best he could that Calf Robe should cling to his coat. Responding to the urging, the injured man grasped tightly and was transported little by little, day by day, in the direction he knew was towards home. Thus the couple inched along until they reached the draw that extends to Fort Benton.

The inhabitants of the village, excited by the appearance of a fearful adversary close to their hearths, raised a clamor, and the grizzly quickly disappeared, leaving Calf Robe with a prayer of thanksgiving for deliverance and a mental kiss for his savior.

This story was related to the author through his interpreter-friend, Dick Sanderville, as told by the son of Calf Robe, an old man living in Heart Butte in the 1930's and a firm believer in its veracity. Sometimes the tale is told with Eagle Plume as principal.

55.4   **East Glacier Park**   **0.0**

At the subway under the railway, U.S. 2 proceeds ahead to Browning, 13 miles, the headquarters of the Blackfeet Indian Reservation with its superb Museum of the Plains Indian. Montana 49, the Blackfeet Highway, starts with the left turn under the subway.

Blackfeet Highway

Montana State Highway 49 from East Glacier Park to Kiowa Junction, and U.S. 89 from Kiowa to Carway, Alberta, on the International Border. East Glacier Park to Kiowa, 11.0 miles; to the St. Mary end of Going-to-the-Sun Road, 31.2 miles; to Carway, 49.8 miles.

Throughout its length, the Blackfeet Highway parallels the front range of the Rockies, snow-white in winter, bizarrely streaked with snow in summer. The road winds over glaciated hills and skips across broad valleys, excavated not by the small streams of today but by tongues of ice thrust from the mountains and by raging melt waters in a waning Ice Age. The route invades grasslands, gay with myriads of wild flowers; penetrates willow marshes; winds through open parks of Douglas fir and limber pines deformed and flattened by storms; twists between thickets of trembling aspen; and passes by groves of venerable cottonwoods and forests of firs and lodgepoles.

Wildlife along the way pursues its day-to-day struggle for life. At times, moose, elk, deer or bear saunter up the right-of-way. Porcupines show up unexpectedly on the pavement. Coyotes slip through the tall grass surging in the wind. Badgers burrow in sunny prairies. Whenever a car approaches, ground squirrels never fail to recall something attractive on the other side of the road, thus scampering to be crushed and become the meal for a hungry scavenger.

Waterfowl dot the faces of ponds and waterholes whose reed and sedge-lined borders are haunts of phalaropes, grebes and snipe. In the willowy thickets, brilliant redstarts and Macgillivray warblers flit in tireless search for insects and are joined in chorus by veeries and catbirds. Visitors often inquire about the magpies, big, handsome birds of the open with flashy, irridescent black and white plumage and long, wedge-shaped tails. Marsh hawks, with conspicuous white rump-patches, glide low over wildflower meadows in an unceasing search for rodents. Both magpies and marsh hawks are common in Waterton Lakes Park. Big, high-flying red-tailed hawks perch for hours on exposed fence posts or snags. Kingbirds nest in the serviceberry bushes and dart forth to harass ravens and hawks that venture too close, so the Indian calls the kingbird "stingy-with-its-berries." By aimlessly strutting about the pavement and disdainfully ignoring passing autos, blue grouse show why people call them foolhens. Black cowbirds, the males with brown heads, perch as bonny companions upon the backs of stock. They swagger fearlessly like self-important personalities between the feet of people and saddlehorses, even, at times, adopting a particular camp by moving in for intimate association with campers.

A traveler assaying the gravelly lanes of the Blackfeet Reservation sees horned larks emerging suddenly and repeatedly, as if out of the very roadbed, flying a short, sinuous course, twisting sharply to face one's car and seemingly dissolving mysteriously into the road again. Or if fancy leads a stroller over the glacial outwash, he can hardly be deaf to the noisy, insistent "kill-dee" or remain indifferent to the broken-wing performance of killdeer trying to lure the intruder away from their territory. These plovers, slightly bigger than robins, are strikingly marked by two black bands across their breasts and by ruddy-golden tails. At dusk nighthawks zoom in and out of the beams of the headlights as they swoop on flying insects. At night the Indians spun tales about this bird of beautiful wings to eager youngsters whose eyes reflected the glimmer of the fire around which they huddled close.

This journey retraces the ancient North Trail used by Indians traveling along the base of the mountains from Central Alberta to Old Mexico. The route gave title to the book, "The Old North Trail," in which Walter McClintock relates his experiences among the Blackfeet early in the century. In places, ruts worn deeply into the ground by numberless travois still remain as vestiges of a vanished age.

MILES FROM EAST GLACIER		MILES FROM CARWAY
0.0	**East Glacier Park**	49.8

The highway begins at the railroad underpass in EAST GLACIER PARK (4795), Montana, although travelers from the east on U.S. 2 can join the route by continuing on U.S. 89 from

Browning to Kiowa Camp at mile 11.9. The Burlington Northern depot, called Glacier Park, serves as the principal entry for visitors arriving by rail from the east. The numerous facilities include good motels, cafes, service stations, shops, taverns and the post office of East Glacier Park, Montana 59434. The National Park Service has a subdistrict office on the highway, 0.5 mile northwest of the depot.

East Glacier Park is located two miles east of the park boundary on the Blackfeet Indian Reservation. Before World War II, the village was a melting pot of west and east, of Indians, cowboys, adventurers, playboys, ranchmen, businessmen and financiers. Traces of this interesting mixture persist although the town has grown from a row of false-front wooden buildings in a sprawl of log huts to a busy, modern tourist center. Before the opening of Theodore Roosevelt Highway over Marias Pass in the thirties, its road connections with Essex and West Glacier across the mountains were 400 miles of seasonal, unimproved dirt roads, via Great Falls and Butte or via the Crowsnest Pass in Canada and Fernie, B.C.

Since the establishment of Glacier National Park, impressive Glacier Park Lodge has dominated the scene. Set on a rise above Midvale Creek west of the depot, its backdrop is a wall of mountain. Indians call the main structure "Big Trees Lodge." The stanchions of its facade and three-story open-raftered lobby are Douglas fir logs five feet in diameter, hauled from the Pacific Northwest over the Great Northern Railroad. A double promenade between beds of bright garden flowers leads to the entrance. Glacier Park Inc., which operates the lodges and cabin camps in the park, has its summer offices in this building. Bus trips in the park start from the lodge entrance and the depot. Arrangements for special transportation are made at the lobby desk. Visitors can drive about the reservation or to dude ranches nearby. Horses may be rented for rides. Hikes can be made to Bald Hill, Bison Mt. and Scenic Point. For other diversions the Lodge operates a 9-hole golf course, swimming pool, cocktail lounge and grillroom in which an orchestra plays evenings for dancing. A barbershop and beauty parlor are in the basement.

The road, running northwest from the depot and the lodge, crosses the golf course, colored a heavenly blue in spring by camas, a lily whose bulbs were a staple food of western Indians. An office of the National Park Service is on the right at 0.5 mile.

The two-story log house across the street from the cluster of National Park Service structures was the studio of John Clark, deaf-mute Blackfeet sculptor and wood carver called by the Indians "Catapuis," or "Talks Not." Some of his larger works are valued in thousands of dollars; samples of his handiwork adorn tables in park facilities as lampshade bases and bookends.

The prominent trapezoidal summit at the right of the reentrant to Marias Pass is SQUAW MOUNTAIN (7353), named for the huge pillar readily discernible on the talus below the summit cliffs. The "OLD SQUAW" is Appekunny argillite which broke from the thrust fault mass and slumped down slippery underlying Cretaceous shales. Colorful Midvale Basin is north of Squaw Mt. In the old days beaters drove game through the narrow entrance, where helpers would lurk to kill it; hence, early settlers called it "The Slaughter House." The summits of BEARHEAD MT. (8406), MT. ELLSWORTH (8581) and adjacent peaks behind the basin are carved from maroon Grinnell argillite.

Since the last Ice Age, Two Medicine River has dug a gorge several hundred feet deep in the forest to the right of the highway. The gorge cuts through upturned, folded and faulted Cretaceous rocks which indicate that 4000 or more feet of marine and freshwater strata were disturbed and pushed northeast by the same forces responsible for the Lewis Thrust Fault.

| 2.5 | Two Medicine River | 47.3 |

Two Medicine River flows through the Marias River into the Missouri. Cottonwoods, locally called balsam poplars, attain great size along the stream, liked by swimmers and picnickers. In early spring twigs of the willows at the water's edge display three distinct shades of orange. The lane to the right leads to the summit of the ridge and the first road built from Glacier Park Station to Many Glacier about 1910.

| 4.1L | Two Medicine Road | R 45.7 |

Automobile route into Two Medicine Valley. LOWER TWO MEDICINE LAKE (4882),

on the left, was formed by the alluvial fan of Fortymile Creek flowing from BISON MOUN-
TAIN (7833) across the valley. The dam at the foot of the lake is part of an irrigation project
started before Glacier National Park was established in 1910. A small auto campground is
across the river.

The highway takes a sinuous course to the summit of TWO MEDICINE RIDGE, locally
called "Looking Glass Hill," because Indians aver that from its summit under certain atmospheric conditions Rising Wolf Mt. shines like a polished black-glass mirror. The road
passes aspen thickets, gnarled Douglas fir, and occasional burned snags. In 1919 a forest fire
denuded all of lower Two Medicine Valley. It was started by a lighted cigarette tossed by a
careless horseback rider.

In early season large yellow flowers of balsamroot brighten the drab herbage as it stirs after
its winter sleep. Purple phacelias, blue penstemons and evening primroses blossom along the
edge of the road in June. Later, Indian paintbrushes, accented by hardy asters, gaillardias and
hollyhocks, cover hills and meadows with gay colors.

7.9	Two Medicine View	41.9

Both Lower Two Medicine and Two Medicine Lakes can be seen from the pullout as they lie
in the typical U-shaped glacial valley. The imposing peak north of the upper lake is RISING
WOLF MT. (9513), after the Indian name of Hugh Monroe, a Scotsman who came to this
region in 1813 and lived with the Piegan tribe. Aptly named RED MT. (9377) is across Dry
Fork Valley to the north of Rising Wolf; its eastern ridge terminates in SPOT MT. (7831),
which is nearest us on the left. MT. ROCKWELL (9272), the biggest mountain to the left of
Rising Wolf, is on the Continental Divide back of Two Medicine Lake. Its northeastern ridge
terminates in SINOPAH MT. (8271), the bold pyramid at the head of the lake. The long ridge
extending north from the summit of Rockwell has a profile of the head, withers and low rump
of a bison bull in the act of getting up, hence its name, conferred by the author, RISING BULL
RIDGE. The colorful red shale slopes south of Rockwell, bisected by the conical, rich-colored
PAINTED TEPEE PEAK (7650), lead to Two Medicine Pass (7440). SCENIC POINT (7522)
on Mt. Henry Trail (96) is the summit of the yellow cliff south of Lower Two Medicine Lake.
HEART BUTTE (6863), 30 miles to the south, is the salient outlier of the front range of the
Rockies. Heart Butte is a center of Blackfeet history and activity.

8.4	Two Medicine Ridge	41.4

Due to erosion and a creep of the soft underlying beds, slumping of early glacial deposits has
produced the sag through which the highway passes. The mountains visible from Spot Mt.
north are BASIN (6920), MAD WOLF (8341) and DIVIDE (8665). The steepness of the
mountain front is due to the Lewis Thrust Fault. The mountain rocks are far more resistant
than the rocks of the plains which erode easily.

The highest parts of Two Medicine Ridge (6288), like Cut Bank and Milk River Ridges
farther north, are capped by early Pleistocene deposits but were not overridden by subsequent
Wisconsin glaciers. Tillite from earliest glaciation is well exposed in a gravel pit to the right
on the crest above the road; it has weathered into pinnacles. That this is older than drift lower

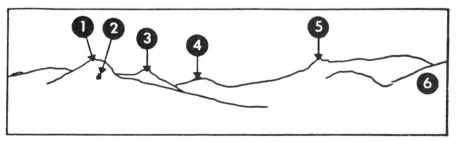

From East Glacier Park: (1) Squaw; (2) the Old Squaw; (3) Bearhead; (4) Ellsworth;
(5) Henry; (6) Bison.

in the valley is inferred from the degree of cementation and of weathering of component materials which are similar to those of adjacent mountain bedrock. Surface layers have been leached of soluble matter, and the conspicuous diorite boulders are crumbly and more altered than those found in younger till. Although not deep enough by several hundred feet to reach the top of the ridge in the Wisconsin stage, Two Medicine Glacier, once freed from confinement in narrow valleys, expanded into a 20-mile wide piedmont glacier which extended 40 miles beyond the mountain front.

10.0 L **Plains Vegetation** **R 39.8**

The ridge to the north has vertical strips of grassland alternating in a conspicuous manner with strips of stunted timber. In this region of scant moisture, thin soil, porous subsoil, high winds and severe climate, trees cannot secure a foothold in sites of excessive exposure, so grassland is the result. However, if they can start in a semi-sheltered location, trees may grow in tortured, twisted shapes, their height and appearance roughly indicating the degree of protection by adjacent environment and accumulation of snow. Their habit conforms principally to prevailing winds. In a favored locale, a group may give enough mutual protection for a thicket to appear which can coddle tender young conifers which otherwise could not persist to an age of hardy self-sufficiency. Certain plants grow where moisture is plentiful, depending on whether it is seasonal or permanent, and whether it is limited to the surface or extends deeply underground. These varying factors determine the sharp delimitations of vegetation seen along the route.

10.5 L **Cretaceous Folding** **R 39.3**

The road cut on the farther side of the curve exposes closely folded friable sandstone and thinly-bedded Cretaceous shales. Both ends of the series terminate in faults. This kind of deformation, common on the plains, was probably produced by forces associated with those responsible for the Lewis Thrust Fault.

10.9 **Roadside Plants** **38.9**

In late summer bright-red, porcelain-like fruits of baneberry shine under the robust cottonwoods as the road curves sharply. The abundant, sturdy herbs are cow parsnips, standing five feet tall; they have large, three-lobed leaves and bear umbels, six or more inches across, of white flowers of two sizes. Indians used the tender shoots for food and the rounded, flat fruits for ceremonials.

11.9 **Kiowa Junction** **37.8**

Montana 49 merges into U.S. 89 coming from Great Falls and Yellowstone. The name is misplaced because the Kiowas have lived in Colorado and Oklahoma since 1840. Ethnologist James Mooney described them as the most predatory tribe of all prairie Indians.

12.9 **Wet Flats** **36.7**

Native iris blooms on the wet flats until July. The rounded knolls on the right mark a stage of retreat of a small glacier formerly occupying Lake Creek Valley while dropping the large limestone boulder to the left of the road at mile 14.7.

15.6 **Cut Bank Ridge** **34.2**

The road climbs Cut Bank Ridge in a series of sharp curves and crosses at an elevation of 5400 feet at mile 15.6.

The prominence on the east is Red Blanket Butte (5646) on which Onistaipokah (White Calf), the last head chief of the Pikuni, was buried. His son, Two Guns White Calf, welcomed visitors arriving on trains at East Glacier Park through the early 30's. He claimed that he was used as the model for the Indian on the buffalo nickel, whom he strongly resembled. The artist, however, has asserted that the face is a composite.

Downstream Cut Bank Creek joins Two Medicine Creek to form Marias River which empties into the Missouri near Fort Benton. Once marked by a big pile of human bones nearby, Blackfeet and Kutenais had a bitter battle before the coming of the white men. The paved road to the right follows the stream past allotted Indian lands to an aircraft landing strip (8 miles) and to Browning (16 miles). The dirt road to the left goes up the valley over open range to the Cut Bank Ranger Station and Campground, 4.0 miles. Located in a mature lodgepole forest, the campground is the most primitive reached by road in the region. Trails 102 and 104 start from the roadhead for Two Medicine and Red Eagle respectively.

18.0   **Milk River Ridge**   **31.2**

Like Two Medicine Ridge, this ridge is covered with pre-Wisconsin drift but was not covered by the last Cut Bank Glacier, which was 700 feet thick at the bridge site; however, ice did spill through the sag to the northwest now used by the road, and extended three miles down Milk River Valley, otherwise free of ice at this point.

The ridge has many limber pines with branches flexible enough to be tied into knots. The dark-brown, deeply-fissured bark of older trees, like that of western white pines, is broken into rectangular blocks. Limber pine cones, three to eight inches long, are generally greenish in color. Mature, lopsided contorted trees are the favorites of photographers for framing distant views or illustrating subjects of character. Specimens up to 50 feet tall with large crowns and heavy trunks grow in Dry Fork Valley, described in the chapter on trails under Cut Bank via Pitamakan Pass, and near Granite Park. A limber pine is difficult to distinguish from whitebark pine, a timberline tree or shrub more common on the west slope. The whitish bark darkens to gray or light brown with aging of the tree. The cones, an inch-and-a-half to three inches long and generally purplish in color, remain closed at maturity. A whitebark pine may be seen on the right of the road at mile 18.4.

18.7 L   **Cut Bank Valley**   **R 31.0**

A splendid view up Cut Bank Valley. Mountains, L to R, are MAD WOLF (8341); EAGLE PLUME (8724); STIMSON (10,142), which is in the Pacific drainage across the Continental Divide; RAZOREDGE (8560) on the Divide; JAMES (9375); and KUPUNKA-MINT or "Shakes Himself" (8797), named for a Kutenai Indian. The trail over Cut Bank Pass and down Nyack Creek was formerly much used by Indians to travel across the mountains. At mile 19.7 the highway crosses MILK RIVER RIDGE (5656).

20.9   **South Fork Milk River**   **28.9**

Named by the Lewis and Clark Expedition because of its turbid white color, Milk River flows northeast into Canada, reenters the United States near Havre and flows east into the Missouri below Glasgow.

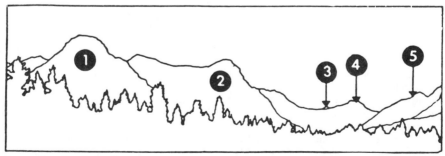

From Cut Bank Valley: (1) Mad Wolf; (2) Eagle Plume; (3) Stimson; (4) Razoredge; (5) James.

The highway climbs St. Mary Ridge, first in a pine forest, then up a grassy slope carpeted with many showy wildflowers. Lodgepole pines predominate in the lower forest nearest the highway, but these soon give way to spruces and firs. In early spring, pasque flowers, carpet pinks, shooting stars and spring beauties put on a lovely floral display; they are followed by bistorts, paintbrushes, bronze and orange agoseris, pink prairie smoke (used by the Blackfeet for sore eyes), geraniums, shrubby cinquefoil and many others.

As the road gains elevation, the vista of the grassy plains ahead presents a classic illustration of the topographic feature termed a peneplain, meaning "almost a plain." The uneroded crests of ridges extending from the mountain front are seen to be coextensive. This is interpreted to signify that before the mountains were uplifted, erosion had reduced the land to one of flat relief. When erosional forces were reactivated through uplift, lowering of the erosional base or change of climate, streams resumed their activity, again cutting into the smooth surface, a process known as rejuvenation. The beveled edges of the flats bordering the streams seen to the southeast indicate that there was more than one stage of peneplanation. Geologists recognize four distinct cycles of erosion in this landscape, possibly correlated with successive advance and retreat of ice. The Lewis Thrust Fault rests upon the highest of these erosional surfaces, believed to be contemporary with, if not an extension of, the Flaxville peneplain in northeast Montana.

DIVIDE MT. is the bold pyramid to the southwest. The three isolated summits of SWEETGRASS HILLS, formerly important to the Blackfeet as lookouts, float in the distant haze of the horizon 80 to 120 miles to the east. These buttes originated from an igneous intrusion which uplifted overlying sedimentary strata, later stripped off through erosion. During the Ice Age they were not locally glaciated or covered by the encircling Keewatin sheet but stood as great nunataks rising 2000 feet above its surface.

The highway reaches its highest elevation (6015) on ST. MARY RIDGE, part of Hudson Bay Divide. Drainage north is through the St. Mary-Saskatchewan-Nelson River system and south into the Missouri-Mississippi River basin. However, the high point of the road is not on the divide proper but on an extending spur.

After passing the high point on St. Mary Ridge, the highway drops slightly to the headwaters of Fox Creek, tributary to South Fork Milk River. A mile farther northwest, the main divide is crossed at an elevation of 5742 feet, in a roadside strip that has been logged by clearcutting.

As it moves into northern exposure the highway plunges into cool spruce-fir forest. A continuous border of beargrass frames the roadway to make a pleasing picture in years of abundant bloom. Early-flowering clematis trails over roadbanks, and vigorous lupines kindle their blue torches in midsummer.

Mountains new to the traveler come into view. MT. SIYEH (10,014), fifth highest in the park, is the first to appear directly ahead of the highway. To its left GOING-TO-THE-SUN MT. (9642) rises into the blue. At mile 27.4, there is an excellent view of its big snowbank, which resembles the head of an Indian looking to the south with the feathers of his war bonnet drooping to the north.

The image, slightly below the summit near the left profile of the mountain, has inspired a pleasant legend, but one Indian claim was woven by white men. In a time of dire stress the Great Spirit descended to live among His People, to teach them arts and crafts, how to get food and how to live. His mission accomplished, the people watched Him return to His home in the sun by way of this mountain. So that the lesson would not be forgotten He caused His image to be impressed in the eternal snow, labelled by the fabricator as the Face-of-Sour-Spirit-Who-Returned-Home-to-the-Sun-When-His-Work-Was-Done.

The point north of the summit, named by the author, is MATAHPI (Face or Person) PEAK (9365). LOGAN PASS lies behind and to the left of Going-to-the-Sun Mt. Other mountains, from right to left, are RED EAGLE (8881), CURLY BEAR (8099) and DIVIDE. SINGLESHOT MT. (7926) is directly ahead across St. Mary Lake.

A good view of ST. MARY LAKE (4484) extending into the mountains to the left and of LOWER ST. MARY LAKE (4471) extending due north at their feet. St. Mary is 292 feet deep, occupying a glacial valley. Its several appropriate Indian names were "Wind Maker Lake," "The Lake Inside," and "Walled-In Lake."

The two lakes are separated by coalescing alluvial fans built by Divide Creek on the south and Wild Creek on the north. W. C. Alden, an authority on local glaciology, estimated the thickness of St. Mary Glacier during the Ice Age to have been 1300 feet at the present park boundary. This was enough to cause it to spill over St. Mary Ridge, creating the gap passed through at mile 25.3. The lower lake, 50 to 70 feet deep, appears to be impounded by the fan built by Swiftcurrent Creek, which also crowds St. Mary River against the eastern bank so that it cuts into soft, friable sandstone of Cretaceous Age. Some believe that East Flattop Mountain is a remnant of pre-glacial topography. If this is true, the region was then of low relief compared with that of today.

Red Eagle Valley south of Red Eagle Mt. is an exemplary glaciated canyon. A rugged peak named ALMOST-A-DOG MT. (8922), after a Piegan Indian, is at the head of the valley to the left of Red Eagle Mt.

It is quite evident that the gently curving 3-lane highway is of fairly recent construction, as it drops to St. Mary and the outwash plain of Divide Creek, here forming the park boundary for four miles.

The chaotic spread of recent detritus evident here includes great boulders and thin, coarse, infertile soil on which sparse vegetation now struggles for a foothold. This is the picture left by the flood of June, 1964, greatest in recent history. An unprecedented winter snow pack was assaulted by warm, heavy rain. At 1:30 a.m. on June 8, the immediate area was reported inundated, with the settlement of St. Mary doomed. Quickly all valleys, even those with seasonal dry forks, were swept by raging torrents which tore away banks and spread over the countryside. Lake basins filled; the surface of Lake McDonald was raised eight feet above normal high level. Park headquarters was isolated as bridges were washed away and electric communications and power were blacked out. A large part of the Great Northern Railway and U.S. Highway 2 were destroyed, as well as the highway bridge at Walton. Dams at Lower Two Medicine Lake and Swift Reservoir south of Heart Butte collapsed. Damage to roads, trails and bridges in the park mounted to $5,431,500 of which $2,250,000 occurred on Going-to-the-Sun Road. Several score Indians perished on the reservation, but no lives were lost within the park. Divide Creek shows clearly the overwhelming power of such flood waters in the mountains. Snyder Creek by Lake McDonald Lodge and the mouth of Boulder Creek on Many Glacier Road in Swiftcurrent Valley are additional examples.

31.2   St. Mary   18.6

Here is the eastern terminus of Going-to-the-Sun Road. Drivers with limited time are urged to visit Logan Pass, 18.2 miles, and, possibly, The Loop, 7.9 miles farther. This spectacular side trip to Logan Pass can be made in approximately two hours. Covering the route twice will not seem repetitive, for the scenes facing the motorist going and returning are completely different.

Accommodations in the settlement meet every immediate need of the visitor. A Blackfeet Arts and Crafts Shop and Travel Alberta Information Station are near the wye. Horses may be rented for trips on the reservation. Whitefish, highly esteemed for their taste and quality, may sometimes be featured on the menus of local restaurants. Consult the log of Going-to-the-Sun Road, miles 49.9 to 50.6, for information on the visitor center, campground and other facilities inside the park.

Leaving St. Mary on its way north, U.S. 89 skirts the eastern shore of Lower St. Mary Lake for its entire length of six miles. Aspen groves, interspersed here and there by cottonwoods, alternate with flower-starred grasslands especially colorful in June.

By the time the tourist season has shifted into high gear at the beginning of July, the earliest flowers have faded and the modest blue of camas has been replaced by flashier hues of midsummer flora. The stage has been taken by buckwheats, cinquefoils, roses, lupines, vetches, geraniums, blazing stars, phacelias, polemoniums, bur forget-me-nots, puccoons, horsemints,

Lower St. Mary Lake. Hileman photo.

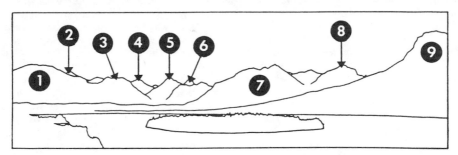

From Lower St. Mary Lake: Thunderbird Island in foreground; (1) Curly Bear; (2) James; (3) Kakitos; (4) Norris; (5) Split; (6) Stimson; (7) Red Eagle; (8) Little Chief; (9) Singleshot.

penstemons, valerians, bluebells, agoseris, fleabanes, yarrows and arnicas. Pasque flowers, well past their season of bloom, bear persistent fruits with long silky hairs forming soft white balls several inches in diameter waving in profusion amidst the host.

By the end of summer blue and purple asters still persist, surviving even the early frosts of autumn; hundreds of handsome flowers on a single, robust plant make a big bouquet long after less hardy flowers have disappeared.

Wherever overgrazing and abuse have not reduced the Great Plains to drabness and weediness, nature still spreads a carpet of multi-colored flowers. Like the precious meadows in the park, which have been spared from use as horse pasture, patches along the road remain as reminders of formerly widespread splendor, mocking apology for development, expedience and progress.

33.9 L   **Air Force Rest Area**   **R 15.8**

Malmstrom Air Force Base recreation area for military personnel.

34.5 L	**Thunderbird Island**	R 15.0

The little island is identified by Piegans with the legend of the thunderbird: a party of Indians once found a large partridge-like bird on the isle; they carried it to their medicine man who declared that it was a thunderbird. Its eyes were always tightly shut, but one day it opened them and streaks of lightning shot out. As it spread its wings and flew away, the flapping reverberated as thunder; so the keepers recognized its identity. Today, whenever there is thunder and lightning, the Indians say the thunderbird is flying.

The panorama of mountains massed behind the deep blue lake is breath-taking. They are identified in the line diagram on the preceding page.

37.2 L	**Public Campground**	R 12.6

CHEWING BLACKBONES CAMPGROUND is operated by the Blackfeet tribe. The noblest profile of CHIEF MT. (9080) looms over SWIFTCURRENT RIDGE to the northwest. In 1854 James Doty named the body of water Chief Mountain Lake. Appropriately named YELLOW MT. (8966) forms the long ridge to the left of Chief Mt.

37.7 L	**Lake Outlet**	R 12.1

A gauging station is at the outlet of Lower St. Mary Lake. Lofty MT. MERRITT (10,004), with OLD SUN GLACIER below its summit, makes its appearance to the west. The glacier, largest visible from the Blackfeet Highway, was named after Natoas, or "Old Sun," a venerable Blackfeet sun priest.

38.5	**St. Mary River**	10.0

The blacktop on the right at the approach to the bridge goes to Duck Lake (5021), 3.0 miles. To the left up SWIFTCURRENT VALLEY, the wall of APPEKUNNY MT. (9068) on the north frowns across at that of WYNN MT. (8494) on the south. The tip of MT. WILBUR (9321) peers over the cirque headwall which connects Appekunny with ALTYN PEAK (7947), guardians over the Many Glacier Hotel. The road crosses the flat, stony, alluvial fan built by Swiftcurrent Creek.

A 13-mile road goes to MANY GLACIER. This is described later in this chapter. Blackfeet Highway continues north through the settlement of Babb, which has a general store, motels, gasoline stations and cafes. The village was named for C. C. Babb, superintendent of the pre-park Milk River Reclamation Project.

Milk River rises in the United States, enters Canada for a short stretch and flows back into Montana near Havre. Its water is essential for irrigation, particularly of sugar beets. Because Alberta farmers were using all of the water, American farmers protested. To adjust the situation and assure ample summer flow, a dam was built in Swiftcurrent Valley, thus raising the level of Sherburne Lake. Its outlet was diverted to flow into Lower St. Mary Lake and then into a canal to supply additional water to Milk River. As the east river bank is a steep and unstable bluff, the ditch was dug on the west bank. It parallels the highway at mile 41.5 where it is higher (4467) than the opposing sag in St. Mary Ridge in which SPIDER LAKE (4436) reposes. The water is transported across St. Mary River by an inverted steel siphon (4438 near mouth) and emptied into the lake, which has Atlantic drainage. The novel aspect about this operation is that water which would naturally drain into Hudson Bay is made to flow ultimately into the Missouri-Mississippi River system and the Gulf of Mexico.

The well-defined parallel benches slanting north on St. Mary Ridge probably correlate with stages of retreat of St. Mary Glacier. Several miles below the site of Babb the ice was still thick enough to spill over and interrupt the smooth crest with numerous rounded knolls. It then spread as a lobe six miles long and six miles wide in Milk River Valley, otherwise free of ice. The glacier moving down Swiftcurrent Valley at the same time probably helped force the St. Mary ice over the divide to create the depression in which Duck and Goose Lakes lie today. Spider Lake, two miles north of Goose Lake, lies in a similar basin; but here St. Mary Glacier had encountered the forward edge of the Keewatin Ice Sheet, which deflected it over St. Mary Ridge.

At the time the mountain glaciers were encroaching upon the plains, continental ice spread from centers near Hudson Bay and buried northeastern North America. The westerly Keewatin Sheet crossed the site of the International Boundary eastward from the mountain glaciers. A dramatic change in the drift provides the evidence. Throughout the length of the Blackfeet Highway the drift is composed of the same kinds of rocks which form the mountains: limestone, diorite and argillite. Northeast of Duck Lake, however, this drift yields abruptly to one brought here by the Keewatin ice from sources more than a thousand miles to the northeast. Keewatin drift is composed of gray and pink granites, gneiss and quartzite, all of which are from bedrock entirely foreign to this region.

To the left of Mt. Wilbur up Swiftcurrent Valley, the even crest of MT. GRINNELL (8851) slopes sharply to a lesser pyramid on its southwest flank. The bold summit farther to the southeast, up the valley between Wynn Mt. and East Flattop, is MT. SIYEH. Going-to-the-Sun Mt., to the left of Mt. Siyeh, appears dwarfed.

41.5 R   **Diversion Ditch**   **L 8.3**

The ditch on the right diverts the water from St. Mary to Milk River. Blackfeet Indians display their buckaroo skills at a rodeo grounds above the road (L).

45.0   **Kennedy Creek**   **4.8**

Named for John Kennedy, known as Otatso or "Walking Stooped," a frontiersman who had a trading post at the mouth of the creek in 1874.

45.1 L   **Chief Mt. Junction**   **R 4.7**

CHIEF MOUNTAIN INTERNATIONAL HIGHWAY turns left for Waterton Lakes. Blackfeet Highway bends northeast over rolling moraine. CHIEF MT. is the impressive landmark to the west.

49.8   **International Border**   **0.0**

At Carway the highway becomes Alberta 2, an excellent paved road. Cardston, 15.0 miles, has a Mormon temple with free visitor guide service provided. In 1887 a band of 41 faithful Mormons made the hazardous trek from Utah to the mouth of Lee Creek in southern Alberta to found this outpost of the Church of Jesus Christ of Latter Day Saints. They named the settlement after their leader, Charles Ora Card, a brother-in-law of Brigham Young. The first winter was very hard; game was scarce and food was scanty. From bare survival their camp has grown to a flourishing town of 3000 inhabitants with many modern facilities for visitors.

Alberta 2 crosses Alberta 5 on the north edge of Cardston. No. 5 goes 35 miles west to Waterton Townsite, providing an alternative route between Waterton and Glacier Parks. On clear mornings and evenings with rosy sky-tints, views of the mountain front are elegant along the way. Higher peaks, Blakiston, Cleveland, Merritt and Chief Mountain, are in the vanguard. Alberta 5 goes 46 miles east from Cardston to Lethbridge (population 46,752), where it connects with Alberta 3 for eastern points. From Cardston, Highway 2 continues north to Calgary (148 miles) and Edmonton (335 miles). Banff is 81 miles west of Calgary on Alberta Highway 1.

Two Medicine Road

East Glacier Park, Montana, to Two Medicine, 12.0 Miles

Two Medicine, along with St. Mary, was the target of the adventurous long before Glacier Park was established; it has always been a favorite with locals as well. According to James Willard Schultz, an authority on the Blackfeet Indians, the name stemmed from a time-honored tradition of erecting adjacent medicine lodges on the river, one by the Piegans, the other by the Bloods. Starting as ''Where-Two-Medicine-Lodges-Were-Built,'' it became simply ''Two Medicine.''

The glacial-scoured trough is exquisite; encircled by highly colored ridges and outstanding peaks, it is graced with a plenitude of peaceful lakes and streams, singing waterfalls, and forests murmuring under lazy white clouds in an azure sky. Its lofty, steep-walled, flower-adorned recesses—Paradise, Aster and Buttercup Parks, Bighorn Basin and unnamed others—have lured searchers for beauty from earliest days. Its wildlife is rich and varied, and it is well endowed with trails which guide to every delightful retreat. A portion of this road is shown on the fold-out map.

4.2	Road Junction

The route follows Blackfeet Highway (Montana 49) from East Glacier Park to the road junction. Bearing to the left from the intersection, Two Medicine Road follows the shore of LOWER TWO MEDICINE LAKE (normal pool elevation 4882). Aspen and spruce reach out towards the plains on moister parts of terraces along the lake. It is evident that much of the area has been burned over in many places a number of times. Grasslands mark the sites of repeated burns. The most recent conflagration, extending from Squaw Mt. up the Dry Fork Valley, was in 1919.

SINOPAH MT. (8271) squats squarely in the valley ahead. It is flanked on the right by RISING BULL RIDGE, pyramidal LONE WALKER MT. (8502) and RISING WOLF (9513). On the left are PAINTED TEPEE (7650), APPISTOKI PEAK (8164), and MT. HENRY (8847).

7.3	Park Boundary

Upon leaving the Blackfeet Indian Reservation, SCENIC POINT (7522) is the tip of the mountain wall south of the lake. Rising Wolf Mt. towers majestically ahead.

Two Medicine Entrance Station

Entrance permits must be shown or purchased from the park ranger stationed here.

9.9 R   **Trail to Running Eagle Falls**

(0.3 mile). This level trail to the base of the falls takes the visitor along a shady forest path which can readily be walked in ten minutes. It is too delightful to be by-passed. See page 91.

The road crosses Two Medicine River over a concrete bridge. After making a hairpin curve, it passes through a lodgepole-spruce forest which gives way to one of pure spruce as it climbs over the face of the Lewis Thrust Fault.

11.6 L   **Trailhead**

A short lane leads to a water tank while also serving as the foot of trail 96 from East Glacier Park. A quarter mile upstream Appistoki Creek, having carved a narrow, tortuous gorge in green Appekunny argillite, plunges over a steep ledge as APPISTOKI FALLS.

11.8 R   **Road to Two Medicine Picnic Area and Campground**

Located on tiny Pray Lake below Two Medicine Lake. Many consider this campground location the most attractive in the park. Photogenic whitebark pines stand between the lakeshore and campground on an open, gravelly flat. Their skewed shapes frame a pleasing scene of outlet, lake and background of rugged peaks. The campground has a campfire circle for evening naturalist programs.

11.9   **Appistoki Creek**

12.0   **Two Medicine Lake**

Two Medicine Lake (5164), a beautiful glacial tarn, is over two miles long and 260 feet deep. A store and fountain serving coffee and sandwiches are at the end of the road. Boats leave on schedule from the dock for the upper end of the lake, from which walks can be taken to Twin Falls, Upper Two Medicine Lake and other sites. Trails 98 and 99 are used for a circuit of the lake. See fold-out map.

From the shore near the lower dock, the peaks (L to R), are: SCENIC POINT (7522), APPISTOKI PEAK (8164), NEVER LAUGHS MT. (7641), GRIZZLY MT. (9067), PAINTED TEPEE PEAK (7650), SINOPAH MT. (8271), LONE WALKER MT. (8502), MT. HELEN (8538), PUMPELLY PILLAR (7620), and RISING WOLF MT. (9513).

Many Glacier Road

Babb, Montana, to Many Glacier, 13.0 Miles.

To the visitor using public transportation and to many others, Many Glacier is the foremost center of activity for park experience. Offering an abundance and variety of easily accessible scenery of superb quality, it is the center of the most convenient trail network. Lakes, streams, flower-starred meadows and cool woodlands lie close at hand. Its mountains crowd around intimately. With careful deliberation, Louis W. Hill, President of the Great Northern Railway (forerunner of the Burlington Northern), selected Many Glacier as the most attractive site for his largest investment in tourism.

Many Glacier Hotel was opened in 1915. Early pictures reveal an atmosphere more pleasing than that of today with its environmental degradation. Concentrated visitor use and vast numbers of pack and saddle horses have denuded flats and rocky ledges of fertile soil, tender herbs and wildflowers. Fires, especially that of 1936, have thinned the primeval lushness which once was the glory of the woodland. Management today is faced with staggering problems of ever-increasing impact by use while it struggles with restoration as well as preservation of the original scene.

Swiftcurrent Valley was the focus of mining fever when the present park strip east of the Continental Divide was purchased from the Blackfeet and thrown open to prospecting on April 15, 1898. The mineral zone extending from the head of Cracker Lake past Grinnell Point to Mt. Wilbur drew many in eager search, first for riches of gold, later for copper. The camp village of Altyn sprang up overnight on Appekunny Flats at the head of Lake Sherburne, only to die almost as quickly a few years later. Sam Somes, the manager of its two-story hotel, discovered oil near the foot of the lake and precipitated an oil boom which lasted only four years despite exaggerated claims of success and spectacular exhibits of purported products. The last digging in a mine shaft took place in the forties on Grinnell Point. In recent years exploration for oil and gas has resumed outside the Park boundaries, in all directions.

0.0   Babb

(4520). From this settlement on the Blackfeet Highway, Many Glacier Road runs southwest directly up Swiftcurrent Valley and into the mountains. Aspen thickets, pine-spruce forests and wildflower glades alternate along the route. The prominent bands on the face of EAST FLATTOP (8356) across the creek are quartzite.

1.6 L   Swiftcurrent Creek

The 1964 flood has restored some flow to the previously dry creek, which empties into St. Mary River below Babb. The jumble of boulders in the creek bed is evidence of the power of the floodwaters which transported them. The ditch diverting water from the creek to Lower St. Mary Lake, a part of the Milk River Irrigation Project, skirts the foot of East Flattop. BOULDER CREEK, tumbling in above the ditch, rises in a cirque below SIYEH PASS (7750), crossed by trail 117 between Sun Point and Many Glacier. Boulder Cirque, once the scene of eager prospecting, is today unmolested wildlife range, as it is rarely visited.

4.7 L   Sherburne Dam

Sherburne Dam, part of the Milk River Reclamation Project, approved prior to establishment of Glacier National Park. Two natural lakes lay on the heavily forested valley floor before

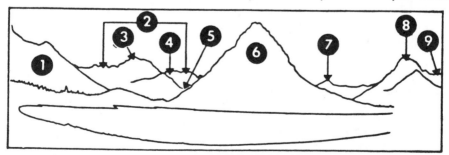

From Swiftcurrent Valley: (1) Allen; (2) Garden Wall; (3) Gould; (4) Gem Glacier; (5) Grinnell Glacier; (6) Grinnell Point; (7) Swiftcurrent Mt.; (8) Wilbur; (9) Pinnacle Wall.

the dam was built. Montana's first oil well was located near the dam below the road.

Relocated for better access, parts of the old road may still be seen in places above the present alignment. The valley floor is mantled with drift lying upon Cretaceous strata like those exposed in roadcuts. The slippery nature of this formation when weathered and wet causes much slumping, which is aggravated by lakelets and pools of water impounded by slide masses on the hummocky slope. In some places the road surface is constantly being pushed upwards by hydrostatic pressure; the bump at Cassidy Curve, a mile upstream, results from this action. Road maintenance is expensive but must be continuous.

7.1 A   Grinnell Glacier

Grinnell Glacier appears prominently on the GARDEN WALL. The glacier today consists of two sectors which sixty years ago formed a single continuous ice mass. The lower glacier, a mile wide and halfmile long, has a surface area of 250 acres and a possible thickness of 200 feet. From a distance it appears as a streak of snow on the mountain wall because one is looking only at the forward edge of the ice. The steep upper section is called THE SALAMANDER. The tripartite band across the Garden Wall resulted from the intrusion of molten igneous rock (diorite) which metamorphosed contiguous limestone layers to a color much lighter than the intrusion itself, which is almost black.

The mountains visible here L to R are WYNN (8404), ALLEN (9376), GOULD (9553), GRINNELL (8851), ALTYN (7947) and APPEKUNNY (9068). SWIFTCURRENT (R) and GRINNELL (L) Valleys are separated by GRINNELL POINT (7716).

7.6   Many Glacier Entrance Station

Entry permits must be shown or purchased from the ranger on duty.

8.5 L   Cracker Canyon and Mt. Siyeh

(10,014). The cliff below the summit is 3000 feet sheer. Turquoise CRACKER LAKE (5910) nestles at the base of SIYEH GLACIER. At the start of the century, a lane was fashioned along the narrow canyon up which an ore concentrator weighing eight tons was moved to Cracker Mine near the head of the lake.

The north face of Mt. Wynn is the front of the Lewis Thrust Fault. The ancient rocks, bounded by cliffs, have been shoved over the weak Cretaceous rocks which comprise the slopes of the valley and which appear as dark gray-black patches here and there on the drift-covered slope. As the soft rocks erode with a gentle sloping surface, support is removed from the tough overlying limestone, so that large blocks break off at a time.

The tip of the thrust fault strata is clearly seen on Mt. Wynn, as well as in the diorite band across the summit cliff of Mt. Siyeh; this sill undoubtedly is an extension of that visible on the Garden Wall. Explorers along the cliff base of Mt. Wynn can readily detect the contact between the two formations differing in age by 3/4 billion years. Surprisingly little alteration in character has been caused by this titanic process. Fossils, especially clam shells, occur in numbers in fresh exposures of the Cretaceous strata.

A secondary thrust fault on the shoulder of Mt. Wynn above Canyon Creek is plainly visible from the road, especially in late afternoon. The strata on top are almost horizontal, while the strata below dip at a sharp angle. The upper strata have slid over the truncated ends of the lower.

10.4   Appekunny Creek

Appekunny Creek draining the cirque between Appekunny Mt. and Altyn Peak. A lofty waterfall drains over the lip of the cirque on the right accessible by a foot trail (166) leading from the bridge to the falls. In 1900 the mining village of Altyn sprawled on Appekunny Flats below the road. Its population once zoomed to almost 200 wild and lawless inhabitants. Early and late in the season, mountain sheep wander to the valley floor, formerly their lambing grounds.

Treasures await the plant lover in the boggy meadows and bottomlands above and below the road. Some migrants of the Transition Zone at the foot of Swiftcurrent Valley and some from alpine heights have strayed into this nook. One tiny bog fed by a spring above the road contains hundreds of grape ferns growing in thick moss under scrub birches. Below Swiftcurrent Falls bunchberries (otherwise absent east of the divide), many bog orchids and various pyrolas formerly grew in a tangle of logs in beaver ponds.

11.4 L   Swiftcurrent Falls

The stream plunges over a ledge of Altyn limestone with the thrust fault line at its base. The dip of the beds is to the southwest. Swiftcurrent Lake (4878) occupies a glacial basin above the falls. The lake used to be larger and the falls were higher than at present. As the stream eroded the lip of the basin, the lake waters retreated, leaving a tilted rim on which the hotel has been built. The bridge above the falls was designed in 1929 by distinguished landscape artist Ferruccio Vitale.

11.5   Road Intersection

The left member crosses the creek above the falls and goes to Many Glacier Hotel, a quarter mile away. This is a large, well-equipped mountain resort hotel with spacious lobby, dining rooms and other amenities. The stone structure on the lakeshore is a water gauging station. The overpass is for saddlehorse parties that assemble at the corral on the far side of the parking lot behind the hotel. Beyond the hotel entrance the road loops to a large parking area.

From the road intersection the route proceeds straight ahead to its terminus, 13.0 miles from Babb. It goes along the north shore of Swiftcurrent Lake to the Swiftcurrent picnic area; the ranger station, which dispenses information; a large campground for cars and trailers; and SWIFTCURRENT MOTOR INN, with cabin facilities, a coffee shop, general store and automobile service station. Other structures between the picnic area and campground are residences for employees. A boat ramp for launching boats is situated on the northwest corner of Swiftcurrent Lake. To retain a serene atmosphere, boating on the lake is restricted to rowboats and canoes, except the authorized concessioner-operated sightseeing vessels.

Naturalists give popular talks at the inn and the hotel and lead guided trips in the field. An outdoor campfire circle for naturalist services is located beyond the campground and the parking area in front of the inn office.

Chief Mountain International Highway

Babb, Montana, to U.S. Customs, Chief Mountain, 18.7 miles; to Waterton, 29.0 miles. Log of route from Waterton to Border, page 56.

This narrative consists of two parts starting at Babb and at Waterton and ending at the border. In the first part mileages indicated are, on the left, Babb to the U.S.-Canada border; and, on the right, in reverse direction from Waterton Park. Conversely, mileages and descriptions in the second part of the description are, on the left, from Waterton Park to the border; and, on the right, from Babb, Montana. In general, best views, described here, lie ahead. A portion of the Canadian part of this route is shown on the map on page 123.

Chief Mountain International Highway is the main artery between the two units of Waterton-Glacier International Peace Park. Built in 1935 on rolling prairie outside the mountains, it traverses highly scenic landscape, affording appealing mountain vistas and offering a delightful variety of forest and grassland. Drivers should be alert for wildlife or livestock on the roadway.

| 0.0 | **Babb** | 39.0 |

Leaving Babb, Blackfeet Highway (U.S. 89) is followed for 4.3 miles to the intersection on Kennedy Creek.

| **4.3 L** | **Intersection** | **R 34.7** |

Chief Mountain Highway (Montana 17) bears left immediately to climb drift-covered slopes. Gas station, trailer court and sign with customs hours are at the junction.

The rounded hills here were buried by Kennedy Creek Glacier during the Wisconsin stage. The glacier merged with St. Mary Glacier below, but some of the ice, when freed from confinement between mountain walls, spilled over Kennedy Ridge east of Chief Mt. to flow down the valley of Lee Creek. As the gap created by this diversion is 800 feet above the present valley floor, an estimate of the depth of the glacier at this point can be obtained.

SHERBURNE PEAK (8578), YELLOW MT. (8966) and CHIEF MT. (9080) to the left, were carved out of the Lewis Thrust Fault block, chiefly by glaciers. Chief Mt. stands on a pediment of dark shales and related sediments which appear as dark patches through the talus at the foot of the cliffs. It is a mountain without roots, an island of ancient rocks afloat in a sea of youngsters. It cannot be called monolithic as it is not fashioned from a single block of stone, for limestone strata have been thrust over each other in minor mountain movements, just as they have on Mt. Wynn (Many Glacier Road, mile 8.5), and on Summit Mt. (U.S. Highway 2, mile 49.1). The upper third of the mountain is composed of undisturbed horizontal, thin-bedded limestone limited at its base by a major thrust plane. Beneath is a chaotic thickness of 100 feet of limestone, fractured and traversed by minor faults, most of which dip 30 degrees southwest, roughly parallel to the bedding planes. Slumping of the hard Altyn limestones of the ridge connecting Chief and Gable Mts. has left two isolated pinnacles resting on Cretaceous shales. The Indians refer to them as Ninaki, the "Chief's Wife," and the "Papoose."

Yellow Mt. presents complexities similiar to those of Chief Mt. The upper part is Appe-kunny argillite separated by a major thrust from crushed and disturbed Altyn beds. In one place 500 feet of strata have piled themselves upon each other to a thickness of 2400 feet. In another place a single set of strata repeats itself no less than nine times within a thickness forming half of the formation exposed.

| **6.1** | **Chief Mt.** | **32.9** |

As seen from the southeast, the mountain shows a narrow crest and vertical east face. From the east the profile appears broad, with a horizontal crest. Much talus has accumulated about the base. On the south slope 3000 acres of lodgepole pines were burned in 1935 by a fire started by hikers.

| **9.0 L** | **Otatso (Slide Lake) Trail** | **R 30.0** |

Otatso Creek Truck Trail to the park boundary, head of Otatso Creek Trail (150), and locked park patrol cabin, 5.0 miles. This road is seldom maintained and frequently impassable to vehicles. From the park boundary the trail goes up the creek 1.3 miles to the foot of GABLE PASS TRAIL (149) at SLIDE LAKE (6030). Trail 149 goes 6.1 miles from the trail junction over infrequented GABLE PASS (7200) between Chief and Gable (9262) Mts. to Belly River Ranger Station.

| **9.3 R** | **Overlook** | **L 29.7** |

The outwash to the east below the overlook (5500) is pitted with kettles filled with water.

PIKE LAKE is about three miles northeast, and St. Mary River, its course marked by trees, is in the distance. The place where the river crosses the international boundary marks the contact between the drift of mountain glaciers and the drift of crystalline rocks carried by the Keewatin Ice Sheet, the only place on the border where this is true.

Lakelets from a few square yards to several acres in size characterize moraine topography east of the park region, but they are particularly abundant along the trace of the Keewatin terminal moraine. A score or more are below the Carway Custom House on Blackfeet Highway, where the ice sheet came to a halt. Scores are along Alberta 5 near the Belly River bridge west of Mountain View. The location of the Keewatin moraine can be determined in this vicinity by the abundance of these tiny lakes.

13.3 L   **Chief Mt.**   **R 26.0**

View of the east face of Chief Mt. and the trace of the Lewis Thrust Fault. The line of separation between the ancient rocks of the mountain and the younger Cretaceous strata over which they slid appears plainly just over the talus slope.

According to legend, Chief Mt. had once been scaled by a young Flathead brave seeking a sacred vision. He fasted for four days and nights upon the summit using a bison skull for a pillow. In 1891 Henry L. Stimson, later Secretary of State under Hoover and Secretary of War under F. D. Roosevelt, climbed the east face with two companions. When they reached the top, Stimson was intrigued to find an ancient, weathered buffalo skull resting there.

14.4 L   **New Service Road**   **R 24.6**

The road leads to an oil well drilled near the park boundary. Many prospect wells have been sunk in the area between the highway and the park boundary.

15.1   **Park Boundary**   **23.9**

Leaving the Blackfeet Indian Reservation, Lee Ridge, extending north from the eastern tip of Gable Mt., is in the foreground. MT. CLEVELAND (10,466) rises in majesty on the right side of the valley. The groves of trees along the highway to this point are aspens; the forests ahead consist mainly of lodgepole pine. Moose may appear in the middle of the road at times, and other wildlife is present.

16.7   **Lee Creek**   **22.3**

The ice of Belly River Glacier in Wisconsin time was deep enough to spill over the ridge beneath Chief Mt. and dig the notch which now serves the highway. It must have been at least 1000 feet thick to accomplish this.

17.8   **Lee Ridge**   **21.2**

On the summit, Lee Ridge Trail (146) follows the crest of the ridge to connect with Gable Pass Trail (149), 6.0 miles. The junction of 146 and 149 is 0.7 mile west of Gable Pass (7200). Spruce are mixed with pines in the forest.

18.6   **U.S. Customs**   **20.2**

To expedite return and avoid confusion and delay, travelers north may check with officials about regulations, documents and import taxes for return to the United States. Travelers entering from Canada must clear with Customs and Immigration.

18.8   **International Boundary**   **20.2**

The wide swath in the forest marks the boundary. As posted on both ends of the highway, customs are open only during certain hours, depending upon the time of the year. Before returning, visitors may check in Babb, Cardston or Waterton Lakes about hours of operation. A suitable monument on the boundary commemorates the establishment of Waterton-Glacier International Peace Park.

As you continue to watch your odometer you will pass various points of interest along the Canadian portion of the highway. Some of these are viewpoints from which extensive views to the south and the west may be seen, but, generally, to enjoy these you will have to stop your car and look back. Consult reverse mileages in the section that follows.

WATERTON LAKES NATIONAL PARK

Waterton Park to Canadian Customs, 20.1 miles; to Babb, Montana, 39.0 miles. See page 53 for description of route between Babb and the International Border.

WATERTON LAKES NATIONAL PARK was set aside by Canada in 1895. In 1932 Waterton Lakes and Glacier National Parks were designated through appropriate legislation by both countries as the first International Peace Park in the world. This designation is a symbol of the peace and amity existing between the peoples of Canada and the United States, in recognition of the fact that for over a century not one fortification, offensive weapon or soldier has been placed along the entire 5500 miles of common border between the two countries.

The highway actually starts near the bridge over Waterton River, but since most of the traffic between the two parks begins or terminates in Waterton Townsite this account includes six additional miles on Alberta 5.

Waterton Lakes National Park, with an area of 204 square miles, is a gem of sparkling mountain landscape. Its ranges, like those of Glacier, rise precipitously from plains which roll eastward across the continent. Its wildlife and vegetation are closely akin to those of its cousin to the south.

Waterton Townsite is perched obtrusively at the foot of Upper Waterton Lake, the only visitor service center in Waterton Lakes National Park. It is a bustling community in summer with all of the customary services of a modern town.

Many visitors are surprised upon finding flourishing towns within the boundaries of Canadian national parks. Their presence represents a difference in policy and interpretation of appropriate use of a natural area from the definition given in the United Nations "List of National Parks and Equivalent Reserves." Historically, their existence is traceable to the archetypal Banff Hot Springs in Alberta's Rocky Mountain National Park (now Banff National Park), which was patterned after Hot Springs, Arkansas, at the time when that was classified as a national reserve, not a national park, and was centered within a city.

MILES FROM WATERTON		MILES FROM BABB
0.0	**Waterton Park**	**39.0**

The townsite is the center of administration and activity in the park. Alberta Provincial Highways 5 and 6 connect it with all parts of Canada; Chief Mountain International Highway offers the most direct road connection with points in Northwest Montana. Rail and air connections are through Lethbridge, 77 miles distant, and daily buses operate in summer via either Pincher Creek or Cardston. Glacier Park Incorporated has daily summer service between Waterton and centers in Glacier National Park.

The park administration center is located on the principal business street of the village, opposite the wharf on Emerald Bay. To reach it from the east turn left on the first street beyond Akamina Highway Junction. The park information bureau is opposite the Prince of Wales

Hotel, across the approach road to the townsite.

Waterton Townsite is the point of departure for auto tours on 50 miles of all-weather roads within the park, including Akamina and Red Rock Canyon Highways; for trips on 105 miles of park trails; for boat rides on Upper Waterton Lake, 485 feet deep; and for trail trips into Glacier National Park.

In addition to hotels, chalets, lodges, bungalow cabins, restaurants, garages, service stations, stores, shops, bank and post office, the town has a photo shop, liquor dispensary, tennis courts, 18-hole golf course, children's playground, motion picture theater and convention center. A large heated outdoor swimming pool and a small wading pool with adjacent shower facilities are near the center of town.

A 35-acre camp for cars and trailers is on the southern edge of town. It is serviced with electricity, modern plumbing, washroom facilities, shower baths, sewage disposal units and kitchen shelters; it receives matron and caretaker attention. There is an amphitheater for daily illustrated talks by naturalists on local subjects.

Waterton Townsite is situated on an outwash fan built by Cameron Creek during the waning Ice Age, when a much greater volume of debris-loaded water scoured the canyon and built the delta in the lake. An example of the tremendous power of such steep glacial streams is no longer present locally, but may be seen in the Illecillewaet River (Glacier National Park, British Columbia) and in the raging torrents of melt waters from the great glaciers of Alaska. The hollow rumble of massive boulders clashing against each other in the roily waters and smashing against rocky channel walls arouses a feeling of dread within the observer. One step into such a maelstrom would quickly doom a victim to instant amalgamation in the icy mix.

Like adjacent valleys, Waterton was sculptured by great glaciers in the Ice Ages. Since the master glacier excavated more vigorously than the smaller Cameron Glacier, upon retreat of the ice Cameron Valley was left hanging on the wall, and Cameron Falls was formed much higher than at present. The erosion of the crest, even now in progress, was much accelerated by the greater flow when Cameron Glacier was in retreat. The bedrock at Cameron Falls, like the lower strata of the promontory of the opposite shore, is composed of limestone, dolomite and argillite belonging to the Waterton Formation, the oldest exposure in the region.

The dark sill of igneous rock bordered by bleached strata on its borders is a conspicuously geological feature in the park. It is readily seen as the horizontal band across the north face of Mt. Cleveland (10,466) at the head of the big lake.

Local Trails

Waterton Townsite is blessed with good short trails. A one-mile village PONY TRAIL starts at the trail bridge over Cameron Creek below the falls; it climbs the north bank and follows the wooded slope behind residences. Crossing Akamina Highway above the intersection, it goes behind the information bureau and park buildings north of Lake Linnet.

BEAR'S HUMP TRAIL starts at the information building and climbs 700 feet up to Bear's Hump, the prominence on Mt. Crandell overlooking the town, 0.8 mile. The name stems from an earlier name for the peak, Black Bear Mountain; the mountain has since been renamed for an early prospector.

The trailhead for a circuit of tiny Lake Linnet is located between that lake and Middle Waterton Lake. Parking, washrooms and picnic facilities are available. This paved path is designated the "Centennial Trail" for the handicapped. Interpretive signs are posted along the route.

BOSPORUS TRAIL follows the shoreline from the picnic area on the north shore of Emerald Bay to the Bosporus and Lake Linnet, 0.8 mile. Bosporus, the lake narrows below Prince of Wales Hotel, is shallow, but horses must swim to cross it most of the season. After crossing and before branching, the trail climbs 400 feet along the promontory between the two lakes. The right branch goes to Crypt Landing and Crypt Lake; the left descends gradually to STONEY FLATS.

The trail up VIMY RIDGE starts three miles from the Bosporus on this trail continuing

Upper Waterton Lake and Townsite with Prince of Wales Hotel. National Park Service photo.

past the Dardanelles, the outlet of Lower Waterton Lake, and on to the Y.M.C.A. camp on Knight's Lake where it meets the trail coming from Chief Mountain Highway, mile 6.4. It is seven miles from Bosporus to the highway by this route.

For detailed descriptions of longer routes consult the chapter on trails.

0.3 L	Junction	R 38.7

Intersection with Akamina Highway, described in this chapter.

0.5 R	Prince of Wales Hotel	L 38.5

Prince of Wales Hotel is on a rocky point on the opposite side of the road. An imposing Elizabethan structure, it commands a vista of lake and mountains, especially that from the wide hotel view-windows. This largest of Waterton's hotels has a gift shop, commodious dining room and tap room and an especially attractive lobby window view of Waterton Lake.

0.8 R	Lake Linnet	L 38.2

1.6R   **Saddle Horse Stables, Picnic Facilities and Youth Camp**

Riding stables are on the right. Just beyond the stables, the road forks. The left fork after a mile forks again to give access on the right to the Dardanelles picnic facilities and on the left to Stoney Flats. From just beyond the stables the right fork provides access to Camp Columbus Youth Camp and picnic facilities on the shore of Middle Waterton Lake, with views west of the Bosporus and Waterton Townsite.

| 1.8 L | Golf Course | R 37.2 |

The 18-hole course is owned by Parks Canada but operated by a private concessioner. Its attractive clubhouse is open to visitors.

| 2.2 L | Blakiston Creek | R 36.8 |

Picnic Shelter and Bridge. Red Rock Canyon Highway branches to the left. A half mile beyond is the trail (R) to the Dardanelles.

| 3.5 R | Settlers' Graves | L 35.5 |

Surrounded by a white picket fence, the graves of John George "Kootenai" Brown and his two wives can be seen on the shore of the lakelet at the end of the descending lane. Brown arrived in the region in 1868 to become the first local white settler. A colorful figure, he is regarded as the first acting superintendent of Waterton Lakes National Park.

| 4.5 R | Lower Waterton Lake | L 34.5 |

Picnic area in a pleasant grove at the lake outlet, the beginning of Waterton River.

| 5.4 L | Entrance Station | R 34.6 |

Visitors must stop at road junction to purchase or show park permits. ALBERTA PROVINCIAL HIGHWAY 6 comes here from Pincher Creek, 30.0 miles, through terrain locally called "badlands." A fish hatchery is passed on the left a half-mile north on this road. Plains buffalo occupy a fenced paddock of a half section west of the road on the park's northern boundary. There are large ponds fed by Indian Springs and cool groves of broadleaf trees. Auto visitors may enter the enclosure to see and photograph the animals, but are strictly forbidden to get out of their cars. Pedestrians and cyclists are not allowed inside the fence. An exhibit overlooks the enclosure just off Hwy. 6.

| 5.7 | Waterton River | 33.9 |

Waterton River is crossed after turning to the right at the Entrance Station. A picnic shelter is to the right on the shore of MASKINONGE LAKE. The name is an Indian term for the large pike which live in the lake.

Straight ahead is Alberta 5 for Cardston, 25 miles, and as an alternative route, to Babb, 48 miles, and Glacier National Park.

Approaching from the east, views of the mountains—Chief, Merritt, Cleveland, Vimy, Blakiston and peaks to the north—are extraordinarily exciting in the clear air of early morning or sunset hours.

Alberta 6, as Chief Mountain International Highway, turns right toward the U.S.

| 6.4 R | Vimy Peak Trail | L 32.6 |

Trail among cottonwoods along the lakeshore connecting with trails to Stoney Flats, Vimy Ridge, and Bosporus.

| 9.9 R | Big Bend Overlook | L 28.8 |

Panorama of Waterton Valley. Beginning on the left and close-by is brown-sloped SOFA MT. (8268), then VIMY PEAK (7825), CRANDELL (7812), overlooking it to the north, ANDERSON PEAK (8700), with the valley of Blakiston Creek beneath it sloping towards Mt. Crandell, the red spike that is the southern tip of crescent-shaped MT. GALWEY (7900) with the high ridge of MT. DUNGARVAN (8500) behind it.

| 11.4 R | Plaque | L 27.5 |

Explains the Lewis Thrust Fault.

| 12.2 R | Plaque and Viewpoint | L 26.7 |

The plaque describes the philosophy of use of Canada's national parks. Water, picnic and toilet facilities are provided here.

| 12.8 | Indian Reserve | 26.2 |

BLOOD INDIAN RESERVE TIMBER LIMIT (a closed area). LOOKOUT BUTTE (5255) on the left. The first view of CHIEF MT. (9080), a remarkable outlier of the front range. The mountain walls to the southwest are scalloped with glacial cirques.

| 13.0 | Glacial Kettles | 25.8 |

The ground is riddled with glacial kettles occupied by ponds. Most of these were formed by

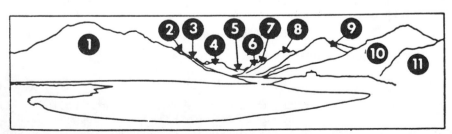

From Lower Waterton Lake: (1) Vimy Ridge; (2) Cleveland; (3) Stoney Indian Peaks; (4) Cathedral Peak; (5) Flattop; (6) Citadel Peaks; (7) Porcupine Ridge; (8) Campbell; (9) Richards; (10) Bertha; (11) Crandell.

melting of blocks of ice carried here with morainal debris. The feature is termed "pitted outwash."

Beaver have been busy in the willow-covered bottoms and aspen thickets. Note the yellow-tipped spikes of trees freshly cut by these sharp-toothed rodents. A beaver hut can be seen on the right; another is a little more than a mile up the road.

Orange Canadian lilies illumine this roadside in June. They are more common farther north but only a few grow wild in Montana. National parks, both in Canada and the United States, forbid picking wild flowers.

| 14.4 R | Mt. Cleveland | L 24.2 |

Looking up the North Fork of Belly River to MT. CLEVELAND (10,466), GOATHAUNT MT. (8641) and MICHE WABUN PEAK (8861).

| 16.4 | Belly River | 22.6 |

Belly River flows through the Saskatchewan River, Lake Winnipeg and the Nelson River into Hudson Bay.

The name may be from the Gros Ventre (Mokowanis) or "Big Belly" Indians who lived on the river downstream.

The road ascends the west slope of MOKOWAN BUTTE (6000) which is remarkably flat-topped viewed either from this highway or from the Cardston highway to the north. It is capped by river gravel which must have been transported by streams from local sources. The mesa shows that it was not overridden by glaciers, although its sides were cut deeply by them. It probably represents an interesting remnant of topography which existed here before the Glacial Epoch. It is the earliest known record of the pre-glacial predecessor of Kennedy Creek, which here built a fine alluvial fan. A plaque explains the origin and use of the Blood Indian Timber Reserve.

BELLY RIVER WAGON ROAD. This lane was once passable all the way to Crossley (now Cosley) Lake, a dozen miles upstream. Before park days, it was used for hauling out logs, and today its trace can still be followed. Belly River is the boundary of the Blood Timber Reserve.

| 20.1 | Canada-U.S. Border | 18.8 |

CANADIAN CUSTOMS AND IMMIGRATION, Chief Mountain Port of Entry. To expedite re-entry, Canadians are advised to check with resident officials before leaving.

CHIEF MT. is overlord of mountains and plains. Indians revered it and saw it as a chief leading his warriors in the field of battle. Piegans call it "Ninnah Istahkoo," Chief of the Mountains, and honored indeed is any notable to whom this distinguished name is given.

Behind Chief is yellow GABLE MT. (9262). The stately glacier-capped eminence to the right is MT. MERRITT (10,004). Trim PYRAMID PEAK (7933) and pointed MT. KIPP (8839) occupy places far up MOKOWANIS VALLEY below Mt. Merritt. Like Grinnell Point at Many Glacier and Sinopah Mt. on Two Medicine Lake, Pyramid Peak dominates the scene in exquisite Mokowanis Valley.

Pass Creek or Red Rock Canyon Highway
Waterton Townsite to Red Rock Canyon Exhibit and Trailhead, 9.4 miles

This short road ascends from a stony flat by a rushing creek in surroundings of flaring color to a focus from which trails radiate to cool retreats.

The road branches off from Alberta Highway 5 after crossing Pass Creek, 1.2 miles northeast from the information bureau opposite Prince of Wales Hotel. A kitchen shelter and the park golf course are on the opposite or west side of the stream. The road climbs immediately to the top of a terrace of glacial outwash strewn with rounded boulders.

Across Lower Waterton Lake the view of the mountains starts with ever present Vimy Peak. Sharp-spired CITADEL PEAKS are in the distance beyond the main lake, with MT. RICHARDS (7800) north of the International Boundary on the west lakeshore. BERTHA PEAK (7613), scarred by avalanches, rises behind the Prince of Wales Hotel. The great wall extending from MT. RICHARDS to MT. ALDERSON (8833) behind BERTHA and ALDERSON LAKES is to the left behind Bertha Peak. The slopes of MT. CRANDELL (7812) across Pass Creek change from gray and red argillites to lighter colored dolomite and limestone nearby.

| 1.0 | Blakiston Valley |

The road changes course from north to west up the valley of BLAKISTON CREEK between Mt. Crandell (L) and BELLEVUE HILL (6929) whose sides are indented by deep gullies. It crosses the trace of the Lewis Thrust Fault, which is here buried under detritus but is clearly apparent at the base of the cliffs on Bellevue Hill, Mt. Crandell and Vimy Ridge across the lake. An exhibit explains the importance of beaver in reclaiming abandoned stream channels, which support a variety of life.

| 2.0 R | Trail |

Trail to the buffalo paddock and Galwey Creek in the northeast corner of the park, about three miles. To the right beyond Bellevue Hill, MT. GALWEY (7900) has gentle lower slopes that climb to a ridge of sharp spikes. The lofty mass of MT. BLAKISTON (9600), highest in the park, looms ahead to the left.

| 3.0 L | Erosional Patterns |

Huge conical fans of slide rock lie between projecting vertical bosses of terrace remnants, making a striking erosion pattern. The swift waters of Blakiston Creek have eroded deeply into the glacial outwash.

| 4.0 L | Exhibit |

Exhibit on the erosion/depositional story of Blakiston Creek and the history of early Indians of the Blakiston Valley.

| 4.5 L | Crandell Campground |

Crandell Campground with 129 sites (no utility hookups) for small trailers or tents. Each site has a raised fire grill, table, tent pad and easy access to a kitchen shelter and washrooms with running water. During July and August nightly programs are offered in the centrally-located interpretive theater.

| 5.0 | Coppermine Creek |

A picnic shelter is on a dirt road that crosses Blakiston Creek (4600) to the Canyon United Church Camp and the start of a one-mile trail to a kitchen shelter on Crandell Lake. The trail skirts the west shore, crosses a low pass (5300) and drops to Akamina Highway and thence to Waterton Townsite, 3.5 miles.

| 6.0 L | Ruby Ridge |

Ruby Ridge (7993) and Ruby Falls. Ahead, a sill of igneous rock in the Helena (Siyeh) limestone near the summit of Mt. Blakiston can easily be discerned because it is darker than adjoining beds, and breaks up into spines by erosion along joints. A similar sill shows even more distinctly among horizontal layers on ANDERSON PEAK (8700) ahead.

7.9 R   Picnic Shelter

Picnic shelter on the creek draining Mts. Galwey and DUNGARVAN (8500).

9.3 L   Confluence

Confluence of Bauerman and Blakiston Creeks. The road goes up Bauerman Creek to the Red Rock Canyon Exhibit and adjacent parking. RED ROCK CANYON has been cut in brilliant red Grinnell argillite by the small stream flowing here from CLOUDY RIDGE (8489) to the northeast. The smooth vertical faces in the canyon wall are structural joints possibly created by stresses set up during periods of mountain movement. Rounded surfaces on the wall are probably remnants of old potholes, so common elsewhere in similar gorges. The paler strips of greenish argillite make a pleasing contrast to the vivid reds, and a somber spruce forest provides an august setting.

The road ends at a parking area but a trail continues along Bauerman Creek. At 2.5 miles above Red Rock Canyon, a trail (R) strikes for GOAT LAKE (6500), two miles farther in the basin on the south side of NEWMAN PEAK (8250), which is on the north park boundary.

Two creeks meet at Twin Lakes Warden Patrol Cabin, 4.9 miles from the trailhead. A trail up the right member leads to LOST LAKES (6200), 1.0 mile, and to CASTLE RIVER DIVIDE (6600), 1.7 miles. The divide, which is the north park boundary, can be followed for two miles to the summit of AVION RIDGE (7997) to the east. The left branch at Twin Lakes Cabin leads 1.9 miles to a kitchen and campground on TWIN LAKES (6500) stocked with rainbow and brook trout.

Just before reaching the lakes, a 0.7-mile spur climbs to SAGE PASS (7000) on the provincial border a half-mile north of Upper Twin Lake. The trail continues south past Lower Twin Lake, climbs over a low unnamed pass (6700) and goes past shallow BLUE GROUSE LAKE (6400) to South Kootenay Pass Trail, two miles from Twin Lakes. The junction is a mile below South Kootenay Pass. The circuit from the Red Rock Canyon trailhead via Twin Lakes and return via Lone Creek (South Kootenay Pass Trail) is 15 miles.

SOUTH KOOTENAY PASS TRAIL starts across the road from the Red Rock exhibit, crosses Bauerman Creek and ascends Blakiston Creek between Mt. Blakiston and picturesque Anderson Peak. At 0.7 mile the trail passes a viewpoint of BLAKISTON FALLS (4900). At 3.2 miles the main trail climbs LONE CREEK CANYON between MT. HAWKINS (8800) and LOST MT. (8240). Much of the trail is in forest as it passes over red or green argillite slopes. At 6000 feet it ascends rapidly by three switchbacks to the junction of the trail to Twin Lakes, some six miles distant, as mentioned above. A short distance beyond this junction, a two-mile trail branches to the left to LONE LAKE (6700) on MT. FESTUBERT (8274). There is a warden patrol cabin, horse corral and primitive campsite. From the Lone Lake Trail junction (R), it is an additional mile and 700 feet of climb to South Kootenay Pass (6903) on the British Columbia border. This pass was a historic trade route used extensively by the Kootenai Indians on their travels from the prairies east of the mountains to the Tobacco Plains in the Flathead River drainage west of the Continental Divide.

Akamina Highway

Waterton Townsite to Cameron Lake, 9.5 miles

Akamina Highway follows bow-shaped Cameron Creek up a picturesque canyon to make a pleasant short drive from Waterton Townsite. It ends at Cameron Lake in a basin squeezed against the Continental Divide. Several inviting trails start from the road for destinations in the mountains.

0.0 L   Waterton Townsite

The highway begins at the broad road junction on the northern edge of town below the Prince of Wales Hotel. It climbs the outwash fan in a broad sweep followed by a hairpin curve.

0.4   Overlook

A good overlook of the village and its surroundings. The complicated structure of Vimy Peak (7825) across the lake is quite evident from this vantage point. The lowest rocks of the promontory extending north to the Bosporus are of Waterton Formation, the oldest in Waterton-Glacier. Cameron Falls, below the road, is also cut in this formation, which is immediately below the Altyn Formation.

Waterton Lake was named by Lt. Thomas Wright Blakiston after Charles Waterton, the English naturalist. Lt. Blakiston was a member of the Palliser Scientific Expedition which in 1858 crossed South Kootenay Pass by an approach from the west.

2.8 L   Waterfall

An attractive waterfall in Cameron Creek. The canyon is assuming gorge character, and the road has dropped close to stream level. The long roadcut ahead exposes strata of sandy dolomite with some gray and green siltstones dipping at steep angles. A little farther, the uniformity of strata ceases abruptly in a thin zone of crushed and broken rubble which marks a fault. Sedimentary layers are folded and abruptly terminated by a minor overthrust above the fault.

3.9 L   Picnic Shelter

Bighorn ewes often come to the highway along here looking for handouts from would-be animal lovers. Because they have learned to depend on unnatural food, they are scrawny and find it hard to survive the rigors of winter. To be really kind to wild animals, visitors should refrain from feeding them. Also, it is *illegal* to feed wildlife in national parks.

4.0 R   Trail to Crandell Lake

Trail to Crandell Lake (5000), 1.0 mile. Visitors may go on foot or on horseback starting from the west side of Crandell Lodge. The trail runs above the highway until it turns for the short 300-foot climb over the low pass (5300) between Ruby Ridge and Mt. Crandell. Kitchen shelters are located at both ends of the lake in which rainbow and brook trout thrive. A round trip can be made to mile 5.0 on Red Rock Highway and around Mt. Crandell back to the starting point, making a complete circuit of roughly 12 miles.

5.4 L   Pullout

High falls in the creek. The gorge is cut in Altyn Formation, mostly buffy dolomite with gray limestone strata and ripple-marked sandy beds.

5.7   Site of Oil City

The first oil well in Alberta was drilled on the canyon wall in 1886. A townsite was plotted, but all that remains today are a few foundation walls and odd bits, including well casings, one of which has a broken drill stem stuck in it.

5.8 R   Lineham Lakes Trail and Lineham Creek

For some three miles this trail ascends on an open, flowery hillside, then passes through open forest near the creek to a 400-foot waterfall. To go farther, a difficult route must be bushwhacked up the cliff to the right. To proceed beyond this point a climbing permit must be obtained free of charge from a park warden or one of the park offices. Three large and two small lakes, stocked with cutthroat, lie above in a charming alpine basin between Mts. Lineham (8900) and Hawkins (8800). These lakes may also be reached by compass routes over high passes from Lone Lake and Red Rock Highway, or via Lower Rowe Lake, each about four long miles distant.

6.5 R   Rowe Lakes Trail; Rowe Creek

The trail ascends in a forest between Mts. Lineham (R) and Rowe (8043). After about two miles a short spur to the left crosses the creek to tiny Lower Rowe Lake (6200). The main trail climbs 3.8 miles along the right branch and via switchbacks to Upper Rowe Lake (7000), stocked with cutthroat.

8.1 L   Little Prairie Picnic Area

Little Prairie Picnic Area with shelter and wood stove.

9.3 R   Trailhead

Foot and horse trail to AKAMINA PASS (5835), 0.5 mile, on the British Columbia line, and down Akamina and Kishinena Creeks to the North Fork Flathead River.

9.5   Cameron Lake

Cameron Lake (5445), northern tip of lake. Exhibits, washrooms and boat rentals; 1.3-mile footpath down the west shore; start of the Summit Lake Trail to the International Boundary, 6.5 miles, and to Waterton Townsite, 14.5 miles, via Boundary Trail (137); also start of trail over Carthew Pass to Waterton Townsite at Cameron Falls, 12.0 miles.

Cameron Lake lies in a glacial basin under FORUM PEAK (7922). The point where British Columbia, Alberta and Montana all meet is 0.2 mile southeast of the summit. The extreme southern tip of Cameron Lake lies in the United States.

MORE THAN 850 MILES OF

TRAILS

IN WATERTON-GLACIER INTERNATIONAL PEACE PARK

Waterton-Glacier is prime trail country. Auto tours, boat trips or short rambles from hotels and chalets yield spectacular thrills, whetting the appetite for the sublime grandeur to be seen and felt in full measure from trails to isolated points. In this chapter frequently used trails are treated in detail starting at centers from which travel normally begins.

Some trails are treated in two sections. For example, the trail between Lake McDonald and Sun Point is divided between an account from Lake McDonald Lodge to Sperry Chalets, which bears the heavier travel, and from Sun Point to Sperry Chalets, on which the traveler faces the spectacular views east of the Continental Divide. Information on some trails used primarily for patrol and fire control is included in the chapter on Highways and Roads. Refer to the index for this.

Trails in Glacier National Park bear official names and identifying numbers, but these numbers do not ordinarily appear on trail signs that clearly mark all important trail junctions. Canadian trails have established names but no identifying trail numbers. To clarify trail descriptions in this book, maps of important trail centers are provided, bearing administrative trail numbers as well as 6000- and 8000-foot contour lines. These maps appear in the fold-out section. The most reliable official data available are used for trail distances.

Larger scale maps are sold at information centers in the two parks. A 1:63360 map of Waterton Lakes Park may be purchased from the Map Distribution Office, Department of Mines and Technical Surveys, Ottawa. A 1:125000 topographic map of Glacier National Park and 1:24000 maps of 7-1/2" quadrangles are sold by the U.S. Geological Survey in Washington, D.C. 20242, or in Denver, Colorado 80225.

Compass users should note that magnetic deviation for the region is approximately 20° E, which means that all compass readings must be increased by 20° to get true bearings. Thus, when the compass needle points to N, 0°, the true bearing is 020 or 20° E of North. The direction of the compass needle pointing to E, 090, is 110° true, or 20° S of East. Deviation varies with location and time. Precise data are included on the topographic maps.

As it is not feasible to describe all natural history features in detail wherever they are encountered on the trail, reference should be made to appropriate chapters and to the index.

Trails from Lake McDonald and Avalanche Campground

Gunsight Pass Trail (52), West Section

Lake McDonald Lodge to Sperry Chalets, 6.4 miles; to Sperry Glacier, 9.9 miles; to Lake Ellen Wilson, 9.1 miles; to Jackson Glacier Overlook, 19.0 miles; to Sun Point, 21.9 miles. See fold-out map.

Before the road over Logan Pass was opened, the Gunsight Pass Trail was part of the popular circuit called the South Circle, which also included trails over Piegan Pass to Many Glacier, over Swiftcurrent Pass to Granite Park, and to Lake McDonald via McDonald Creek. The present alignment up Snyder and Sprague Creeks on the sides of Mt. Brown and Edwards Mt. was built in the fall of 1933, but reconstruction was necessary after the floods of 1964. Travel time to the chalets can be as little as two and one-half hours, but hikers who are not in top physical shape should plan to at least double that amount of time. Several more hours are required to climb to the glacier. The vertical climb is 3432 feet from Lake McDonald to the chalets, with an additional 1500 feet to the glacier. Since the trail to the chalets has southern exposure and is out of the forest much of the distance, travel is best early in the morning or in late afternoon. The trail to the glacier also is more pleasurable at these times, especially if one expects to see mountain goats.

Several trails begin in common across Going-to-the-Sun Road from the McDonald Lodge parking strip, going straight ahead past the old sewage disposal plant. At a junction just past this area, the Avalanche Trail (56) branches left past the horse corral to Avalanche Campground; Trail 52 to Sperry Chalets and Glacier and Gunsight Pass continues straight ahead.

For the first mile Trail 52 rises in a forest of red cedars, hemlocks and larches. Red cedars disappear first, then the others, as their places are filled by white pines, Douglas firs, spruces, true firs and random lodgepole pines. Big cottonwoods grow near the creek. Lower dead branches, especially on larches, bear heavy growths of black witch's hair lichen. Shrubs increase as one climbs and include most of the common species found in the Canadian Life Zone. Red and black raspberries, as well as thimbleberries, serviceberries and tasty huckleberries grow beside the trail and bear good fruit in season. At lower elevations the thick growths of devil's club along the stream contribute an Alaskan aspect to the forest.

Wildflowers are few in the dense woods; twin flowers, bunchberries, pyrolas, pine drops and saprophytic Indian pipes are among interesting species found early in the season. Flowerless plants include trailing club mosses and various fungal heart rots whose many fruiting bodies appear as conchs on tree trunks.

Winter wrens, Cassin's finches, several kinds of wood warblers, Steller's jays, flickers, nuthatches, woodpeckers and thrushes are common. Black bear and deer may be seen and occasionally some rarer mammal such as pine marten; but animal life in general, aside from pine squirrels and chipmunks, is not conspicuous in heavy forest.

Rock formations along the route are, in order of appearance, greenish Appekunny argillite, red Grinnell argillite around the chalets and on the high cirque walls of Gunsight and Edwards Mts., and buff Helena (Siyeh) limestone and dolomite forming the summits of Gunsight and Jackson Mts.

1.7 miles from Sun Road, Mt. Brown Lookout Trail (49) begins a steep 3.7 mile zigzag course to the lookout (7478) on a ridge below the summit. A tenth-mile farther on trail 52, Snyder Lake Trail (50) parallels Snyder Creek 2.6 miles to lower Snyder Lake, while trail 52 drops on the right to cross Snyder Creek at Crystal Ford. Trail 52 meets Snyder Ridge Trail (45) on the far side.

At the ford the trail to Sperry turns upstream, briskly climbs the ridge extending westerly from Edwards Mt. and enters the drainage basin of Sprague Creek.

For the next two miles the trail idles in easy ascent of a few hundred feet in open forest until,

3.8 miles from the road, two sharp switchbacks startle it into dogged assault of the glacial wall on Edwards Mt. Another 0.9 mile farther BEAVER MEDICINE FALLS is the beautiful plunge of Sprague Creek nearby.

The country opens with altitude; the slopes are covered with beargrass, giving a magnificent display in opulent years. There are increasingly numerous blossoms of other plants; false hellebore, columbine, larkspur, lupine, fireweed, false forget-me-not, red and purple penstemons, red monkeyflower, paintbrush, butter-and-eggs, arnica, tall ragwort, goldenrod and showy fleabane. The lower limit of the Hudsonian Zone (6000) is on the cirque floor below the chalets which break into view appearing tantalizingly close, but are a last long weary mile farther and 600 tiring feet higher. At 6.0 miles the trail crosses Sprague Creek by a footbridge.

Upstream, 0.2 mile above the bridge, trail 51 turns to the left, bound for Sperry Glacier, while the right fork, trail 52, turns and climbs to the chalets, 0.2 mile farther and to Sperry Campground, 0.2 mile above the chalets.

Beyond the chalets and campground, trail 52 goes over Lincoln and Gunsight Passes to its junction with the Piegan Pass Trail (113) just below Deadwood Falls on Reynolds Creek. Various exit routes from there are described under Trails from Sun Point, Gunsight Pass Trail (52), East Section.

The nature of a compound cirque is well illustrated at Sperry. A short distance above the lowest switchback is the wall over which BEAVER MEDICINE FALLS plunges. Another cirque wall is surmounted by the chalets. A third wall encircles the basin northeast of the chalets. Smaller cirques are higher, entered on the way to the glacier.

Near the chalets, forests have thinned to isolated groups of whitebark pines and stunted subalpine firs. Shrubby plants are prostrate and spreading, but white and purple heathers, kalmia, dwarf huckleberry and alpine willow are naturally low-growing. Flowering plants are brilliant: glacier lily, beargrass, cinquefoil, chickweed, white catchfly, buttercups, globeflower, anemone, yellow columbine, larkspur, milk vetch, alpine fireweed, various saxifrages, blue gentian, stickseed, blue phacelia, Jacob's-ladder, heliotrope, monkeyflowers, alpine penstemon, elephant's-heads, paintbrush, yellow arnica and showy aster. Attractive rock ferns grow on cirque walls with maidenhair, parsley and lace ferns outstanding.

The open environment provides splendid opportunity to see and study wildlife: marmots, pikas, black bear, snowshoe hares, Columbian and golden-mantled ground squirrels, alpine chipmunks, weasels, deer and, especially, mountain goats. Birds, although fewer in numbers and species, are easier to see: there are many nutcrackers, jays, siskins, white-crowned sparrows and crossbills. A little higher, rosy finches, ptarmigan and pipits appear, while golden eagles soar over the highest cliffs.

Sperry Glacier Trail

Horses are not permitted on Sperry Glacier Trail (51) which begins 0.2 mile below the chalets. The trail bends in a great arc gouged out of a rose-purple wall before climbing the narrow defile between Gunsight and Edwards Mts. and passing through FEATHER WOMAN FALLS which showers the passerby with mild, refreshing spray.

After touching the intensely folded and contorted strata forming the cliffs of Edwards Mt., the trail oscillates with increasing altitude from one side of the glacial staircase to the other. A sheer argillite wall blocks the head of the cirque. Views become expansive, embracing the trail to Lincoln Pass (6050) on the wall in back of the chalets and, in the distance, Flathead Valley and the peaks of the Flathead Range topped by Great Northern Mt. (8705) with Stanton Glacier. This is the haven of mountain goats. Busy pikas bleat plaintively in the talus; fat marmots slouch on rocky shelves in the warm sunshine.

Two exquisite gems, FEATHER WOMAN LAKE (7538) and AKAIYAN LAKE (7720), lie in the narrowing acclivity. Below them is AKAIYAN FALLS.

Akaiyan and Feather Woman are principal characters in one version of the legend of the beaver bundle, the most powerful medicine possessed by the Blackfeet. Medicine bundles are collections of sacred objects revealed to the originator in dreams and visions, who passes them down to another owner, who then becomes charged with the rigid care and strict maintenance of the bundle, as well as with the mastery and precise performance of an elaborate accompanying ritual. Bundles are opened only on solemn occasions, like the Sun Dance, to call on superhuman aid. Transported traditionally only by dog travois and never carried on the warpath, the beaver bundle served the vital purpose of calling buffalo and the cultural necessity of sowing and harvesting tobacco. During the ceremony lasting hours or days, each object animated with supernatural power is removed in turn with circumspection, waved in demonstration with chanting, and placed before the ritualist seated on the ground.

In the early 30's, Ksis-tau'-a-na (sis is as in sister; rhymes with cow; -a- is a short AH!; na rhymes with -a-; a strong accent is on the second syllable as indicated), or Bird Rattle (sometimes called Bird Rattler) possessed a beaver bundle which was always suspended from a tripod outside his painted tipi. In his log cabin on Cut Bank Creek six miles north of Browning, the bundle was hung on the west wall above Bird Rattle's ceremonial seat. As in a tipi, this is always opposite the door which must face east. By some, Bird Rattle is regarded as the last esteemed Blackfeet medicine man.

With prayers and incantation, the owner of a bundle would ceremoniously untie the elk thongs enclosing it and hold aloft each item of its contents; perhaps a beaver claw, beaver teeth, the foot of a crow, a fish vertebra, kinnikinnick, a sacred buffalo stone or *iniskim* which is a curiously-shaped fossil ammonite found on the plains. Each had appropriate songs and prayers: "Beaver! I take! It is powerful!" "Give me of thy medicine, oh buffalo!" "Oh Morning Star! Oh Seven Stars! All of the stars! I call on you for help!" Streaked with vermillion clay, suppliants knelt before the medicine man, while he prayed for alleviation of woes or for strength and success on a forthcoming venture.

Before the assembled tribe, on a cold February day in 1930 during the annual Blackfeet Winter Fair, Bird Rattle and his wife, Samosi or Goes-After-Water, formally and overtly adopted the author as their son, giving him the name "Ninaistako," Chief Mountain. In characteristic manner, he proclaimed that the peak, Chief Mountain, like their new son, best symbolized Glacier National Park and its ranges to the Blackfeet people. Thereafter, he always hailed the author as *Ksisknochkoa,* my white son, or as *Ninaipokah*, the chief's son.

The author was once introduced by a group of entertainers to an assembly of visitors at Many Glacier Hotel with "Us Indians believe Ninaistako is just as good as any one of us," which, coming from the proud Blackfeet, is a compliment indeed. Years later, Bird Rattle passed on to his white son a small bundle wrapped in red calico with strict injunction never to open it without proper ceremony. This sacred object has been presented to the Smithsonian Institution in Washington along with other gifts received for participation in ceremonies for President F. D. Roosevelt, Crown Prince Olaf and Crown Princess Martha of Norway, Chief Justice and Mrs. Harlan Fiske Stone, and FBI Director J. Edgar Hoover.

Once at the close of a sweatlodge ceremony, the author was beckoned to kneel before Bird Rattle, who proceeded aloud to pour out his heart in earnest plea in the assertive Blackfeet tongue. All the while copious tears streamed down his cheeks as he smeared broad bands of red paint across the author's brow. Later, interpreter-witness Reuben Black Boy disclosed what the chief remarked after the ceremony: "I did not know to whom my son wishes me to pray, and for what he sought petition, so I prayed the best I know how to the Giver of All Good that he grant my son wisdom and those things which are good." And what better prayer might be uttered?

Above the lakes, 3.1 miles from the chalets, a stairway has been blasted in a chimney in the headwall. Before the 30's, access to the top was via a steel ladder placed nearby.

Tiny, rock-bound GEM LAKE, formerly called Lake of the Seven Stars, rests on top of grassy COMEAU PASS (8000), named after a settler who explored routes about 1890 and pioneered in guiding parties to the glacier. Among these were groups under Professor Lyman B. Sperry of Oberlin College, Ohio, who, in 1895 or 1896, bestowed his name on the glacier, previously called by the Kootenais, "Son Ice."

The sharp red pyramid to the left is the LITTLE MATTERHORN (7886) which rises above Snyder Basin. The deep basin of AVALANCHE LAKE, 3500 feet below the rim, is to the north. Beyond the basin, from left to right, appear HEAVENS PEAK (8987), MT. CANNON (8952), BEARHAT MT. (8684), REYNOLDS MT. (9125), the peaks of the Garden Wall and Logan Pass, MT. SIYEH (10,014) and GOING-TO-THE-SUN MT. (9642).

Sperry Glacier itself is no longer visible from Comeau Pass, but is reached in 0.9 mile via a route marked with rock cairns over bedrock terraces covered with loose glacial till. Even during the height of summer, foggy and/or wintry weather conditions often prevail at this elevation and may temporarily obscure the route; proceed with caution.

Sperry Glacier

Not many years ago, Sperry Glacier completely filled the cirque between Gunsight and Edwards Mts. The mammoth glacier spilled over Comeau Pass and over the gap north of Edwards Mt. into Snyder Basin. The sector of ice left on Edwards which is protected by the shadow of the mountain was detached from the main mass in 1919. It has torn away from the cliff, creating a bergshrund. The edge of the ice is steep and covered with perennial snow. The main mass of the glacier remaining today is shut from view from Comeau Pass by a spur of Gunsight Mt.

On the west side of the cirque, the vivid maroon pavement, banded with white quartzite, has but recently been smoothed and polished by the glacier. Glacial processes of quarrying and stoping are clearly demonstrated: blocks become loosened along joints, are broken away, and moved distances from a fraction of an inch upward. Melt water is tinted red. Subglacial streams have scoured narrow, tortuous channels up to several feet deep in the floor which are exposed as the ice melts.

The surface of the glacier appears smooth while buried under a snow layer in early season, but becomes deeply crevassed and covered with slush and streams of melt water by midsummer. Moulins, tables, dust wells, seracs, bergshrunds and other features develop as the season progresses. The most interesting are farthest away, near the front of the glacier, where there are huge moraines, marginal caves, turquoise lakelets dammed by ice or drift and rivers gushing from beneath the ice. Often ponds are chosen as homesites by water ouzels.

The ice of the glacier reveals its exquisite blue-green color wherever it is sufficiently thin, but the face of the glacier is banded; each dirty streak is the exposed edge of a former surface soiled with debris and marks a year's increment of ice. Similar banding is seen on the walls of ice caves and crevasses; some of the caves may be followed under the glacier for more than a hundred feet, but this is a highly hazardous stunt.

Walls of caves may be covered with a veneer of rock powder, the product of abrasion since clear ice is behind the coating. Larger rock fragments frozen in the matrix serve as grinding tools and are strewn at random on the floor, which is smooth, striated and highly polished. A varnish of powder is sometimes streaked on rock faces, in places bearing rich brown color. Here and there a rock lies at the lower end of a striation or groove which it has dug, like a tool dropped by a workman, to be picked up for further use as the ice advances and grips it once again. Where ice projects above the bedrock, the surface shows that it has been modeled and fluted by irregularities.

On the far side of the glacier, the cirque wall reflects intense heat of the sun, creating a titanic moat a hundred feet deep. This is a novel feature. The glacier rounds a spur of rock and spreads out slowly beyond it, leaving a marginal depression that reveals stratified ice several hundreds of feet long: there are no streams or lakes in the bottom of the trough, drainage being subglacial. The bedrock of the mountain wall and the glacial floor is Helena (Siyeh) limestone.

The lofty, narrow piles of till beyond the glacier have uneven crests and impound turquoise lakes of gletschermilch (glacier milk). The cores of these moraines are largely of ice. Along most of its front, the glacier is melting backward so rapidly that the ice rests on bare rock; but in a few places it pushes against moraines. Outer moraines are already much weathered, so that some bear a scant cover of soil, hardy shrubs and plants. Attractive alpine lady ferns grow on loose rock in dense clumps a foot to a yard wide, appearing at their best against a background of Grinnell argillite.

Even though it looks very safe, one should not tempt fortune by going upon the glacier without necessary equipment and a competent guide. One should not go alone and must be properly shod and equipped with ice axe, crampons and rope. Stay far away from dangerous crevasses and wells and remember that snow masks treacherous pitfalls. The big moulins and yawning crevasses do not open up and become obvious hazards until well into August.

A person of good endurance can hike from Logan Pass to Sperry Glacier, but as a safety precaution, cross-country hikers should report to park officials before and after making the trip. The entire route is in open country without technical difficulties, but as it is arduous, it should be undertaken only by toughened, experienced hikers. Beyond Hidden Pass a route is picked along the west shore of Hidden Lake and up the headwall below BEARHAT MT.

Gunsight Mt. can be climbed along the ridge west of Sperry Glacier without ropes or guide. The view from the summit is exceptionally grand and widespread. One should, however, exercise the usual precaution of testing all hand and foot holds to make sure they are firm. The temptation to glissade down steep snowbanks should be resisted by novices, as fatalities have resulted from this practice.

Edwards Mt. is most easily climbed starting a short distance north from Comeau Pass and picking a route up the talus and low cliffs to the gentle crest of the ridge which extends east from the summit.

Mt. Brown Fire Lookout and Snyder Lakes

Lake McDonald to Mt. Brown Fire Lookout via trail 49, 5.4 miles; to Snyder Lakes via trail 50, 4.4 miles. See fold-out map.

Two rewarding, moderately long trails break off from Gunsight Pass Trail (52), 1.7 miles above Lake McDonald Lodge. It is possible, although not recommended, for a hiker to combine visits to the two destinations in a long, 16-mile day. The portion of the route over trail 52 is described earlier under Trails from Lake McDonald, Gunsight Pass Trail (52), West Section.

Mt. Brown Lookout Trail (49) climbs immediately by a long series of steep switchbacks from its base in the dense forest. With elevation come distant views. The lookout (7478) is 5.4 miles from the lodge. Though fireguards are no longer stationed at the lookout, outside the upper catwalk, park backcountry rangers have posted a copy of an old logbook which welcomes visitors and describes the way of life of previous fireguards. Also provided is a registration booklet for hikers to sign and record their own comments on trail conditions, weather and wildlife.

The summit of Mt. Brown (8565) is a mile northeast of the lookout. Since the ascent presents possible hazards, climbers should first consult experienced rangers or a park climbing guidebook for the most accessible route.

Snyder Lake Trail (50) branches to the left off Gunsight Pass Trail (52) 0.1 mile above the base of Mt. Brown Trail (49). The ascent, by contrast, is on a gentle slope a hundred feet or more above Snyder Creek.

The forest changes gradually from one dominated by larches to white pines, then spruces and Douglas firs. Snowberry and huckleberry bushes are common. Holly, oak and male ferns and club mosses abound in moister maple-alder wetland. Occasional moose appear, and a pine marten, with head cocked at varying angles, may peer from a lodgepole bough in inquisitive scrutiny of the intruder. Woodland birds enjoy the shadows of the brush-lined stream.

The trail ends abruptly at Snyder Lake (5200), cradled in a basin collared with great, blocky talus. The serene water holds small westslope cutthroat trout. Large spruces provide shady sites for pitching tents in the nearby campground across the outlet, but no wood fires are permitted.

A larger, more beautiful lake (5574) reposes in the basin beyond the waterfall at the head of the lake, but there is no passage to it by trail so the hiker must cautiously clamber over and around the big boulders to reach it. The easier route is to the right side of the lower lake, choosing as a target the break in the cliff above a slide of broken rubble. The left slope is tougher because of the dense brush.

The magnificent headwall around the upper lake is crowned by the spike of LITTLE MATTERHORN (7886) with the abyss of Avalanche Basin on the other side.

Fish Lake

Lake McDonald Lodge to Fish Lake, 2.4 miles. See fold-out map.

Fish Lake, a rewarding half day outing from the Lake McDonald Lodge area, lies along the

Snyder Ridge Trail (45) 0.5 mile from its junction with the Gunsight Pass Trail (52) at Crystal Ford. The portion of the route over Gunsight Pass Trail is described earlier under Trails from Lake McDonald.

After leaving Crystal Ford, trail 45 enters a mixed forest of white pines, larches and hemlocks. The forest floor is covered by heavy duff with frequent windfalls and felled trees. Many different species of mosses, crustose lichens and occasional slime molds may be distinguished on rocks and rotting logs. Green-bearded lichens grow in profusion on living trees. The numerous, large rectangular holes in the boles of dead cedars were chipped by pileated woodpeckers, in search of insects and their larvae. The stringy, fibrous nature of the wood contributes to the unusual shape of the openings.

Fish Lake is a small, shallow, warm body without direct inlet or outlet, deriving its water from Sprague Creek by seepage. Yellow pondlilies grace the surface. These plants are widely distributed from the Dakotas to Alaska, and their seeds, "wokas," were much used by coastal tribes for food. Uncommon bog-loving plants, including the insect-eating sundew and sweet-scented ladies-tresses, a small white orchid, grow in wet land along the shore. Red-legged and tree frogs are abundant near the edge of the water. Hybrid cutthroat trout also live in the lake, but fishing success tapers off during the summer as the water warms.

The lake basin is gradually being filled by an interesting quaking bog of sphagnum moss and sedges in the process of forming peat. Deposits have been dated back 1500 years by their pollen content. A thick layer of black muck rests on the lake bottom.

West Lakes and Camas Creek Trails

North Lake McDonald Road to Trout Lake, 3.5 miles; to Arrow Lake 6.9 miles; to Camas Lake, 10.5 miles. See fold-out map.

West Lakes Trail (9) formerly went 51 miles all the way up the valley of the North Fork Flathead River to the foot of Kintla Lake. It paralleled the Inside North Fork Road at higher elevation and passed below the long finger lakes of the Livingston Range. Segments of the trail have been obliterated by blowdowns and floods or closed because of lack of maintenance funds or use. Most traversable sectors are mentioned at appropriate points in the log of Inside North Fork Road. This description concerns itself only with the southern end of the trail, from Lake McDonald over Howe Ridge, and with connecting Camas Trail (39) which continues up the floor of Camas Creek Valley.

The trailhead for West Lakes Trail (9) is above Lake McDonald lakeshore, 0.8 mile beyond Lake McDonald Ranger Station. It is conveniently reached by car, leaving Going-to-the-Sun Road at mile 12.3. The narrow, unimproved single lane has been widened at the trailhead to provide parking for a few cars.

At the start trail 9 climbs Howe Ridge in heavy forest. At 0.8 mile and an elevation of 4200 feet, four short switchbacks carry it rapidly upward 200 feet. Just below the crest, at 2.3 miles, Howe Ridge (Fire) Trail (37) branches to the left to the head of Howe Lake Trail (38), a brushy, lightly-maintained 6.4 miles; and to mile 4.8 of the Inside North Fork Road, 9.6 miles. Howe Lake Trail (38) drops from the trail junction (37, 38) to Howe Lake, 1.7 miles and to mile 7.3 of the Inside North Fork Road, 3.7 miles.

Trail 9 reaches the broad crest of Howe Ridge at 5140 feet, then descends gently in woods before making a headlong plunge of 600 feet by six switchbacks to the verdant floor of Camas Creek Valley and a junction with Camas Creek Trail (39), 1.2 miles farther. The bare mountain ahead is Rogers Peak (7320). Turning downstream, trail 39 continues for 6.9 miles, first above Rogers Lake (3793) which cannot be seen from the trail, then in open, inviting forest to the northwest of Rogers Meadow and past the site of Rogers cabins and an early homestead, finally past Christensen Meadows to the Inside North Fork Road, mile 9.3.

Up valley from the trail junction of 9 and 39 at the foot of Howe Ridge near the outlet of Trout Lake (3903), Camas Creek Trail (39) goes a short distance to open forest on the lakeshore, the scene of a fatal incident with a grizzly in August 1967. Camas Creek Valley is prime grizzly range; one must always be alert NOT TO STARTLE, ENTICE OR ANTAGONIZE THESE POWERFUL BEASTS.

The trail along Trout Lake is in timber, but enters meadows above the lake, going 3.4 miles to Arrow Lake (4070). The trail then ascends 3.6 miles along the north shore of Arrow Lake to terminate at the foot of Camas Lake (5076). Infrequent maintenance beyond Arrow Lake may make trail-finding a challenge. Fishing (fly fishing only) can be very good in all of the lakes mentioned. Day use of Camas Creek Valley is encouraged; camping is permitted only at the designated site at Camas Lake.

Trail 39 traverses great moose country, and one should be wary of approaching these animals too closely or of taking them by surprise, for they have, on occasion, charged and chased intruders up trees. Elk may appear; their bugling in early autumn is a concomitant melody of the valley. Otters are sometimes seen at play in the creek; and a rare treat is to come upon a lynx or bobcat unexpectedly. Pine marten are not easily disturbed if one's movements are deliberate; quiet approach and rapt observation can yield the thrill of an encounter with rarer wildlife.

Sacred Dancing Cascade Circuit
(McDonald Falls, Sacred Dancing Cascade and Johns Lake)
Round trip from Lake McDonald Lodge, 5.0 miles. See fold-out map.

McDonald Creek Trail (59) starts on the North Lake McDonald Road, 0.2 mile west of the road bridge over Upper McDonald Creek. To reach this bridge by vehicle turn on the unsigned, paved road at mile 12.3 of Going-to-the-Sun Road. Hikers from Lake McDonald Lodge can follow Avalanche Trail (56) for 1.4 miles from its start across Going-to-the-Sun Road from the main lodge parking strip to connect with the Avalanche Cutoff Trail (258). Trail 258 slants 0.5 mile across Sun Road at mile 12.2 to the North Lake McDonald Road and a short walk to the above-mentioned bridge.

To avoid a stretch of trail 59 that is seasonally very muddy or dusty from horse use, hikers can follow a footpath about 50 yards west of the bridge. This unsigned trail stays closer to McDonald Creek and Paradise Canyon, skirting the lip of McDonald Falls before rejoining trail 59. (The almost forgotten name, "Paradise Canyon," applies to the colorful box canyon of Upper McDonald Creek, downstream from the falls.) Trail 59 continues upstream 0.3 mile to a junction at the footbridge at Sacred Dancing Cascade. From there trail 59 formerly extended up the valley as part of a loop called the South Circle Trip, between Lake McDonald, Granite Park, Many Glacier, Sun Camp and Sperry centers. Now much of the trail has been abandoned for various reasons: the fire of 1936, the flood of 1964, and decrease in use because of the proximity of the transmountain road. From the footbridge trail 59 continues 2.5 miles up the valley, passing a backwater oxbow of McDonald Creek. Deer, bear and other animals, including moose, may be met in the delightfully cool forest. Wild hollyhock appear to prefer the freshly-turned rock along the trail, the flower spikes making a pink streak on the wall in blossomtime. A few scattered Douglas firs grow to large size and have thick heavily-furrowed bark. Engelmann spruce and fir become very large. Trail 59 ends along McDonald Creek across from a viewing platform on the Sun Road north of Moose Country.

Across the footbridge from trail 59, to complete a circuit back to their starting point, hikers can choose between two linking trails. McDonald Creek Cutoff Trail (57) used by guided horse parties crosses Going-to-the-Sun Road through an underpass, then climbs 0.7 mile to join Avalanche Trail (56). Since trail 57 receives heavy horse use, hikers may prefer to take the graded walk up from the footbridge to Sun Road at mile 13.0, then cross the road to Johns Lake Trail (259). In 0.4 mile trail 259 joins trail 56. Following trail 56 down the valley, hikers can either return to McDonald Lodge or take trail 258 back to the North Lake McDonald Road or bridge. For a description of trail 56, see below.

Avalanche Trail
Lake McDonald Lodge to Avalanche Campground, 5.9 miles. See fold-out map.

Avalanche Trail (56), following the base of Mt. Brown and out of sight of the road, is the main route for hikers and horsemen from Lake McDonald to Avalanche Campground. The walk is nearly level and may be covered in two to three hours.

Starting with the Gunsight Pass Trail (52), trail 56 shortly turns to the left. The site of the sawmill used during the construction of the hotel in 1913 was near the start of the trail. The first mile is through a beautiful stand of western red cedars, with a gradually increasing proportion of larches and hemlocks.

Many dead larches are evident, but the cause of death is not apparent. The trunks are heavily riddled with holes drilled by woodpeckers in search of beetle larvae; the appearance of the bark suggests that the birds were not disappointed. Parallel horizontal lines of smaller holes circling hemlock boles are the work of yellow-bellied sapsuckers which lap exuded sap and entrapped insects with their brushlike tongues.

The hemlocks along the trail are heavily infested with Indian paint fungus (*Echinodontium tinctorum*). Scattered through the forest are occasional large cottonwoods and a few northwestern paper birches. Yews are common in the undergrowth, while alders and dwarf maples are occasional. Heavy duff and many windfalls cover the forest floor. Mosses and ferns are abundant. Olive-sided flycatchers, varied thrushes, red-breasted nuthatches, purple finches, warbling vireos, several species of wood warblers, winter wrens and many other birds may be seen and heard along this trail.

Trail 258 to the head of Lake McDonald slants to the road on the left 1.4 miles from the lodge, and continues to the terminus of West Lakes Trail (9) and of McDonald Lake Trail (43) down the northwest shore of that lake. It is part of Sacred Dancing Cascade Circuit described on page 73.

Avalanche Trail (56) continues straight ahead without crossing the road. In 0.1 mile, McDonald Cutoff Trail (57) angles obliquely to McDonald Creek and trail 59, 0.7 mile. Beyond the trail junction, Douglas firs, lodgepole pines and white pines grow on a warm, open slope; the floor is covered with a thick mat of beargrass and kinnikinnick, the latter used by Indians for smoking.

The forest quickly resumes its previous dense character. Three-tenths mile past the junction of trails 56 and 57 a small pond to the left of the trail offers a chance to find ducks of various kinds. A little farther are several interesting outcrops of limestone with thin fracture planes suggestive of shales. Just beyond is Johns Lake (3340), a small warm pond much like Fish Lake. It is rimmed with a gradually expanding sphagnum and sedge bog, in which several species of club moss, sundew (*Drosera rotunifolia*), and other interesting plants may be found. The forest of lodgepole pines, grand firs and spruces comes close to the water's edge to make exploration somewhat difficult, since there is no trail around the lake. Invertebrates in the lake include freshwater leeches.

Just beyond the lake the trail forks, the left branch (259) leading 0.4 mile to the road, then crossing McDonald Creek to McDonald Creek Trail (59). It is part of the Sacred Dancing Cascade Circuit described elsewhere. The fork to the right is Avalanche Trail.

A few large trees grow near the trail. A hemlock near 4.6 miles measures 42 inches in diameter, while at 5.0 miles, there is a stand of solemn giant red cedars. The interspersed boulders, the resilient mossy banks, pipsissewas, Indian pipes poking up their naked stalks, and above all, the cathedral stillness give the forest a hallowed atmosphere not unlike that of the stately redwoods of the West Coast. The lane nearby was cleared from Going-to-the-Sun Road, mile 14.5, in order that "thousands may see," but incipient damage and concern for the life of the trees quickly caused it to be blocked to wheel traffic; now it is dedicated only to the searcher for quiet nooks and for intimate knowledge of the beauty of McDonald Valley never to be grasped from an automobile.

At 5.9 miles the trail skirts Avalanche Campground on the left. To go to Avalanche Lake, 2.0 miles, continue another hundred yards to Avalanche Creek and follow trail 60 on its near bank. This trail is described separately. The creek can be crossed by a footbridge below its gorge nearby. On the opposite bank, self-guiding Trail of the Cedars, described below, proceeds on a boardwalk downstream 0.3 mile to Going-to-the-Sun Road and the entrance to Avalanche Campground, mile 16.6.

Avalanche Creek Trail

Avalanche Campground to foot of Avalanche Lake, 2.0 miles; to end of trail, 2.8 miles. See fold-out map.

Millennia ago a deep glacier pushed down Avalanche Canyon, abrading, plucking, smoothing and polishing the ancient rocks and fusing with the glacier that filled McDonald Valley. After the glacier melted, it left the high-walled, U-shaped canyon of today. A huge cirque at its head was quarried into purple-red walls a half-mile high over which a half-dozen silvery waterfalls now tumble. Deep, blue Avalanche Lake (3905) reposes in a solemn forest on the floor of the basin. Though it is not visible from the lake, Sperry Glacier lies on the shelf above the lake and in the shadow of Gunsight Mt. (9258) where it carves and abrades the mountain block as did its predecessor in past ages.

Avalanche Creek Trail (60) through this incredible canyon offers a beautiful short trip from McDonald Valley. The climb of 500 feet is gradual, requiring about an hour each way.

Near the foot of the trail and only a few hundred yards from the campground, Avalanche Creek races through a colorful gorge with walls 50 feet sheer, worn smooth and concave by pebbles gyrating in the swirling, frothing water. The rock is maroon Grinnell argillite, bright and fresh in the stream but near the banks mottled with the gold of lichens and emerald of mossy cushions kept verdant by the incessant spray. The drooping hemlocks shroud the gorge in shade so deep that it is a cool retreat on the hottest summer afternoon. Water ouzels complement the singing waters and fly merrily up and down the gorge.

It is well to view the gorge both from its mouth, which can be seen to best advantage from the footbridge downstream and from the rim, paralleled by the trail a few paces distant. (Beware of approaching too closely, as moss-covered logs and boulders can be very slippery.)

Avalanche Trail (56) reaches Avalanche Creek from Lake McDonald after passing through vaulted cathedral aisles of giant cedars. Immediately after branching off 56, trail 60 climbs to the rim of the gorge of Avalanche Creek which it follows throughout the entire course around the base of Mt. Brown. For the first mile it passes beneath hemlocks and larches with haphazard cedars and paper birches. Large cedar snags, scarred by fire and exceeding in girth any now living, are scattered at random. At one place a fallen cedar has rejuvenated, with several vertical branches growing vigorously from the prostrate bole and persisting apparently without independent root systems.

The songs of numerous birds fill the air; tracks of many animals are evident in the path. Snowshoe hares, pine squirrels and chipmunks scamper in and out of cover. Butterflies, mostly checkerspots and mourning cloaks, flutter among the flowers or bask in spots of sunshine. Cones of trees are sprinkled everywhere; flowering plants are common: beargrass, queen cups, pyrolas, columbines, arnicas, fireweeds, harebells and bunchberries.

As the trail climbs, the dense forest dissolves into an open stand of birches, cottonwoods and dwarf maples, with random larches and subalpine firs. Glimpses of the magnificent strata of the canyon and the fine cirque at its head unfold here and there. The entrance of the rugged canyon which drains Hidden Lake appears on the left. Small fragments of diorite are scattered beside the trail.

The trail glides into a dense stand of mature hemlocks heavily loaded with goatsbeard lichens, in which varied thrushes are almost certain to be seen or heard in company with Swainson's thrushes. Passing over a small open stretch, another almost pure stand of hemlock is reached, heavily infested by Indian paint fungus and loaded with strands of streaming beard lichens.

Since the 1964 flood the trail has been relocated near the creek as it weaves among maples, smaller shrubs and false helebores to the edge of the lake. The trail extends along the southwest shore terminating at the upper end of narrow, elongated and clear Avalanche Lake (3905). The lofty waterfalls at its head come from Sperry Glacier, out of view above the headwall. Small westslope cutthroat trout provide good early season fishing, especially at the inlet. Because this fish is a native species, the possession limit is two.

Trail of the Cedars

Going-to-the-Sun Road to Avalanche Creek Trail (60), 0.3 mile. See fold-out map.

Trail of the Cedars (256) is a self-guiding, handicapped-access nature trail along the north bank of Avalanche Creek across from Avalanche Campground. Its boardwalk affords a level, shady stroll in deep forest dominated by murmuring red cedars which "stand like the Druids of old with beards that rest on their bosoms." Interpretive signs describe some of the features of the area. The trail may be entered from the upper or east edge of the campground.

Trails from Going-to-the-Sun Road

McDonald Creek-Flattop Mt. Trails

Going-to-the-Sun Road to Packers Roost, 0.7 mile; Packers Roost to Fifty Mountain via Flattop Mt. Trail, 11.4 miles. (Packers Roost to Flattop Campground, 0.1 mile off the main trail, is approximately 6.5 miles.)

From mile 22.8 of Going-to-the-Sun Road, a gravel lane 0.7 mile long drops to Packers Roost (3800), starting point of the McDonald Creek Trail (63). Nine-tenths mile upstream from Packers Roost, Granite Park Trail (62) branches off to the right where in 0.8 mile it meets the half-mile spur from The Loop, (Sun Road mile 24.7), a favored route for hikers. Between the junction with trail 63 and the Loop spur, trail 62 fords a creek just above a small waterfall; the crossing can be seasonally hazardous for hikers.

Almost a mile above the Granite Park trail junction, trail 63 crosses Mineral Creek on a suspension bridge which is dismantled during the offseason. Two-tenths mile west of the bridge, Flattop Mountain Trail (66) begins, branching from the abandoned continuation of the McDonald Creek Trail.

Trail 66 briskly climbs the narrow defile of the creek; four short switchbacks in a quarter-mile have a grade said to be 27 percent, possibly the steepest in the park. The vertical south face of the opposite canyon wall is the formidable prow of Flattop Mt.

After 1800 feet of rise in two miles, the surrounding aspect suddenly changes to a broad upland of meadows interlined by straight rows of trees growing on ledges, so that they appear to have been planted to frame passage for the trail. Flattop Campground Trail (283) goes 0.1 mile on the right to Flattop Campground.

Proceeding north in almost a straight line, the trail becomes fainter with distance; its course is marked here by orange tree markers or cairns (three or four flat stones piled one on top of the other). After passing the highest elevation (6855), it starts a downward and eastward course zigzagging from one forested ledge to another as it drops 600 feet toward Kipp Creek. It traverses the Continental Divide three times with imperceptible ease and crosses a crystal cold tributary of Kootenai Creek before reaching Fifty Mountain Campground and meeting the Highline Trail (121) from Granite Park.

Flattop Mt. is a singular feature, hemmed in by two parallel mountain ranges: Lewis on the east, Livingston on the west. The hard limestone strata of the Lewis Range dip southwest to pass under Flattop Mt. They reappear in the Livingston Range dipping to the northeast, i.e., in the opposite direction. During the uplift and overthrust, once horizontal beds buckled while sliding northeast to form a broad, shallow downward fold or syncline, which is Flattop Mt., now deeply incised by glaciers and streams.

The soft red argillites of the Snowslip Formation covering Flattop Mt. lie above limestone similar to that appearing on the tops of surrounding mountains. These strata were protected to a degree by the sill of diorite and flows of Purcell lava, outcrops of which completely circumscribe Flattop and West Flattop Mts., as well as the basin between Kootenai Peak (8542) and Redhorn Peak (8128) to the northwest.

The ranges on both sides as seen from Flattop Mt. contribute most spectacular scenery, in particular the wall from Mt. Kipp (8839) to Logan Pass and beyond, the icy mass of Vulture Peak (9638), and the never-never jumble of the Kintla group.

Strata of mountains west and south of the major axis of the syncline are intensely folded. In particular low Nahsukin Mt. (8294), on the Continental Divide to the right of Vulture Peak and due west from Fifty Mountain Campground, has a series of greatly contorted complex folds.

The Continental Divide shifts from the Lewis Range to the Livingston Range while coursing 20 miles along the north edge of Flattop and West Flattop.

Trails to Granite Park

Granite Park from Packers Roost, 5.1 miles; from The Loop, 4.0 miles. See fold-out map.

Three trail routes connect Going-to-the-Sun Road with Granite Park. Two are described here, a third in the next section. The lowest, generally used by horse parties, starts at Packers Roost. See Going-to-the-Sun Road, mile 22.8. After following McDonald Creek Trail (63), described earlier, for 0.9 mile, it climbs northwesterly as Granite Park Trail (62), 0.8 mile, to meet the spur from The Loop at an elevation of 4297. The route is lined with huckleberry and serviceberrry bushes with fruits relished by bears as well as hikers.

A fine view of The Loop and its busy visitors is presented at 5200-foot elevation. The celebrated views of mountains and environment for which Granite Park is noted gradually unfold.

Above the sharp switchback two miles above the spur trail junction, a cross section of highly colored Purcell lava makes its appearance. Flow lines, pillow structures and glacial striae and polish are pronounced.

The chalets come into view on the edge of a cliff against the skyline above, as the trail forks 200 feet below them. The left fork leads to Granite Park Campground, a patrol cabin and the Highline Trail (121) to Fifty Mountain and Goat Haunt. See Trails from Many Glacier, North Circle. The right hand member leads to the chalets.

A second route to Granite Park starts at The Loop. See Going-to-the-Sun Road, mile 24.7. It travels almost on contour to cross, by footbridge and a hairpin curve, a narrow gorge and sparkling stream which tumbles down from Granite Park. Water ouzels revel in the dancing spray. In 0.6 mile, the spur joins Granite Park Trail (62) described immediately above.

Short Walks from Granite Park

See fold-out map.

The vicinity of Granite Park holds many delights for the sojourner with free time on his hands. The country is open, with expansive views of valleys and ranges. Distant streamlets shimmer like silvery ribbons. The air is fresh and invigorating, stimulating deep breathing and an urge to discover and observe.

In early morning chill, valleys are filled with billowy fog, as, in an earlier geological day, they once were filled with earthy matter now eroded away. The mountain summits, resplendent in the clear air, pierce the downy blanket like rocky islands in a sea of cloud. Their noble forms, sculptured in fine detail, stand forth with each line sharp, undisturbed by haze or heat wave.

Wildlife, timberline birds in particular, and alpine gardens are attractively near at hand. The geological background story is clear and simple. Its interpretation is unfolded in accounts of the North Circle and other trail approaches to the area.

North of the chalets, the southwest ridge of Swiftcurrent Mt., easily reached by Highline Trail 121 in a span of minutes, is a point of vantage from which to enjoy the sun setting behind the Livingston Range. Swiftcurrent Pass (7285), 0.9 mile above the chalets on trail 157, with a small rock-paved basin on the northeast, is an inviting spot for visitors. Sheltered by a rim on the west and south, snowbanks persist here through the warm days of July. Trees are stunted; other vegetation is sparse. A mile northeast of the pass, the Swiftcurrent Pass Trail 157, after hugging the sunny north incline, reaches the crest of the acute eastern ridge of Swiftcurrent Mt. The overlook extends down rock-walled Swiftcurrent Valley past the chain of lakes with Swiftcurrent and Sherburne Lakes dangling on the far end. Morainal kettles sparkle in the distant rolling plains. The ledged southeast rim of the basin affords a view of Swiftcurrent Glacier and the west face of Mt. Grinnell (8851).

It is a short attractive walk from the chalets up the low prominence (7680) south of Swiftcurrent Pass which also overlooks Swiftcurrent Glacier and down Swiftcurrent Valley. The broad summit is a good place to search for ptarmigan broods.

The 2000-foot zigzag up Swiftcurrent Mt. (8436) goes to the fire lookout on the summit. No more extensive view in the park can be obtained with less effort in such a short climb and distance. Swiftcurrent Lookout Trail (158) starts on Swiftcurrent Pass and climbs on open rocky slopes. It is 2.3 miles from the chalets and campground to the lookout which is manned at times of high fire hazard.

Chalets guests may choose a longer day's trip north on the Highline Trail (121). Ahern Pass junction is 4.5 miles from the chalets. From the junction Ahern Pass Overlook Trail (125) goes 0.4 mile to Ahern Pass. Hardy hikers may be enticed to scramble cross country from the pass to the notch above Iceberg Lake. For this, see the description under Trails from Many Glacier, the North Circle.

A prime favorite with Granite Park visitors is the walk to the Grinnell Glacier Overlook (7560), a gap in the Garden Wall, 1.6 miles distant, and requiring, on the average, less than three hours. Starting on Highline Trail (121) to Logan Pass, 0.8 mile from the chalets, the Garden Wall footpath (127) climbs steadily over loose rock, diagonally to the saddle. From here one looks down on The Salamander, the main mass of Grinnell Glacier, the bergshrund or great crevasse which lies between the ice and the headwall, and down Grinnell Valley. The Logan Pass country, Lake McDonald trapped in a narrow trough, and the grand peaks of the Livingston Range are seen in the opposite direction.

The rock in the saddle is a great dike cutting across beds of Helena (Siyeh) limestone at a steep angle. The trace of the dike appears as an inclined shelf which can be followed until it disappears beneath the cover of Purcell lava upon which the chalets are built. Whether this dike was the source of the lava is not known; although the compositions are identical, actual continuity between the dike and flow has not been discovered.

From the saddle an unmaintained goat trail continues along the wall, edging the cliffs and squeezing tightly against them in places. A half-mile south, a second gap is reached which overlooks Swiftcurrent Lake and Many Glacier Hotel which cannot be seen from the first saddle. Alpine flowers, including blue columbines and alpine fireweeds, alpine birds and mountain goats make appearances here.

Trails from Logan Pass

Garden Wall or Highline Trail

Logan Pass to Granite Park Chalets, 7.6 miles; to Fifty Mountain Campground, 19.5 miles; to Goat Haunt, 30 miles; to Many Glacier Hotel, 17.4 miles. See fold-out map.

Highline Trail (121) is very popular as it starts conveniently at Logan Pass (6646). It offers sweeping views, crosses the interesting algal and igneous (diorite) members of the Helena (Siyeh) Formation and is gouged, in part, out of sheer cliffs. It passes gnarled trees, veterans of icy storms, invades the haunts of mountain goats, bighorns and wolverines and is above timberline throughout most of its length. It passes over snowbanks even in late summer. It winds through flower beds with solid bloom and climbs to the home of showy alpines. Although parallel with the highway, far below and mostly out of sight, it is eminently attractive and merits its popularity.

The trail is a remnant of a once famous route between Sun Point and Granite Park, but the three miles from Siyeh Creek to Logan Pass are now abandoned. Trail 121 forms part of an open-jaw circuit, with return from Granite Park Chalets to Going-to-the-Sun Road at The Loop, mile 24.7, a journey of 4.0 miles over Granite Park Trail (62) and Loop Spur Trail.

Trail 121 starts north of the road at Logan Pass. After crossing the meadow of glacier lilies, monkeyflowers, wild heliotropes, windflowers, globeflowers and gentians, it is chiseled out of the limestone cliff called "The Rimrock" on Pollock Mt. This is just above the igneous band which can be traced by the eye along the Garden Wall and on Clements and Oberlin Mts. on the opposite side below Logan Pass. In places, the trail is hewn from this resistant rock, as well as out of its associated algal band, so that close examination of these geological members is possible.

This alignment is reasonably level for three miles until a broad switchback carries it up to 7274 feet after passing over the saddle (7000) between Haystack Butte (7486) and Mt. Gould (9553), both of which can be climbed from here. A less perilous climb is made over loose shale rock to the gap west of Gould, on the other side of which lies the remarkable block of glacial ice called Gem Glacier, visible from Many Glacier. See Trails from Many Glacier, Grinnell Glacier Trail.

The cols on each side of the saddle back of Haystack Butte are the result of glacial sculpture, and one can infer that a wall once extended here which was consumed by cliff glaciers from both sides. The butte and saddle are all that are left of this arete. Haystack Butte is a low horn similar in origin to Reynolds, St. Nicholas, Kinnerly and other more celebrated pinnacles. A moraine remains unaltered north of the summit of the butte, indicating that the last ice disappeared only a few decades ago.

As the trail climbs, the open slopes are elegant with plumed stands of beargrass, nodding to the passerby in years of good bloom. True forget-me-nots, alpine columbines, alpine fireweeds and other gems brighten scree slopes, otherwise bare, with the celestial brilliance of alpine blossoms. Open slopes are frequented by mountain goats and bighorns. Bear and deer come here on hot days, presumably to escape torment from insects. Nutcrackers, eagles and mountain-loving birds make this their airy home.

At 6.8 miles from Logan Pass, trail 127 slants (R) up the loose slide rock to the Grinnell Glacier Overlook, at a saddle in the Garden Wall. Continuing on trail 121, as one crosses a low rise, a flowery park unfolds, whose floor is the ancient lava which was extruded at the time when these regions were beneath a sea.

Granite Park Chalets pop into plain view as they perch on the rim of a prominent lava ledge at one's feet. See Trails from Many Glacier, North Circle, Many Glacier to Granite Park. Granite Park Chalets is open July 1 to Labor Day. Lodging and meals are available. Reservations must be made in advance at Belton Chalets, West Glacier, Montana, 59936, or by telephone (406) 888-5511.

Hidden Lake Trail

Logan Pass to Hidden Lake Overlook, 1.5 miles; to Hidden Lake, 3.0 miles. See fold-out map.

Anyone with the slightest inclination to walk and an hour or two to spend should make this delightful journey. The hike is near timberline, beginning in flowery gardens set in groves of subalpine firs, and climbing up gentle ledges to the rock moraine of Clements Glacier. At Hidden Lake Overlook, only 1.5 miles away, the trail comes to a viewing platform (7140) several hundred feet above sapphire waters, sparkling in a basin hewn out of Bearhat (8684) and Reynolds (9125) Mts.

A description of Logan Pass is included in the log of Going-to-the-Sun Road, mile 32.6. Trail 120 to Hidden Lake starts behind the visitor center as a self-guiding trail. Much of the route to the Overlook is over a boardwalk, constructed to alleviate the adverse impacts that great numbers of visitors were having on the delicate alpine vegetation. For the sake of fragile beauty, please refrain from straying off the walkway. As is true throughout the park, pets are not allowed on the trail.

The lowest ledges up which the trail climbs show the fossil algae described at miles 23.7 and 26.1 of Going-to-the-Sun Road. Below, the broad bench to the left and south of the pass is called HANGING GARDENS because of the wealth of its wildflowers each spring. Snow many feet deep remains into summer on the broad slopes below CLEMENTS MT. (8760).

Clements Mt. can be scaled from the saddle between it and MT. OBERLIN (8180), following a mountain goat trail to the nose of the peak and ascending one of the chimneys on the northwest face. A direct assault on Oberlin is relatively easy, but avoid the hazards of the steep snowslopes below the saddle unless properly equipped with an ice axe or other means of arresting a precipitous plunge. Reynolds Mt. can be climbed from the southwest, although the climb is more difficult than that of Clements. Much of the rock in Waterton-Glacier is not firm or trustworthy; great care should be taken assaying for firm holds. All climbers attempting ascents in the Logan Pass area should register out and in at the visitor center.

The sides of Clements, Oberlin, Pollock and Reynolds offer splendid opportunities for seeing mountain goats, sometimes at close range. More rarely bighorns put in an appearance. Bear are often seen, and sometimes a coyote or wolverine. Marmots and ground squirrels are friendly and common, although the former go into hibernation before the park season closes. Early in the season one may frequently find burrows that ground squirrels have dug through the snow patches. Clark's nutcrackers, water pipits, ptarmigan with broods, rosy finches, fox sparrows, white-crowned sparrows and golden eagles are among the birds most frequently seen.

The trail climbs toward the moraine that circles the bed of former Clements Glacier. Today a few patches of ice remain beneath the cliffs and become visible when the snow cover has melted. Several low gaps in the moraine permit closer study. It will be seen that much of the heterogeneous rock making up the mound is very angular and does not show the faceting, polishing and striations expected in glacial-borne material. When the basin is filled with snow in wintertime, the slide rock from the cliffs shoots over its surface and comes to rest against the mound. The resultant mixture of slide rock and true glacial drift is given the name "pseudo-moraine." Some plants, such as carpet pink, grow upon it. Since the glacier has disappeared only recently, the bedrock above the moraine shows freshest evidence of glacial work: grooves and striae, smoothed and rounded edges, bright polish and a brown surface stain. Next to the trail are gray-buff limestone and dolomite of the upper Helena (Siyeh) Formation. Extending most of the way up Clements and Reynolds Mts. are the pale reddish and greenish argillites of the Snowslip Formation, with the top quarter of these peaks consisting of the yellowish weathered dolomites of the Shepard Formation.

St. Mary Lake can be seen from the trail as it crosses the outer edge of the moraine. There is a shallow pond on the gap between Clements and Reynolds Mts. 500 feet above Logan Pass. It dries up completely each midsummer, leaving the bottom mud ripple-marked and cracked, illustrating how similar features were impressed in muds near ancient shores to be exposed in park argillites today.

The trail leads to a viewing platform above Hidden Lake (6375). BEARHAT MT. (8684) is to the south. Hidden Lake drains down a rugged canyon into Avalanche Creek. A footpath dropping to Hidden Lake is used mainly by fishermen.

After fording the lake outlet it is possible though strenuous to hike crosscountry to Sperry Glacier and to Sperry Chalets. The distance is over 12 miles, half of which are without established trail and involve an aggregate of some 3000 feet of climbing. NOTIFY RANGERS BEFORE STARTING AND AFTER COMPLETING THIS TRIP. The chalets must be notified *in advance* if accommodations are desired.

Trails from Sun Point and Sunrift Gorge

Sun Point is a bold promontory of red Grinnell argillite on the north shore of St. Mary Lake and Going-to-the-Sun Road, mile 40.6. The name is in common use for Going-to-the-Sun Point. A famous Swiss-style hostelry sprawled here in the early days, but the structures, now all razed, were victims of time and change. Visitor facilities are now located at more spacious Rising Sun. The large empty parking area is a reminder of past use and popularity.

Nine majestic peaks encircle Sun Point: left to right are RED EAGLE (8881), MAHTOTOPA (8672), LITTLE CHIEF (9541), CITADEL (9030), GUNSIGHT (9258), FUSILLADE (8750), REYNOLDS (9125), GOING-TO-THE-SUN (9642) and GOAT (8826). A viewfinder is located on a spur trail just off the Sun Point Nature Trail, a short distance from the parking lot. A plaque nearby sketches the story of Going-to-the-Sun Chalets.

The four principal park formations compose the mountains. Helena (Siyeh) limestone, with the dark ribbon of igneous rock, is seen on the upper parts of Little Chief, Citadel and Going-to-the-Sun Mts. Grinnell argillite is well exposed on Red Eagle, Goat and the lower slopes of Going-to-the-Sun. Appekunny argillite appears on lower slopes of Goat Mt. Altyn limestone forms the cliffs of the Narrows of St. Mary Lake. The angle to which the beds have been tilted by the uplifting forces is evident upon the walls bordering the lake.

The effects of glacial erosion appear everywhere. The U-shape of St. Mary Valley is very pronounced. A fine example of a cirque on Little Chief is directly across the lake from the Point. Virginia Creek, between Little Chief and Citadel, occupies a typical hanging valley.

Sun Point is one terminus of a wonderful 50-mile Inside Trail from East Glacier Park via Scenic Point and Two Medicine, Pitamakan and Triple Divide Passes and Red Eagle Lake. Jackson Glacier Overlook at mile 37.3, St. Mary Falls Trailhead at mile 39.3, Sunrift Gorge at mile 40.0 and the Sun Point Parking Area at 40.6 are convenient along Going-to-the-Sun Road for starting or ending a trail journey.

Baring Falls and Sunrift Gorge

Sun Point to Baring Falls, 0.8 mile; to Sunrift Gorge, 0.8 mile. See fold-out map.

The classic walk from Sun Point is along the lake to Baring Falls and Sunrift Gorge. The trail forks after 0.6 mile, the right-hand member (117) leading under the roadway to the gorge, 0.2 mile. See Going-to-the-Sun Road, mile 40.0. The left member (113) passes Baring Falls, 0.2 mile.

For many years, water ouzels, or dippers, have built a mossy, dripping nest behind the falls so that they must dash through the spray to reach it. Chunky, wren-like birds with short, pert tails, ouzels are slate gray in color and somewhat smaller than a robin. As they tarry briefly on projecting stones or totter restlessly along the edge of water, they constantly dip up and down on bending legs. It comes as quite a surprise to discover this little land bird actually flying to a pool or dashing mountain stream and walking on the bottom to get the caddis fly larvae on which it feeds. Whether floating upon the surface or flying at great speed just above, ouzels never venture far from lakes and streams. The dark eye, already obvious because of pronounced white lids, flashes the more into notice as a white nictitating membrance keeps flicking momentarily across it. An excellent singer, its melodious song is rarely heard by visitors, for it sings sweetest and oftenest in mid-February, accompanied by the howl of wintry winds and the gurgling of a rivulet down an icy pavement.

Beyond Baring Falls trail 113 may be followed to Florence Falls, 6.1 miles, and Gunsight Lake, 7.5 miles, or via trail 109 to St. Mary Falls, 1.6 miles and Virginia Falls, 2.3 miles.

Piegan Pass Trail

Sun Point to Gunsight Pass Trail (52) junction, 3.2 miles; to Siyeh Cutoff junction, 5.8 miles; to Preston Park, 7.3 miles; to Many Glacier Hotel, 17.4 miles. See fold-out map.

Piegan Pass Trail (113) ascends St. Mary Valley to Reynolds Creek, 3.2 miles, described later in this chapter under Gunsight Trail. At the fork, take the right-hand trail. A small waterfall, Deadwood Falls, is above the trail junction. Trail 113 climbs steadily 1.3 miles from the junction to pass near the viewpoint for Jackson Glacier, Going-to-the-Sun Road, mile 37.3 (5284). It goes up a sloping ledge on Going-to-the-Sun Mt. in spruce-fir forest.

At 5.8 miles from Sun Point and an elevation of 6295 feet, the trail meets Siyeh Bend Cutoff (115) coming 1.2 miles from the road crossing of Siyeh Creek, Going-to-the-Sun Road, mile 35.5. This cutoff affords a shortcut to hikers bound for Siyeh and Piegan Passes.

At 7.3 miles, Piegan Pass Trail (113) reaches Preston Park. Trail 117 (described elsewhere), over Siyeh Pass and around Going-to-the-Sun Mt., goes up the creek on the right. Trail 113 to Piegan Pass, 1.8 miles, and to Many Glacier, swings to the left around the head of the valley. For description, see Trails from Many Glacier, Piegan Pass Trail.

Siyeh Pass Trail

Sunrift Gorge to Siyeh Pass, 5.6 miles; to Preston Park, 7.6 miles.
Siyeh Creek at Going-to-the-Sun Road, mile 35.5 to Preston Park, 2.7 miles; to Siyeh Pass, 4.7 miles; to Sunrift Gorge, 10.3 miles. See fold-out map.

A great part of Siyeh Pass Trail (117) is in open country passing over richly colored rocks in the shadow of legendary Going-to-the-Sun Mt. It climbs above 8000 feet, the highest point reached by any established trail in Waterton-Glacier and provides a good view of Sexton Glacier, a cliff glacier with an exciting ice fall. Wildlife is abundant in the vicinity, and the hiker should keep alert, for he is trespassing in the domain of grizzlies.

From the highest point on the trail, distant views embrace Goat, Red Eagle, James, Mahtotopa, Split, Norris, Little Chief, Pinchot, St. Nicholas, Stimson, Almost-a-Dog, Matahpi and Going-to-the-Sun Peaks. The bulk of Mt. Siyeh blocks views north.

The counterclockwise direction used in this description is recommended so that Sexton Glacier, Baring Basin, and the pass lie ahead of the traveler. The clockwise direction, however, is easier, starting 1200 feet higher from the east side of Siyeh Bend Bridge (5850) on Going-to-the-Sun Road, mile 35.5, ascending Piegan Pass Trail to Preston Park and then over Siyeh Pass down to Sunrift Gorge. The trail may be included as a leg of a Many Glacier trip, although the journey of 17.7 miles between Sunrift Gorge and Many Glacier via Siyeh Pass is a long one.

Leaving the gorge, trail 117 winds through twisted Douglas fir. Though not visible, the gorge of Baring Creek is always near (L) with its fantastic shapes cut in argillite. The trail rises steadily over open beargrass slopes on the east side of the defile between Going-to-the-Sun and Goat Mts. At its head the canyon expands into Baring Basin. A lofty waterfall graces the side of Going-to-the-Sun Mt. across the valley.

The higher mountain meadows are enriched by many alpine blossoms in a setting of bright red rocks. In the heyday of the chalets, parties made Baring Basin and summit of Goat Mt. destinations for a day's outing, but the inclination has worn thin and the trail section up Goat Mt. has fallen into decay. Buffalo skulls and antelope bones found on the grassy slopes indicate that these animals once used this range. The narrow red summit of Goat Mt. overlooks Goat Lake, a half mile directly below.

Above Baring Basin, trail 117 persists in unbroken ascent of the headwall by one switchback after another. On the left, the tier of ledges on Going-to-the-Sun Mt. is a good place to spy mountain goats; and, above, Sexton Glacier lies on a shelf surrounded on three sides by sheer walls over 1000 feet high. From time to time great masses of ice break off and crash with reverberation over the brink of a precipice. Melt water plunges as chalky waterfalls beneath the snout of the glacier; good lateral moraines extend along its left side; and the band of igneous rock stands out prominently behind it.

The main trail climbs by many short switchbacks to an unnamed col with windswept Siyeh Pass (7750) immediately ahead and below. Because of persistent snowbanks, the trail does not traverse the pass proper but climbs to an elevation of 8150 feet on the south shoulder, from which a good view extends northeast down Boulder Canyon to the rolling plains of Alberta. Two lakelets lie below in a rocky pocket to the west.

The trail drops rapidly from its high point by two short series of steep switchbacks, then coasts beneath subalpine larches and fir in the broad col to Preston Park (7000).

At Preston Park, trail 117 connects with Piegan Pass Trail (113) going to the right to Piegan Pass and Many Glacier, and, to the left, to Siyeh Bend on Going-to-the-Sun Road or down St. Mary Valley to Sun Point and Sunrift Gorge. See Trails from Many Glacier, Piegan Pass Trail for a description of trail 117 from Preston Park over Piegan Pass.

Gunsight Pass Trail, East Section

Sun Point to Florence Falls, 6.7 miles; Gunsight Lake, 8.1 miles; Jackson Glacier, 9.9 miles; Lake Ellen Wilson, 12.8 miles; Sperry Chalets, 15.5 miles; Lake McDonald, 21.9 miles. See fold-out map.

The Gunsight Pass Trail (52) is of highest excellence among Glacier's trails. It glides through cool woods, along dashing streams and beside beautiful waterfalls; crosses two mountain passes and broad subalpine flats where snow lingers through summer and wildflowers blossom in profusion; rims exquisite glistening lakes, zig-zags over shale slopes, and scratches a course across perpendicular cliffs. Extensive views are everywhere. Wildlife is plentiful; no trip in the park affords surer chance of encountering mountain goats face-to-face.

Several locations on Going-to-the-Sun Road are convenient for the start or finish of a trip on the trail:

1. Trail 113 starts officially by the parking area at Sun Point near road mile 40.6, leads up

the lakeshore 3.2 miles to junction with trail 52.

2. Hikers may start from Sunrift Gorge at mile 40.0 dropping down Baring Creek 0.2 miles to trail 113.
3. The Gunsight Horse Trail Cutoff (279) at mile 39.4 drops 100 feet to trail 113 in 0.1 mile.
4. At mile 39.3 is St. Mary Falls Cutoff Trail (261) which intersects trail 113 in 0.3 mile.
5. The most popular alternative for hikers is to start at Jackson Glacier Overlook, mile 37.3. From here trail 113 drops 300 feet in 1.3 miles to the eastern terminus of trail 52.

Starting at Sun Point parking area, the route moves high on the north shore of St. Mary Lake, past the junction of trail 117 (R) to Sunrift Gorge and Siyeh Pass. At 0.6 mile, it crosses Baring Creek below Baring Falls, then climbs above St. Mary Lake along the edge of fine red bluffs which form the crest of Baring Falls. The open slopes of maroon rocks are habitat of contorted trees and distinctive plants. Cutoff trails 279 and 261 join 113 near the head of the lake. At 1.8 miles the trail forks, trail 109 leading (L) to St. Mary Falls, 0.5 mile, Virginia Falls, 1.2 miles, and Red Eagle Lake, 13.1 miles. See description of Inside Trail, segment from St. Mary to Sun Point.

The floor of St. Mary Valley is swampy in many places, so that trails are constructed with a corduroy of rough lumber. Although the kinds of forest trees seen are those common to the east side of the range, a few vagrant individuals occur of species otherwise found only west of the Divide. A hemlock, red cedar or white pine appears rather out of place in this company, so ragged compared with the lush host in McDonald Valley. Yew, a Pacific shrub, is better adapted and occurs in greater numbers.

A major trail junction is at 3.2 miles from Sun Point. The right fork is trail 113, for Many Glacier via Piegan Pass or for return to Sunrift Gorge via Siyeh Pass. See Trails from Many Glacier, Piegan Pass Trail. The left fork, designated from this point as Gunsight Pass Trail (52), is the route to Sperry Chalets and Lake McDonald.

After crossing the bridge over Reynolds Creek below Deadwood Falls, trail 52 edges St. Mary River bottom lands, filled with willows and water-loving plants. Tiny Mirror Pond on the left reflects the splendor of Citadel and Dusty Star Mts. Elk may appear suddenly anywhere in the vicinity. At 5.9 miles from Sun Point, spur trail 54 presents an attractive side trip as it leads 0.8 mile to the right to Florence Falls, below the eastern tip of Fusillade Mt. (8750). Twin Lakes nestle in a cirque above the falls beneath the beetling north wall of Fusillade. To reach them, one must climb a mile through the brush on the south side of the creek.

From the foot of the sharp spire of Fusillade Mt. trail 52 leaves the forest and ascends a slope covered with alder, mountain ash and other shrubs. Fine views of Blackfoot and Jackson Glaciers, Mt. Jackson (10,052) and Gunsight Pass lie ahead. Behind, the bare north face of Citadel Mt. (9030) glares across St. Mary Valley. Siksika Falls is the great waterfall below Blackfoot Glacier.

The trail climbs over the rim of a steep-walled, rocky bowl in which Gunsight Lake rests beneath Gunsight Pass. A patrol cabin and campground are near the lake outlet.

The clear blue waters of Gunsight Lake, one of the jewels of the park, are the home of vigorous, fighting rainbows. The wall of Gunsight Mt. on the north shows a series of closely folded pink argillite strata over which a half-dozen streams from melting snowbanks sinuate in picturesque beauty. On the south the lofty ramparts of Mt. Jackson are studded with small ice masses. It is possible to climb Fusillade Mt. from the lake outlet for a superb view down St. Mary Valley.

The trail branches after it crosses the outlet of the lake. Spur trail 53 on the left continues south for 1.8 miles, heading straight towards Jackson Glacier. This secondary trail is steep and not for horses which should be left at the hitchrack near the campground. Trail 53 climbs on a sharp pitch to an elevation of 6000 feet. Upon reaching the edge of timber, it gradually fades a quarter of a mile below the great northern lateral moraine of the glacier. The exact location of the trail as it leaves the forest should be carefully noted to facilitate return upon completing exploration. The rest of the journey is over wet, sloping, moss-covered rocks which make for slippery footing.

Jackson Glacier was once a part of Blackfoot Glacier from which it became separated in the early thirties. It was called Siksikaikwan Glacier in earliest reports. Siksikaikwan, meaning "Blackfeet Man," was the Indian name of William Jackson (1858-1892), grandson of Hugh Monroe and an army scout and mountain guide for George Bird Grinnell, who named the mountain and glacier after him.

When the park was established, Blackfoot Glacier was a massive icefield straddling the Continental Divide on both sides of Blackfoot Mt. and stretching from Mt. Logan to Walton Mt. Along with Jackson Glacier, Harrison and Pumpelly Glaciers were part of this extensive sheet. As the mass dwindled, it broke up into smaller glacierets, leaving Jackson Glacier as a narrow tongue in the col on the east slope of Mt. Jackson.

It is easy to climb to the head of the col for a fine view of Walton Mt. (8926), spectacular Harrison Glacier and the head of Harrison Valley. The extensive snow field or neve near the top, partly consolidated by alternate freezing and thawing, gradually changes into ice to give birth to the glacier. In late summer the glacier is much crevassed; only those experienced and properly equipped should venture upon it.

The main remnant of Blackfoot Glacier with its many crevasses and ice caves lies on Blackfoot Mt. to the east. It is imperative that parties have proper equipment and glacier savvy before attempting to traverse this glacier, possibly the most challenging in the park.

A suspension bridge crosses the outlet of Gunsight Lake but is dismantled late each fall to prevent damage from heavy snowpack. Early and late season hikers should check with St. Mary rangers to learn if the bridge is usable.

After parting company with Jackson Glacier Trail (53), Gunsight Pass Trail (52) turns abruptly right and climbs relentlessly up the steep northeast face of Mt. Jackson. In lower reaches it is lined with thick brush, mostly alder, but a mile from the outlet it had to be carved in a sheer limestone cliff. It has often been reconstructed and repaired in the past, exemplifying the difficulty of trail construction and maintenance in the high country. Only a half-dozen switchbacks break the long course to the summit.

Because the trail is in the shadow of a lofty mountain, combatting snow is a continual task. Trail crews are constantly kept busy shoveling new tread, arched upward because the snow softens and creeps slowly down the slope. Parties must exercise great care in crossing steep banks, for horses break through rotten snow and become greatly distressed. It is always wise to dismount and lead horses across such hazards.

Several small glacierets, hidden from the eye by huge ridges of debris, rest on the left above the trail. Walkers may climb the slopes of loose rock to reach them—an easy venture, for they often lie only a few hundred yards off the trail. Because of the narrowness of the defile between Gunsight and Jackson Mts., views down the valley are limited, but they extend to Hudson Bay Divide and the Great Plains. On the right the west face of Citadel Mt. presents a formidable wall. Across the densely wooded valley floor, the transmountain road creates an ugly scar as it slashes through the velvety forest near the base of Going-to-the-Sun Mt.

Gunsight Pass (6946) is a rounded notch in the Continental Divide resembling the rear sight of a gun. The arched summit of Gunsight Mt. may be regarded as a fore sight. Views from the pass are magnificent. Like silvered mirrors, Lake Ellen Wilson and Gunsight Lake lie immediately below. They are tightly flanked by chromatic walls towering 4000 feet. Belton Hills, peaks of the Flathead Range and broad Flathead Valley shimmer in the distant haze to the southwest.

The views and a stone shelter cabin on the summit make the pass an inviting place to stop for lunch but no overnight camping or wood fires are permitted. Goats are numerous and generally close by. With patience they may be photographed at very short range. Scrub birch, more commonly associated with swampland at lower elevations, grows on bare slopes near the pass. It can be recognized by its sticky glandular twigs and spatulate leaves, less than an inch long, with scalloped margins.

Trail 52 swings from side to side of the col as it drops 1000 feet from the pass to Lake Ellen Wilson (5929), a deep blue tarn full of lively brook trout and a happy place to enjoy lunch or to camp, but no wood fires are permitted. Many come here to fish and to pass pleasant hours.

A spur to the campground is 1.7 miles below Gunsight Pass and 2.7 miles from Sperry Chalets. As the trail nears the lake from Gunsight Pass, it is showered by a waterfall in a rivulet rising in a snowy pocket high on Jackson's parapet.

Near the head of Ellen Wilson and 150 feet above the lake surface, trail 52 bends with the shoreline and starts the climb to Lincoln Pass (7050). The path to the shore and campground leaves the main trail a short distance beyond the falls.

Nearing Lincoln Pass a vista of Lincoln Lake is disclosed in the cirque 2000 feet below. Lincoln Lake is flush against the sheer walls over which the 1344-foot Beaver Chief Falls drops, one of the most spectacular in the park. A brief glimpse of the falls appears from the trail, but for a fuller view, it is rewarding to walk a few paces to the left among scattered prostrate trees to the brink of the rocky platform. An overlook occurs just before making an abrupt turn to the right for the last half-mile ascent to Lincoln Pass.

Wild and rugged grandeur fills the region. Huge blocks of bright red argillite, tumbled from Gunsight Mt., are strewn casually here and there. Sturdy whitebark pines frame many an enticing view. Mountain goats find this country to their liking; it is one of the best places along trails to see them. Pikas busy themselves in rock slides everywhere; their plaintive bleats are heard more frequently than the animals are seen. Wildflowers are in profusion wherever scant soil yields a foothold.

Passage over the long southwesterly shoulder of Gunsight Mt. is through a shallow gap. The low prominence on the southwest is Lincoln Peak (7440), easily and often climbed from the pass.

On the north side of the pass, Sperry Chalets lies in its picturesque setting in a mighty cirque. A placid lake with campground nearby nestles on a ledge above the chalets and reflects the spires of conifers bristling on the shore. Deer and bear sometimes appear in the basin. The trail drops between blocks of broken slide rock and soon has the traveler at the door of the friendly hostelry.

SPERRY CHALETS: Excellent meals and limited rustic lodging are available July 1 to Labor Day. Advance reservations must be made at Belton Chalets, West Glacier, MT 59936. (406) 888-5511.

Trails from East Glacier Park

Inside Trail

East Glacier Park Ranger Station to Two Medicine Lake via trail 96, 10.6 miles; to Cut Bank Campground via Pitamakan Pass, 27.5 miles; to Red Eagle Lake via Cut Bank Campground and Triple Divide Pass, 39.1 miles; to St. Mary via Cut Bank Campground, 46.6 miles. See fold-out map.

A veteran of Glacier Park trails once enumerated brilliant facets of park experience: the high country, forests, streams, wildflowers. He reflected that, superlative though each one is in its own right, the truly supreme impression—durable, gratifying—comes from the expanse of plains rolling endlessly eastward as seen from some high point on the mountain front. Winds and storms are their complements and have molded them, and he who reflects recalls subconsciously Muir's "The winds will blow into you their own freshness and the storms their energy while cares will drop off like autumn leaves."

Points of vantage are many on the Inside Trail from which to gaze over "The Big Sky Country," thus stirring emotions of "don't fence me in!" The long-standing name for this route was applied to the inner or mountain way from East Glacier Park to St. Mary via Two Medicine, Cut Bank and Red Eagle Lake. The name, Outside Trail, referred to the patrol route used by rangers along the base of the mountains from East Glacier Park to the International Border. Large segments of the Outside Trail have been abandoned because cars have replaced horses, and access roads now serve instead.

East Glacier Park to Two Medicine (10.6 miles)

To enter the Mt. Henry section (96) of the Inside Trail, start from the East Glacier Ranger Station and turn left at the corner one block north. Hotel guests may reach this same street by walking northwest a half-mile on the dirt road along the far side of the golf course. A half-mile from the highway the street forks. Bear right past another section of the golf course to the trailhead on the right.

For the first several miles the trail passes through scattered aspen groves, crossing Fortyone Mile Creek 3.5 miles from the ranger station. The base of the yellow limestone cliff on the left is the trace of the Lewis Thrust Fault.

Fortymile Creek is crossed a mile farther at a good luncheon spot. Hikers may be treated to the sight of golden eagles or prairie falcons hunting over the surrounding terrain.

At 7.5 miles SCENIC POINT (7522), a prominence over Lower Two Medicine Lake, affords a fine view of RISING WOLF (9513), SPOT (7831), and RED (9377) MTS. to the north. The vista includes Two Medicine Ridge; remnants of the so-called "Flaxville" Peneplain, the valley occupied by Two Medicine Glacier in the Ice Age; and other geological features described under the Blackfeet Highway.

The bare slope on the south leads to the top of MT. HENRY (8847). There is no trail, but the pitch is gentle and even; the distance is two miles from trail 96, 0.7 miles southwest of Scenic Point.

Two Medicine Lake (5164) is seen from trail 96, with MT. HELEN (8538) and its long eastern knife-edge terminating in red PUMPELLY PILLAR (7620). The trail descends 1800 feet gradually by a dozen switchbacks to APPISTOKI FALLS in Appistoki Creek which makes a tortuous passage in a narrow gorge cut in Grinnell argillite. The trail reaches Two Medicine Road at mile 11.6, just above the intersection of the campground and lakeshore spurs.

Two Medicine To Cut Bank Via Pitamakan Pass

Two Medicine Campground to Oldman Lake, 5.5 miles; to Pitamakan Pass, 6.9 miles; Cut Bank Campground, 16.7 miles. Pitamakan Pass Trail (102) is part of the Inside Trail route, formerly linking East Glacier with St. Mary.

Cut Bank Pass was the most celebrated of Indian crossings over the mountains. A Blackfeet Amazon, Pitamakan or Running Eagle, is said to have led raids over it to the Salish-Kutenai homeland, although some authorities question this legend and even aver that Pitamakan was a man. In October 1853, a Flathead guide led engineer A. W. Tinkham, of the exploration party of Washington territorial governor Isaac I. Stevens, across the pass in the belief that it was Marias Pass. Geologist Raphael Pumpelly crossed it in 1882-83 while exploring the region. The trail over the pass fell into disuse and was almost abandoned.

After the region became a national park, travel on the Inside Trail between Two Medicine and Cut Bank became popular, and the lesser saddle east of Mt. Morgan over which it passed became known as Cut Bank Pass in conversation, in literature and finally on maps. The error has now been officially corrected, but some outdated literature and maps may confuse the hiker. To summarize, Cut Bank Pass is on the Continental Divide where it should be, and Pitamakan Pass is attached to the saddle over which trail 102 crosses. Cut Bank Pass Trail (80) runs from the junction of the Dawson Pass Trail (99) to Nyack Creek as described under Hwy. 2, Nyack, mile 11.5. The trail from Two Medicine to Cut Bank Campground is Pitamakan Pass Trail (102).

Trails 102 and 99 (to Dawson Pass) start at the bridge over the Two Medicine River near Two Medicine Campground. They immediately separate upon crossing, 102 turning to the right to proceed downstream. It circles the east shoulder of Rising Wolf Mt. in a lodgepole-fir forest and enters the edge of a 1919 burn that shows how long it can take forest to recover when growing on an inhospitable site. The trail crosses Dry Fork Creek on a footbridge and meets, at 1.6 miles, the Dry Fork Trail (266) coming upstream from Two Medicine Entrance Station on Two Medicine Road, 2.6 miles distant, an alternative approach.

Trail 102 now turns left to ascend Dry Fork Valley in groves of aspen, alder and willows, and through a richness of wildflowers. RISING WOLF MT. (9513) poses a mighty wall notched by hanging valleys on the left. A beautiful waterfall high on the mountain is one of the many along the way. Sparkling lakelets on whose shores the feet of man have rarely trod are tucked below cliffs and snowbanks in the lofty pockets. The bright red cliffs and ledges of Red Mt. (9377) are on the north.

As the trail leaves the burned area and begins its climb in earnest, an unusual open forest of twisted whitebark pines is entered, so unlike any other forest along the well-traveled trails of the park it is in itself worthy of a visit. To the southwest FLINSCH PEAK (9225) appears on the Continental Divide. YOUNG MAN LAKE (6960), an exquisite tarn, lies in the cirque below Flinsch Peak, above the wall over which a fine waterfall plunges. OLDMAN LAKE (6646), 0.6 miles below trail 102 on a good path, nestles under the shoulder of MT. MORGAN (8781). The name refers not to a senile gentleman but to Napi, Old Man, a legendary Blackfeet demigod. Some misunderstanding person applied the names "Young Man" and "Boy" to lakes nearby as foils to "Old Man." Big gamey trout in Oldman Lake attract many an angler to this place.

The wild, spectacular trail climbs steadily on exposed slopes to PITAMAKAN PASS (7600), merely a low point on a long hogback extending east from Mt. Morgan to an un-named knob (8193). The north cliff below the pass is a sheer drop to PITAMAKAN LAKE (6805). The lakelet above and to the left of Pitamakan Lake is named The Lake of the Seven Winds (6969), in reference to the capricious air currents in this lofty setting.

The trail follows the crest westward from Pitamakan Pass for 0.2 mile, then divides. Pitamakan Pass Trail (102) descends to the north. The left branch forks again 0.2 mile farther on the ridge, becoming Dawson Pass Trail (99) on the left, Cut Bank Trail (80) on the right. Trail 99 continues in brisk ascent for 0.3 mile to PITAMAKAN OVERLOOK (8050) on the north shoulder of Mt. Morgan for exciting views north and west. The expensive task of building a horse trail to link the overlook with Dawson Pass began in the 30's, but had to be dropped for lack of funds. However, the spectacular trail on the west flanks of Mt. Morgan and Flinsch Peak can be followed today on foot. It is 9.4 miles to Two Medicine from the overlook. See description of Dawson Pass Trail.

Trail 80 angles off trail 99 as a faint trace on loose scree 0.4 mile to CUT BANK PASS (7900), 0.2 mile north of Pitamakan Overlook. Crossing the pass, it makes a steep, rocky 3200-foot descent along mossy ledges and through heavy forest to Nyack Creek Trail (73) on the floor of Nyack Valley. It is 21.8 miles from Cut Bank Pass to a ford on the Middle Fork Flathead River at Nyack. See U.S. Highway 2, mile 11.5. Views from Cut Bank Pass are outstanding, well worth an extra effort by travelers over Pitamakan Pass. See page 32 for more details.

From Pitamakan Pass, trail 102 drops down a precipitous slope to Lake of the Seven Winds in a barren basin, then to Pitamakan Lake in a veritable flower garden on the upper fringe of the Hudsonian Zone. This is a pleasant lunch stop. Snowbanks linger through most of the summer. The encircling walls are good places for seeing mountain goats; bighorns often appear on gentler slopes; deer and elk come up from lower valleys to summer in green pastures here.

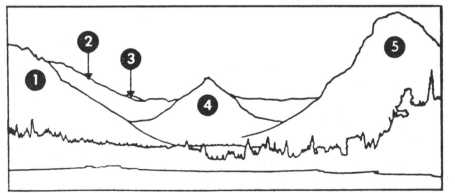

From Two Medicine: (1) Never Laughs; (2) Grizzly; (3) Despair and Two Medicine Pass; (4) Painted Tepee; (5) Sinopah.

KATOYA LAKE (6368) lies a quarter-mile off the main trail and is not visible from it. "Katoya" is Blackfeet for sweet fir, a kind of subalpine fir which bears needles esteemed by Indians as incense for ceremonies and as perfume and a sachet for garments.

Trail 102 drops down benches in the glacial staircase as it follows the North Fork Cut Bank Creek northward to MORNING STAR LAKE (5763), lying between the craggy wall of the Continental Divide and the steep slopes of Red Mt. A campground is near the inlet.

A mile and a half north of Red Mt. EAGLE PLUME MT. (8724) is next in the eastern ridge, which ends in BAD MARRIAGE MT. (8350), named by former Superintendent Eivind T. Scoyen after a Blackfeet brave. MEDICINE GRIZZLY PEAK (8315) is to the west.

Passing down a long meadow at the foot of the west talus slope and crossing a creek with a large waterfall visible from far downstream, 2.5 miles from Morning Star Lake, trail 102 passes below Atlantic Falls in Atlantic Creek, which flows from Triple Divide Peak to the northwest.

At the base of Bad Marriage Mt., 5.9 miles below Pitamakan Pass, Triple Divide Pass Trail (104) is met coming from the Pass.

Trail 102 bears right, following the pleasant wooded valley. It is rewarding to explore the marshy bottom land of alders, willows, grassland and ponds, and watch for wildlife including elk and bear, as well as goldeneye and harlequin ducks, snipe, sandpipers, curlews, marsh hawks, dippers, savannah, white-crowned and chipping sparrows, yellow and yellow-rumped warblers and nuthatches. Trail 102 terminates 3.9 miles downstream by Cut Bank Campground and ranger station, at the upper end of Cut Bank Road coming from Blackfeet Highway, 5.0 miles downstream.

Cut Bank to Red Eagle Lake Via Triple Divide Pass

(Cut Bank Campground to Medicine Grizzly Lake, 6.0 miles; to Triple Divide Pass, 7.2 miles; to foot of Red Eagle Lake, 15.5 miles.)

Triple Divide Pass Trail (104) has strong appeal to park visitors since it passes nearest the summit of Triple Divide Peak (8020), but it also yields a bonus of excellent scenery, variety and fishing.

The route from Cut Bank to Red Eagle Lake combines parts of trails 102 and 104. The south terminus is near Cut Bank Campground (5200) at the end of Cut Bank Road. The first 3.9 miles are a part of trail 102 described in the preceding pages, going up wooded Cut Bank Valley, with the bold cliffs (8484) of Razoredge Mt. ahead.

The summit to the left (southwest) is MEDICINE GRIZZLY PEAK (8315), named for a grizzly that haunted the valley at the turn of the century. The reputation of this big, ferocious beast spread far and wide until stories about it grew to fabulous proportions. Great medicine or power was ascribed to the animal by the Blackfeet, who were loath to go into the valley because of its presence. The Indians called for the help of U.S. Biological Survey lion hunter, Chance Beebe of Columbia Falls, who finally killed the bear after an exciting episode of relentless pursuit in which man and beast matched wits and interchanged roles in stalking each other. For years, Mr. Beebe displayed the record pelt on the living room of his home, never boasting, but praising the unbelievable cunning of his adversary.

At 3.9 miles, trail 102 turns left up the canyon of North Fork Cut Bank Creek on its way to Pitamakan Pass and Two Medicine. It is only 0.2 mile up this trail to sylvan Atlantic Falls, well worth a detour.

Triple Divide Pass Trail (104), climbs the wooded terrace on the right. Atlantic Creek Campground lies 0.4 mile above the junction with 102. Three-tenths mile farther, Medicine Grizzly Trail (260) branches off trail 104 to go 1.4 miles in mature forest and meadows up Atlantic Creek to MEDICINE GRIZZLY LAKE (5536), which reposes close to the bold northeast wall of RAZOREDGE MT. (8560), an arete conspicuous from far out on the plains. The lake contains rainbow trout.

With perhaps the steadiest grade in the region, trail 104 climbs a relentless 2.6 miles up the hot, unshaded southern flank of Mt. James (9375). Parts of the older trail, used until the 30's, are visible below this route. TRIPLE DIVIDE PASS (7397) is at the top.

The view south from the pass reveals two small lakes on a bench on the west side of Medicine Grizzly Peak, but does not include Medicine Grizzly Lake. The view north embraces an exciting glacial headwall with NORRIS (8882) and SPLIT (8792) MTS. projecting above it.

SINGLESHOT MT. (7926) appears north of St. Mary Lake, but Red Eagle Lake cannot be seen.

The low summit to the northwest towards which the trail has been heading is TRIPLE DIVIDE PEAK (8020), the culmination of continental drainage. It is, in this respect, one of the most distinctive mountains of all North America. From its apex waters drain down Atlantic Creek, eventually to reach the Gulf of Mexico. Across the ridge to the left, water flows southwest down Pacific Creek ultimately to mingle with the blue Pacific at the mouth of the Columbia River. To the right, on the other side of the pass, water drains from this peak down Hudson Bay Creek in its course to Hudson Bay. No other peak in North America has drainage into three seas so distant and through watercourses as long as the three river systems: the Missouri-Mississippi, the Columbia, and the Saskatchewan-Nelson. Here is the meeting of the three major divides of North America: the Atlantic-Pacific, the Pacific-Hudson Bay, and the Hudson Bay-Atlantic. But for all of its importance, Triple Divide Peak is not high, since it is only a spur of Norris Mt. to the northwest. The steep face of Triple Divide Peak to the west can be climbed using caution.

Crossing the pass the trail drops by switchbacks down the east face of Hudson Bay Creek cirque. The present trail was constructed about 1930; previously it followed the crest of the long moraine beneath the big snowbank on the opposite wall, passed two small ponds and edged the brink of a fearsome cliff. The glowering face of Split Mt. is ahead. The diorite sill so conspicuous in many parts of the region forms the floor of the pass. The wall between Norris and Split Mts. is a good place for spotting mountain goats. Bighorns are often seen on the slopes of Mt. James, while marmots pop up cautiously to inspect the passing hiker.

The trail crosses Hudson Bay Creek 1.5 miles from the pass, below a waterfall in a stream flowing from a cirque lake on the west. The trail continues down the west bank of the creek as it drops from the Hudsonian Zone, with dwarf subalpine fir, to the Canadian Zone, with dense forest. Following a winding course, Trail 104 eventually crosses a suspension bridge near the confluence of Red Eagle and Hudson Bay Creeks.

A campground at the head of RED EAGLE LAKE (4722) is reached a mile farther on. This lake is famous throughout the whole Northwest for its big, fighting cutthroat, with some rainbows and hybrids also present.

The sharp prow of ALMOST-A-DOG MT. (8922) rises in the west; the bright slopes of Red Eagle Mt. are to the north. KAKITOS (cocky-toes), Blackfeet for star, is southeast of the lake. On a topographic map its contours suggest a three-pointed star. A second campground is 0.9 mile down the lakeshore, near the outlet and the site of Red Eagle Camp, a once delightful hostelry.

Red Eagle Lake to St. Mary (7.7 miles)

Red Eagle Lake occupies a rocky basin near the edge of the Lewis Thrust Fault block. It is similar to Swiftcurrent Lake in origin, with underlying beds dipping to the southwest. The falls and gorge at the outlet of the lake are worth a detour.

Red Eagle Trail (107) crosses the rocky ledge which restrains the water of the lake. It passes through lavish meadows, gay with flowers, which place it among the most popular trails in the park. A few even consider it the prettiest because of its meadows. Beyond the wildflower gardens it enters a dense coniferous forest under which honeysuckle, buffalo berries, Oregon grapes and mountain lovers grow.

A mile below, a spring of clear, cold water bubbles from beneath dripping moss at the edge of a meadow where buckthorn bushes (*Rhammus*) grow abundantly. This plant is a close relative of California buckthorn which provides a mild laxative, the cascara sagrada of commerce. The black, three-seeded fruits are very bitter. Despite its name, the plant has no thorns. Here and there an aspen grows big and sturdy in the wetlands. The spruce have a bluish cast demonstrating the difficulty of distinguishing by sight an Engelmann spruce from the blue spruce in a borderline specimen.

The trail drops down the steep bank, 2.6 miles below the lake, crosses Red Eagle Creek and forks. The member to left, 109, goes around St. Mary Lake to Sun Point, 12.3 miles distant.

A mile below the trail junction, trail 107 recrosses Red Eagle Creek (4560) on another suspension bridge and ascends the steep bank of dark Cretaceous rocks underlying the mantel of glacial drift on the frontal plain. The suspension bridges at these two fore-mentioned places and the one above Red Eagle Lake are dismantled off-season to prevent damage from snowpack.

On top of a grassy knoll (4760), the trail meets the old road leading 3.8 miles to the foot of St. Mary Lake. This winds through meadows of wild hay, the grazing grounds of large herds of elk, and among thickets of twisted aspen and limber pines scattered upon flowery pastures. Mountain lions are occasionally viewed from the trail, but pose no threat to hikers. Near the lake a dens forest of gnarled Douglas firs, fashioned in the fury of storms, has grotesque beauty.

Trail 107 terminates at the historical, refurbished 1913 Ranger Station, site of occasional interpretive activities, but generally unmanned. Just beyond, the blacktopped road to the right leads to the Hudson Bay District Office in a park residence and utility area. Going-to-the-Sun Road is reached halfway between St. Mary Visitor Center/Ranger Station and the park boundary.

St. Mary to Sun Point

(St. Mary to Virginia Falls, 14.4 miles; to St. Mary Falls, 15.1 miles; to Sun Point, 17.4 miles.)

The shadowy route along the southeastern shore of St. Mary Lake is sometimes referred to as Many Falls Trail. It can be entered from Red Eagle Lake Trail, 5.1 miles south of St. Mary, or 2.6 miles below Red Eagle Lake. In reverse direction, departure is from trail 113, the trail from Sun Point to Many Glacier. See description later in this section for exits which can be used for this latter purpose.

Starting from the St. Mary 1913 Ranger Station, Red Eagle Trail (107) is followed for 5.1 miles to its junction with St. Mary Lake Trail (109). See earlier description of the trail from Red Eagle Lake to St. Mary.

St. Mary Trail (109), the right member, climbs briskly up the opposite bank to an old lodgepole forest whose uniform age indicates a fire of long ago. It crosses a flat-topped rim under the northeast point of Red Eagle Mt., then drops to the shore of ST. MARY LAKE (4484) at a site once known as Red Eagle Landing.

In the days before the construction of Going-to-the-Sun Road, a launch plied with scheduled regularity between St. Mary and Going-to-the-Sun Chalets. It stopped at the landing to discharge or receive hikers. A hoisted yellow flag was the signal for a requested pickup. Here alders and willows grow to tree size about 25 feet tall.

A few hundred yards down the lake, a gray sandstone cliff juts above the water. It is made up of thin laminae alternating with thicker strata, not composed of the hard ancient gray-green argillite which forms the cliff of Red Eagle Mt. nearby, but a soft, young, Cretaceous rock over which the mountains have ridden. An interesting feature of this cliff is the fact that the vegetation that covers it forms a tiny plant society distinct in itself. Mats of creeping juniper sprawl and kinnikinnick cascades over ledges. Legumes and river birches not found in the encircling forest make a home here among agonized Douglas firs and lodgepoles, a fantastic, distorted company.

From the landing the trail skirts the south shore of the lake over Altyn limestone. The section to VIRGINIA FALLS, built since 1930, was one of the causes for the decline of Red Eagle Landing. The old burn mentioned earlier reaches the lakeshore here. The rock is highly quartzitic indicating that it is very hard. Mountain lover and spotted saxifrage plants find it to their liking, for they thrive here. Beyond the Altyn slide rock is finer scree of green Appekunny argillite heavily covered with lichens of green gold. Plaintive bleats betray the presence of pikas in the broken slide rock.

Half a mile farther an open shore provides a splendid view of the Narrows and Going-to-the-Sun Mt. (9642). A few limber pines grow near the shore. The trail, cut in Appekunny argillite, crosses a creek below a waterfall tumbling from the summit of MAHTOTOPA MT. (8672) to the left. It then climbs a cliff to the ledge which crops out across the lake as SUN POINT.

There is a good view of LITTLE CHIEF MT. (9541) ahead. After passing beneath several small waterfalls, the trail climbs a green argillite cliff at the head of the lake, giving the first view of the bastion of CITADEL MT. (9030). A few white-barked paper birches grow left of the trail, surprising because these trees are rarely found east of the range.

The bridge over VIRGINIA CREEK passes beneath VIRGINIA FALLS in a woodland

Lake McDonald. Danny On photo.

St. Mary Lake. Kathy Ahlenslager photo.

Two Medicine Lake from Scenic Point. Becky Williams photo.

Climbing to tunnel on Crypt Lake Trail. Marilyn Casteel photo.

Ptarmigan Falls. Marilyn Casteel photo.

Belly River country. Larry Williams photo.

Some days are like that! Marilyn Casteel photo.

Naturalist party on Iceberg Lake Trail. Kathy Ahlenslager photo.

Taking a break on Sperry Glacier Trail. Marilyn Casteel photo.

Pumpelly Pillar. B. Riley McClelland photo.

Boulder Pass Trail. Glacier National Park photo.

Going-to-the-Sun Road above the Loop. Clyde Lockwood photo.

dell, adding to the charm of the setting. The falls lies at the end of a hanging valley which extends almost five miles between Citadel, Little Chief, Almost-a-Dog Mts. and Mt. Logan. The creek below the bridge has cut a colorful gorge in red argillite, making a delightful luncheon stop.

After leaving Virginia Creek, ST. MARY RIVER is crossed 0.7 mile farther, below ST. MARY FALLS, cut into Grinnell argillite. The river here is a raging torrent in a narrow chasm; people should not scramble over the rocks along the brink, because a slip into the stream would be fatal.

Half a mile beyond, Piegan Pass Trail (113) on the valley floor is reached. Going-to-the-Sun Road is 0.3 mile directly above on trail 261; hikers to St. Mary or Red Eagle Lake may meet or leave their cars in the parking space there.

As the trail nears the head of St. Mary Lake, it climbs a red bluff from which the view down the lake is framed in a picturesque setting. It crosses BARING CREEK, 0.7 mile beyond, below BARING FALLS at the mouth of a narrow gorge. It is 0.6 miles from Baring Creek to Sun Point.

Trails from Two Medicine
See also Trails from East Glacier Park, pages 85 - 91

In the heyday of rail travel sixty years ago, Two Medicine was a most popular destination of park visitors, especially of those pressed for time. Two Medicine is only a dozen easy miles from the East Glacier Park railroad station. Its pleasant, rustic chalets, one of which is now the campstore, were always filled to capacity in July and August.

Celebrities, among whom were President Franklin Roosevelt and Crown Prince Olaf of Norway and his wife, Crown Princess Martha, were drawn by its colorful scenery. It was a favorite destination for the parties of Howard Eaton, pioneer leader of backcountry saddlehorse trips early in the century. Author Mary Roberts Rinehart described its charms in her book *Through Glacier Park in 1915*.

Today a network of trails still gives ready access to its features. Frequent launch service on Two Medicine Lake augments travel facility. Two Medicine is a station on the Inside Trail between East Glacier Park and St. Mary. Travelers between East Glacier Park and Two Medicine use Mt. Henry Trail (96). Travelers for Cut Bank and beyond start on the Pitamakan Pass Trail (102). These two trails are described on page 86. An alternative route for hikers to Cut Bank Valley is via Dawson Pass on trail 99 (page 94).

Running Eagle (formerly "Trick") Falls Trail
Two Medicine Road to Running Eagle Falls on trail 257, 0.3 mile. See fold-out map.

It is only a 10-minute walk on the north bank of Two Medicine Creek from the road bridge, mile 9.9 on the Two Medicine Road, to the falls. Most buses stop at the bridge long enough to permit this short walk.

The trail is in shady woods of spruce, fir and cottonwood. The abundance of shrubs includes black and red twinberries, elderberry, mountain ash, maple, chokecherry, spiny currant, spirea, thimbleberry, serviceberry, huckleberry, menziesia and snowberry. Midway a foot bridge permits the walker to cross Dry Fork Creek.

At times of high water Running Eagle Falls is a conventional waterfall. Paneled by conifers backed by the purple summit of RISING WOLF MT. (9513), it is a favorite with photographers. As the season progresses and the flow of water plunging over the brink of the cliff decreases, an opening below, until now hidden by high water, becomes exposed. By late summer the flow over the cliff has decreased to a trickle, for the cave carries most of the water.

The Indians called this cascade Pitamakan or Running Eagle Falls, for a Blackfeet maiden who had a great adventure here, related by James W. Schultz in his book, "The Dreadful River Cave." For more about this remarkable woman, who reputedly led braves on the war-path, see the trail description of the Inside Trail, Cut Bank via Pitamakan Pass.

The falls presents a mode of formation of a natural bridge. The water discharging through the cave has seeped through fissures originating upstream in limestone, which is slightly solu-ble. As the stream grades its bed a rock arch may be left spanning the chasm, provided the cave is enlarged with time to carry the entire volume.

The ledge over which the water falls is part of the Lewis Thrust Fault block. An outcrop of sandstone with characteristics of local Cretaceous rock is beside the stream a hundred feet below the falls. It appears to be in place; if this is so, it follows that the thrust fault line must be located between the falls and this rock.

Two Medicine Pass Trail

Two Medicine Lake (lower dock) to Paradise Point, 0.6 mile; to Aster Park, 2.0 miles; to Cobalt Lake, 5.7 miles; to Two Medicine Pass, 7.9 miles. See fold-out map.

Trails 98 and 87 to Two Medicine Pass offer a most colorful trip, a favorite of old chalet days. Although peaks are not as high as elsewhere in the Lewis Range, they are highly colored and have sharp knife edges. Flower meadows in lofty basins, deeply colored lakelets and many waterfalls in argillite gorges are points to tarry for pleasure and reflection.

The start of trail 98 is in the forest near the parking circle by the lower boat dock. It climbs gently among Engelmann spruces, lodgepole pines and subalpine firs to 100 feet above the lake. At 0.2 mile, a footpath leads 0.4 mile to the right to Paradise Point, an attractive pebbled promontory with a sweeping view of the lake from its foot to Sinopah Mt.

Another footpath, now abandoned, breaks off the main trail several hundred feet beyond that to Paradise Point. This was a part of the well-worn, blazed main trail until beavers flood-ed the swale so that the route had to be relocated through a large meadow around the huge im-pounded pond seen from the trail 0.2 mile farther on.

Reentering the forest one approaches Aster Creek, along which are numerous animal trails that go down to the lakeshore, a half-mile away. Aster Park Trail (101) starts left shortly after crossing Aster Creek and climbs steeply by switchbacks 700 feet in 0.7 mile to elevation 5840 on the west bank. Aster Creek has cut a fantastic gorge in Appekunny argillite, steep-walled on the east side. It lunges for several hundreds of feet in a series of five cascades showing the pothole erosion characteristic of stream cutting in argillitic rocks of the park. It is 2.2 trail-less miles from the end of the trail to Aster Park (6890) where the carefree wanderer can roam at will among flower-rich loveliness. The elevated basin is shut in by MT. HENRY (8847) on the east, MT. ELLSWORTH (8581) at its head, and NEVER LAUGHS MT. (7641) to the west.

Trail 98 follows the lakeshore on a fairly level grade. A fine open meadow on Paradise Creek is reached 0.7 mile beyond Aster Creek with a good view of Sinopah Mt. and the higher red-dish MT. ROCKWELL (9272).

Trail 98 reaches an important junction at 2.3 miles from its start and 0.3 mile after crossing Paradise Creek over a suspension bridge, which may be dismantled off-season. From this junc-tion trail 98 continues to the right as part of the circuit around the lake, with connections to trails to Twin Falls, Upper Two Medicine Lake and Dawson Pass.

At the trail junction the route to Two Medicine Pass, now trail 87, takes off to the left. It goes up the west bank of Paradise Creek. Rockwell Falls is a popular destination, 1.1 miles above.

The forest becomes more open above the falls as trail 87 rises by a dozen short switchbacks on the flank of Painted Tepee Peak. Lovely COBALT LAKE (6570) lies 2.3 miles above Rockwell Falls.

After the Cobalt Lake spur junction, the trail curves close to the wall of Rockwell with an easier grade to the saddle on the divide (7300), from which a fine view of Upper Park Valley unfolds. EAGLE RIBS MT. (8290) and MT. DESPAIR (8582) rise in the south. VIGIL

Author George C. Ruhle on horseback, 1970, near Pitamakan Pass. Mel Ruder photo.

PEAK (8593) and CAPER PEAK (8310) are west across Park Creek. Back of Vigil Peak is Mt. St. Nicholas (9376), its jagged cliffs and crags silhouetted against the sky in an awesome sight. Mt. Ellsworth (8581) is to the east with Mt. Henry (8847) behind it and APPISTOKI PEAK (8164) a little to the left.

After gaining the notch south of Rockwell, the dim trail proceeds southeastward along the crest to the prominence (7682) above Cobalt Lake recently designated CHIEF LODGEPOLE PEAK, after the late Frank Guardipee, an Indian who served long as a park ranger. The peak culminates a faint path leading to Painted Tepee Peak. It is no trick to go a mile and half to the end of the ridge for a view of the valley.

Trail 87 continues southeastward along the Continental Divide from the crest of Chief Lodgepole to Two Medicine Pass (7400). From the pass the trail leads down to Park Creek, from which trail 86 goes upstream 2.3 miles to Isabel Lake (5715), six miles from Two Medicine Pass. There is no established trail to AURICE LAKE (7325) lying in the western shadow of Mt. Rockwell. Park Creek Trail (85) goes 11.4 miles down Park Creek to trail 67 along the park boundary opposite Essex on the Burlington Northern Railroad. See log of U.S. Highway 2, mile 25.0.

Dawson Pass

Two Medicine Campground to Dawson Pass via Trail 99, 6.7 miles. See fold-out map.

The foot of trail 99 to Dawson Pass is at the footbridge below the outlet of Pray Lake near Two Medicine Campground. The trail forks after crossing the bridge, the right hand member being trail 102 to Cut Bank. Trail 99 turns left, skirting Pray Lake. It then follows the north shore of Two Medicine Lake, above whitebark and limber pines, whose contorted shapes indicate the severity of the climate.

The trail crosses a slope stripped bare of trees by avalanches which crash down Rising Wolf Mt. in late winter. The opening affords a fine view of mountains around the lake including, left to right, APPISTOKI (8164), ELLSWORTH (8581), NEVER LAUGHS (7641), PAINTED TEPEE (7650), SINOPAH (8271) and LONE WALKER (8502).

Serviceberries, shrubby cinquefoils and wild roses grow on the slope with willows and aspens grading into cottonwoods along the edge. Beyond is a forest of lodgepole pines and firs with occasional Douglas firs and spruces, and an understory of huckleberries, menziesias and mountain ashes. A stand of pure spruce follows next with menziesias and mountain ashes underneath.

At 2.7 miles the trail gently climbs a shrub-covered slope with SINOPAH MT. in full view at the head of Two Medicine Lake. 3.3 miles from the campground in a forest of lodgepole and fir, trail 265 parts to the left to Twin Falls, 0.3 mile; the upper dock, one mile; and trail 98 on the south shore, for return down the lake. By using the launch service and joining trail 99 at this junction, the trip to Dawson Pass can be shortened by two miles. From its junction with 265 the route to Dawson Pass bears to the right and climbs up mossy, rocky slopes facing the thin wall terminating in PUMPELLY PILLAR (7620) ahead. RISING BULL RIDGE (7680) and red MT. ROCKWELL (9272) are to the left.

Ahead a stand of pure firs with a dense undercover of menziesias grows above a sun-drenched ledge. Meadow rue, ragworts, and false hellebores blossom on open slopes; above are spruces. A short trail leads to NO NAME LAKE (5925) nestled under the wall of PUM-PELLY PILLAR.

The grassy slopes and lush flower meadows of BIGHORN BASIN beneath DAWSON PASS (7598) are the home not only of bighorns but of other wildlife as well. MT. HELEN (8538), in full view to the left, is connected by a narrow ridge to DAWSON PASS. On the right the slope to the summit of FLINSCH PEAK (9225) appears so gradual that one is amazed to discover that it rises 3000 feet above the basin. The view to the west from Dawson Pass reveals Upper Nyack Valley and the impressive mass of MT. PHILLIPS (9494) with tiny LUPFER GLACIER in a pocket on the east face.

Trail 99 turns up the ridge of the Continental Divide. MT. STIMSON (10,142) dominates the scene in the west. For one seeking high places it is a relatively easy 2.5 mile climb along the slope of Flinsch Peak to the summit of Rising Wolf Mt. (9513), taking off from the trail at the switchback, one-half mile above the pass.

Dawson-Pitamakan Pass Trail. B. Riley McCelland photo.

Twin Falls

Upper Boat Dock on Two Medicine Lake to Twin Falls, 0.9 mile. See fold-out map.

Twin Falls is formed by paired cascades on an argillite ledge separated by an island in the course of an unnamed tributary of Upper Two Medicine Creek, which drops from the south face of Rising Wolf Mt. and drains Bighorn Basin. The falls is a favorite destination of walkers from the launch, Rising Wolf, which plies up and down Two Medicine Lake several times daily from the lower dock at the end of Two Medicine Road near the campstore.

From the dock the foot trail enters a forest and in 0.1 mile meets trail 98 which has come up the southwest shore of the lake.

At 0.5 mile, the trail to Twin Falls crosses Two Medicine Creek and enters a grassy meadow with many wildflowers abloom in earlier season. Towering above the trail is the red, needle-like prow of Pumpelly Pillar, a feature of Two Medicine Valley. A 0.2 mile link to the right connects with Dawson Pass Trail (99) following the north shore from the lower end of the lake. It is 3.1 miles to Two Medicine Campground and 3.4 miles to Dawson Pass. The trail to Twin Falls bears left to a junction. The short right-handed member leads 0.1 mile to the falls. The trail straight ahead continues 1.3 miles to Upper Two Medicine Lake.

Upper Two Medicine Lake

Lower boat dock of Two Medicine Lake to Upper Two Medicine Lake via the south shore, 5.5 miles; upper boat dock to Upper Two Medicine Lake via trail 98, 2.2 miles; upper boat dock to Upper Two Medicine Lake via Twin Falls Trail, 2.2 miles; Two Medicine Campground to Upper Two Medicine Lake via the north shore, 4.7 miles. See fold-out map.

Upper Two Medicine Lake is a convenient destination for a short journey using the morning boat trip to the upper dock and returning in the late afternoon; or the launch trip either way may be combined with a trip over either the north or south shore trails. The upper lake (5500) is beautifully cupped within cliffs of bright red argillite, RISING BULL RIDGE extending toward it from MT. ROCKWELL (9272) on the south; then L to R, are LONE WALKER (8502), HELEN MT. (8538) and PUMPELLY PILLAR (7620).

Vegetation is sparse, shaded by the lofty mass of Mt. Rockwell. Mountain goats are common on cliffs around the lake. Pikas live in the rock slides. In September, this retreat rings with the bulgling of elk. The water, though warm, is full of good brook trout and some rainbow.

The official trail to the lake is 98, the initial 2.5 miles being described earlier in this chapter under Two Medicine Pass. From the junction with Two Medicine Pass Trail at 2.4 miles, trail 98 crosses the talus which crowds the lakeshore beneath Sinopah Mt., named after Sinopahki or Swiftfox Woman, Blackfeet wife of Rising Wolf. Buffy gray swifts, or kit foxes, are shy little animals that live on the high plains at the base of these mountains and are becoming rare. Trail 98 meets the 0.1 mile trail from the upper dock then goes 0.8 mile to the Twin Falls junction. From here it goes 1.3 miles to the lake through increasingly more open country on the north bank of Two Medicine Creek.

Around Two Medicine Lake

Circuit, 7.5 miles. See fold-out map.

A circuit around Two Medicine Lake (5164) may be made in either direction from the lower boat dock or campground. Dawson Pass Trail (99) is followed along the north shore 3.1 miles to trail 265 which links to trail 98 for return around the south shore.

Travelers from the lakeshore by the lower dock follow trail 98 as described under the Two Medicine Pass Trail for the first 2.4 miles, then as described under the Upper Two Medicine Lake Trail.

Trails from Many Glacier

The North Circle

Many Glacier Hotel to Many Glacier Campground and Swiftcurrent Motor Inn via lakeshore and road, 1.3 miles; Many Glacier Campground to Granite Park via trail 157, 8.5 miles; Granite Park to Fifty Mountain Campground via trail 121, 11.9 miles; Fifty Mountain to Goat Haunt on Waterton Lake via trail 122, 10.5 miles; Goat Haunt to head of Glenns Lake via trail 131, 16.2 miles; Glenns Lake to Many Glacier Hotel via trail 158, 16.8 miles; North Circle Circuit, Many Glacier to Goat Haunt and return, 64.0 miles. See fold-out map.

Sixty years ago the North Circle trip, whether on foot or on horseback, was one of the most popular vacations in the West. Half of its distance is above timberline, with superior scenery, flowers, wildlife and diversity of attractions. Chalets and camps were spaced for convenient one-day travel, but the camps are no longer in operation because of insufficient patronage. Usually travel over the North Circle is done in a clockwise direction, because shorter distances are covered in the first days. Yet the reverse direction is more rewarding, especially as one faces the spectacular scenery at the head of Mokowanis Valley.

Many Glacier to Granite Park

Swiftcurrent Pass Trail (157) climbs 2300 feet up Swiftcurrent Valley to Swiftcurrent Pass (7185). Saddlehorse parties start at the corral above Many Glacier Hotel, cross the access road and Swiftcurrent Creek, then on trail 152 slant across the campground road 0.1 mile beyond and climb gently as they pass over a residual moraine on the slopes of Altyn Peak.

At 1.0 mile from the start, trail 152 to Iceberg Lake, Ptarmigan Lake and Belly River forks to the right. Trail 157 passes north and west of Swiftcurrent Motor Inn. Hikers from the hotel area may follow the lakeshore or the campground road past the ranger station and across the parking strip in front of Swiftcurrent Motor Inn, thus avoiding the climb over the moraine on

Altyn Peak. After crossing a footbridge over Wilbur Creek (4928), the foot route joins saddle trail 157 to go up the valley. Note that 1.3 miles can be whittled from the distance to Granite Park by departure from the campground area.

Lodgepole pines on Swiftcurrent Lake and the valley floor are the first stage of natural reforestation following the 1936 fire. See the log of Going-to-the-Sun Road, mile 24.7. The trees are runty as growth is very slow on exposed sites east of the Continental Divide.

Grinnell Point is to the left, across the valley. Mountain goats frequently are seen on the steep walls of the peak. The little lake beyond the campground is Fishercap (4925) after the Indian name for George Bird Grinnell. The colored summit to the right of Wilbur Creek is Mt. Henkel (8770). The trail skirts a ledge of bright red Grinnell argillite, the second formation above Altyn limestone on which Many Glacier Hotel is built.

The next lake to be reached, Redrock, two miles above Swiftcurrent Lake, is named after the color of the formation. Redrock Falls is at the head of the lake. An elongate series of lakes above the falls is named Bullhead Lake after the Bullhead Mine, located on the spur of Mt. Wilbur during the mining days. A suspension bridge across a tributary creek may be dismantled off-season.

Now the aftermath of old fires is left behind; willow thickets along the water ring with the rich melody of white-crowned and fox sparrows, the Te Deum of sparkling July mornings. Warblers and goldfinches join in the merriment.

North Swiftcurrent Glacier, a thin strip of ice, lies on a ledge in the broad basin above, on the right of the summit of Swiftcurrent Mt. The depression is especially inviting to hikers seeking solitude and close acquaintance with the inquisitive, trustful mountain goats, for few people invade this remote area. Mt. Wilbur offers a challenging climb to be undertaken only by experienced climbers. One July 4 night, glacier guide Leo Seethaler and the author made a foolish ascent to set off flares on the summit for the entertainment of hotel guests. When they reached the top at 11 p.m., a diaphanous cloud fortunately settled, so the lights in the valley could not be seen. Otherwise this absurd stunt might have established a precedent.

Trail 157 winds up the face of the 1400-foot rock pillar on the right by a series of long switchbacks. Parties usually stop to rest before making the long hot climb to the top of the bare prominence. A half dozen waterfalls tumble in shimmering grandeur from Swiftcurrent Glacier above. Mountain ash replace willows as the most abundant shrubs. Pink spireas blossom beautifully in midsummer. Here and there are corydalis, diffusedly branched plants with golden yellow flowers allied to Dutchman's breeches and bleeding hearts.

Five miles from Swiftcurrent Lake, a dike of igneous rocks cuts across the beds of limestone; its heat while molten bleached and partially crystallized adjacent limestone. A sill, perhaps 75 feet thick, is crossed higher on the trail. The angularity of rock fracture made trail construction difficult and produced a surface unpleasant for hikers and horses. This igneous rock forms the floor of the basin below Swiftcurrent Pass and is responsible in part for the prow of Swiftcurrent Mt. around which the route winds, affording sweeping views of the valley and Great Plains. Eight lakes are visible, the most distant being Duck Lake, 16 miles away. Wranglers call the sharpest point "Devil's Elbow," because at that place many horses were lost in the days when trails were narrow and precarious. The sill itself can easily be traced with the eye around the wall of the defile and across the flank of Mt. Wilbur. Slickensides and algal fossils are prominent geological features easily seen in this vicinity. The trail crosses a massive bed of dolomite built by crowded colonies of algae. Their uniform development and the purity of the rock which they formed indicate that they grew in a quiet sea into which few sediments were carried. The band of igneous rock appears below the thick gray ledge of dolomite on Mt. Grinnell, but above it, on Mt. Wilbur, the rise in position by the rock while molten was apparently accomplished through the dike crossed by the trail.

The trail now climbs diagonally across a slope covered with prostrate subalpine fir. Because snow may linger here all summer, a tread sometimes must be freshly shoveled periodically until August. Buttercups, carpet pinks, dryas, heathers, wild heliotrope, saxifrages and alpine erigerons are in bloom in July. A fine panorama of the Livingston Range is visible from SWIFTCURRENT PASS (7185), as well as a remarkable view down the valley up which the trail has come. The flanks of HEAVENS PEAK (8987) glisten in the southwest. LONGFELLOW PEAK (8904), with a permanent snowbank on its northern shoulder, is in the west. VULTURE PEAK (9638), Vulture Glacier, and the high mountains above Bowman and Kintla Lakes are in the northwest.

A climb of 1.4 miles by short switchbacks on Swiftcurrent Lookout Trail (158) up the bare, even profile of SWIFTCURRENT MT. affords a spectacularly extensive view. Besides the panorama seen from the pass, there are bird's-eye views of Mt. Jackson (10,052), Gunsight Mt. (9258), Sperry Glacier, Logan Pass (6680), the Garden Wall, McDonald Valley and Mt. Wilbur (9321). A fire lookout is on the apex of Swiftcurrent Mt.

Trail 157 twists as it drops 500 feet to the junction with Highline Trail (121) and to GRANITE PARK CHALETS (6650). This overnight stop is located on relatively even upland, surfaced with lava that poured from the earth when this region was beneath a sea. The rocks now composing the summits of the Garden Wall and surrounding peaks were subsequently deposited in this sea as ooze.

As the lava spread, it twisted, burned and pushed masses of clay upwards from the sea bottom and carried them along with it. Cooling under water was rapid, leaving a lumpy blue-greenish gray surface. The pillowy and ropy structure of the present surface resulted from flowage. Steam tubes and gas cavities or vesicles in the liquid were filled with white crystalline calcite after cooling, so that now they look like almonds in a dark cake. The rock is therefore described as amygdaloidal. It is durable and weathers slowly so that scratches and grooves made by glacial ice millennia ago are still prominent on the surface.

Granite Park to Fifty Mountain.

HIGHLINE TRAIL (121) comes to Granite Park Chalets (6650) from Logan Pass, 7.6 miles and continues to FIFTY MOUNTAIN CAMPGROUND, 11.9 miles northwest of the chalets. It received the name Highline because it is mostly near timberline with unbroken views of distant mountains. It was opened in 1929 to avoid a 2800-foot descent to Mineral Creek followed by a long climb up Flattop Mt. (6872).

McDonald Valley cuts deeply into Flattop Mt., which separates McDonald and Waterton drainages between the Lewis and Livingston Ranges. The crest of Flattop is a broad area of low relief which was the floor of a valley existing before present valleys were established. Dissevered remnants of the older valley are preserved as benches, including the area called Granite Park, that between Heavens Peak and Glacier Wall and that north of Fifty Mountain. The appearance of this ancient valley can be visualized by imagining the present valleys filled to the benches with several thousand feet of erosible material. The beds on the sides dip decreasingly towards the axis of the valley, indicating that this is a broad synclinal trough which determined precedent drainage.

Starting at the chalets, trail 121 coincides for a few hundred yards with trail 157 from Swiftcurrent Pass. It passes above the ranger patrol cabin northwest of the chalets, then swings sharply northeast around a sharp ridge on Swiftcurrent Mt. The purple or brown Purcell lava upon and from which the chalets are built is well exposed at this site.

The Granite Park flow is the most southerly exposure of Purcell lava and related basalt. It is exposed around the edges of Flattop Mt. and is prominent at Boulder Pass and the easternmost ridge of the Boundary Mts. In most places, the lava appears above the Helena (Siyeh) and below the Shepard Formations, constituting what geologists term a "horizon marker." Note

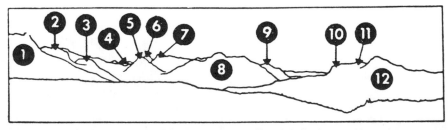

From Granite Park: (1) Gould: (2) Garden Wall and Pollock; (3) Haystack Butte; (4) Logan Pass; (5) Oberlin; (6) Reynolds; (7) Clements; (8) Cannon; (9) Brown; (10) McPartland; (11) Vaught; (12) Heavens Peak.

the concentric flow lines where molten rock bubbled through breaks in a partly hardened surface.

The texture of the Shepard Formation above the lava indicates that the seas in which it was formed were becoming shallower and conditions for growing limy deposits were nearing an end. Interesting rock specimens may be found in the talus above the trail. Some filled crevices suggest mud cracks but lack clear signs that they ever emerged and dried in the sun. The dolomite becomes increasingly mixed with clay and sand, signifying shallowing of the sea and rising of the land surface from which these impurities originated.

Some of the fragments are quartzite: they come from the highest layers and sometimes show cross ripple marks formed as the direction of the wind changed, so that succeeding waves were sent at angles to preceding waves. Such observations give evidence about winds, currents and depths existing when deposits were laid down.

The Mt. Shields formation lies above the Shepard. Mainly formed in shallow water that dried up completely at times, this argillite gives the color to the flaming summits of peaks above Kintla Lake.

Three miles from the chalets the trail turns east sharply on a cirque wall. Great depths of snow form the so-called Ahern Drift and linger through summer. This is the last stretch of trail to be opened in summer and the first to be blocked by new snowfall in early autumn. It is kept passable during the period of use by repeatedly arching new tread, which constantly moves downslope, the center moving fastest. As the snow becomes rotten, breakthroughs are common. Despite precautions, the steep face of the bank is treacherous for both man and beast, so utmost caution should be exercised. Snowbridges collapse without warning.

Beyond the snow, the trail descends diagonally across the sill of diorite which is a prominent feature on the mountain walls at Many Glacier. Extensive bare patches mark the sill as it dips to Mineral Creek on the valley floor.

At 4.5 miles from the chalets, a 0.4 mile spur (125) leads to Ahern Pass (6100) for a view of Helen Lake (5085) and Belly River Valley extending far to the northeast on the plains of Alberta. Beyond the pass is a lofty, steep-faced snowbank which prevents safe descent to the valley, but a scramble can be made along the rim of the wall to the northwest for extended views from other angles. It is more rewarding, however, to climb 1200 feet in a half-mile in the opposite direction to a notch in the Pinnacle Wall cupping Iceberg Lake. The view from the top includes Swiftcurrent Lake and Many Glacier Hotel. Like the wall back of Helen Lake, the cirque wall of Iceberg Lake, including the forbidding north face of Mt. Wilbur, is lofty and sheer, yet mountain goats may be seen frolicking with nonchalance upon it. The highest pinnacle of the wall (9145), 0.4 mile south, was picturesquely named "Crazy Gray Horse," in the 30's by Superintendent Eivind T. Scoyen after a fabulous Blackfeet race horse that made many a betting brave "go for broke." Instead, the unimaginative name "Iceberg Peak" was accepted by topographers, but don't look for icebergs on it!

The intersecting dike causing the low notch in the wall can be traced in an almost straight line from the opposite side of Iceberg Lake, in a notch on the eastern shoulder of Wilbur, near the tip of Grinnell Point across Swiftcurrent Lake from Many Glacier Hotel, in the notch above Falling Leaf Lake on Allen Mt. and to the east side of Canyon Creek. This trace is the heart of a mineral zone that attracted early prospectors and that gave Mineral Creek its name. One of the claimants was Mrs. Nat Collins of Choteau, Montana, the "Cattle Queen," next to "Calamity Jane," the best known woman of Montana pioneer days. For almost a quarter of a century after the park was created her cabin was a landmark on the Swiftcurrent Pass trail above Wilbur Creek. Cattle Queen Creek, below and west of Ahern, was named for this picturesque woman.

In 1895 Lieutenant George Ahern successfully led a detachment of cavalry across the pass, later to bear his name, but most attempts to cross it with horses have ended in disaster. As it is not in line with park travel, it is the only prominent pass in the Lewis Range without a trail over it.

Leaving Ahern Creek the main trail (121) maintains a level grade at 6800 feet as it swings west around Ahern Peak (8749). Enroute it recrosses the igneous sill as well as the vertical dike which outcrops in the notch north of Iceberg Lake and which is 60 feet thick here. In former days there was some prospecting in the dike where it reappears on the northwest side of the mountain.

Good views open of the peaks along the Garden Wall, at Logan Pass and behind Sperry Glacier. The splendid summits of the Livingston Range are always in sight across Flattop Mt. Everywhere the trail offers good places to see mountain goats, bighorns and deer, and sometimes to favor with the rarer privilege of watching a big mountain coyote stalk its quarry of rodents. Travelers have also reported seeing gray timber wolves, wolverine or mountain lion. Soaring golden eagles are hoisted high by updrafts over the mountain wall, which affords them secure nesting sites. The picturesque trees along the trail are whitebark pines.

The trail turns abruptly north and drops rapidly 1000 feet by four switchbacks 1.3 miles west of Ahern Creek crossing, meanwhile crossing Cattle Queen Creek at the 6200-foot contour where hikers should beware of rotten snow bridges. It swings around another low ridge, then starts a gradual climb to 7400 feet on the Continental Divide which switches at this point from the Lewis to the Livingston Range. As the trail nears the head of Mineral Creek, massive diorite boulders are strewn about every which way. Beyond the high point, a 0.4-mile spur (124) climbs to an elevation of 7750 on the crest of Mt. Kipp for an astounding view of Sue Lake (7145) with Mokowanis Valley beyond. The sharp spire of Pyramid Peak (7933) is to the northeast; Mt. Merritt's fluted sides and jagged crest (10,004) are to the east. Mt. Cleveland (10,466) and Stoney Indian Peaks (9350), a serrate knife-edge, rise to the north. Trail 121 descends a mile on the southwestern talus of Mt. Kipp which here poses as a solid wall. Halfway down, the trail makes a sharp switchback to FIFTY MOUNTAIN (6700), an open park of short, much-branched spruce on ice-cold Kootenai Creek. A campground is located here.

Fifty Mountain is the meeting place of trails; 121 just described from Granite Park, 122 from Waterton Valley and 66 from Packers Roost in McDonald Valley via West Flattop. Hemmed between the two superb mountain ranges, the campground location is fantastically beautiful. The dominant peaks to the west include Heavens, Longfellow, glacier-ringed Vulture, Rainbow and Carter of Cerulean Ridge and the giants of the Kintla-Boulder Pass country. The Lewis Range is a castellated wall from Cathedral Peak past the Garden Wall and Logan Pass to the Blackfoot Glacier assemblage.

Fifty Mountain to Waterton Lake (Goat Haunt)

A sloping, lava-covered flat, like that on which Granite Park Chalets is built, stretches northward from Fifty Mountain Campground. It is beautifully clothed with grass and myriad flowers. On the northeast the talus slopes up to a sheer thin wall between Kipp and Cathedral Peak (9041), which appears from the campground to have an even crest. The nearest mountain to the west is Kootenai Peak (8542). Bench Lake (6780), unseen and seldom visited, lies in the great basin scooped out of the southeast side of the mountain.

From the edge of Flattop Mt., trail 122 drops by switchbacks through a grove of whitebark pines into a forest of big subalpine firs. The sill of igneous rock and the associated algal reef of the Helena (Siyeh) Formation are met on the descent to Waterton River.

Leaving the highland the trail drops over a hot slope covered with mountain ash, alder and yew. In summer red raspberry bushes furnish refreshment until the valley floor is reached. At 4.5 miles, trail 122 is joined by the Waterton River Trail (130) which goes 2.3 miles upstream to a locked patrol cabin. At 5.6 miles Stoney Indian Pass Trail (131) from Belly River and Many Glacier is met at Pass Creek.

At the footbridge over Camp Creek, 7.9 miles from Fifty Mountain, a path goes 1000 feet in the forest to the left to a small campground on shallow Kootenai Lakes. It is a good idea to take a peek to see if any moose are lurking in this marshland even if one does not plan to make a longer stop.

Camp Creek is the author's favorite route (no trail) for an ascent of Mt. Cleveland (10,466). The adventure presents no technical difficulties, requiring only moderate stamina, common sense and a full-day's time. The lower course is through timber and brush and is the most strenuous part of the trip. The usual access is up the main or south fork of Camp Creek to the notch (8650) to the left (north) of Stoney Indian Peaks. The shorter route up the north fork is more precipitous and dangerous. The peak can also be climbed from Stoney Indian Pass, avoiding the strenuous fight through timber at lower elevations. One can also start from

Glenns Lake on trail 131 by ascending Whitecrow Creek. *Make certain to register at a ranger station before starting any ascent.*

The summit view from Mt. Cleveland is the most widespread in Waterton-Glacier. On clear days it extends 150 miles northwest to the famous matterhorn, Mt. Assiniboine (11,870), on the southwest boundary of Banff Park. On one ascent of Cleveland, the author found droppings of a grizzly encysted by beetle larvae on the very summit.

Until the middle thirties, an old log cabin stood at the left of the trail on the north bank of Camp Creek. This was the home of one of the picturesque rangers who were the park protective force in 1910. Because of his avowal "to die with his boots on," he carried the somber name, "Death on the Trail" Reynolds. He vies with Kootenai Brown of Waterton Park fame as the best known character in Waterton Valley history.

The mixed forest is of spruce, subalpine fir, lodgepole pine and Douglas fir, with cottonwoods growing in damper sites. Local wildlife is rich. Deer, moose and bear are common; grizzlies show up now and then. The bugling of elk tingles the ear in the crisp air of autumn twilight. Lynx and mountain lions have been surprised by a party suddenly popping on the scene. Members of the marten family are reported in this valley more frequently than in any other place in the park.

Evidence of beaver activity along the trail and on Waterton Lake is a highlight for the observer. Beaver dams, ponds, meadows, canals and lodges can be seen on all sides. In places it has been necessary to relocate the trail because beaver ponds flooded it, and beaver enjoy the right-of-way in the park. Trail 122 ends at the Goat Haunt Ranger Station, 10.5 miles from Fifty Mountain Campground.

A pair of ospreys often nest on top of a snag near the mouth of Waterton River; another pair have had their home several hundred yards below the boat dock. Some years a pair of bald eagles nest on snags along the lakeshore. Keep well away from any nest to avoid disturbing the birds. Other birds are numerous and include warblers, juncoes, siskins, grosbeaks, thrushes, hawks, owls, dippers and waterfowl. Particolored flocks of crossbills appear sporadically, the irregularity as yet unexplained.

From Goat Haunt Ranger Station, Waterton Lake Trail (135) goes northwest about 0.4 mile to the horse crossing of Waterton River. A pleasant, uncrowded campground lies directly across the river, but hikers must continue upstream, passing the junction of the Rainbow Falls Trail (196), which goes 0.5 mile to the falls. Just beyond the junction, hikers on Trail 135 cross Waterton River on a suspension bridge, dismantled off-season to avoid damage from heavy snowpack. Less than half-mile past the bridge exciting Boulder Pass Trail (6), a steep ascent, starts up Olson Valley. Waterton Lake Trail follows the west shore to the International Boundary, 3.7 miles and continues about six miles more to Waterton Townsite in Canada.

Seven-mile long Waterton Lake (4196), 317 feet deep, is pinched between serried, glaciated peaks. It is almost bisected by the International Boundary. Spiny Porcupine Ridge is a hallmark of the region. Mt. Cleveland stands as a sentry with its north face a perpendicular 6200-foot precipice. Prince of Wales Hotel obtrudes like a lighthouse at the foot of the lake.

The locality at the head of the lake is loosely termed Goat Haunt after GOAT HAUNT MT. (8641), rising above it on the east.

Just behind the employees' bunkhouse Goat Haunt Overlook Trail (134) begins in a grassy meadow and climbs one mile through a mixed forest affected by mountain pine beetles. From the overlook excellent views are provided of Waterton Lake, Porcupine Ridge and the Sentinel towering over the Olson Creek Drainage.

Two-tenths mile east on the pebbly shore is Goat Haunt Landing, with an L-shaped dock for boats in daily service from Waterton Townsite. An exhibit shelter faces the dock. The exhibits explain the concept of the International Peace Park, the geology and ecology of the area and similar subjects. The Coat of Arms of Canada and the Great Seal of the United States, carved in bold relief, flank the entranceway. At the left of the building two swastika-shaped structures of four units each provide overnight shelter for trail hikers. In summertime a naturalist is stationed here to give information and popular talks and to conduct trips afield.

In days gone by Goat Haunt was a principal stopover for saddle parties and hikers on the North Circle. A log and stone chalet with a long picture-veranda faced the lake at dockside. With decline in popularity after World War II and deterioration with age, the structure was razed in 1952.

Waterton Lake (Goat Haunt) to Cosley Lake (Ptarmigan Trail Junction)

Stoney Indian Pass Trail (131) promises adventurers interesting engagement. It makes for easy access to wild high country with associated delights. It offers the intimacy of eminences around Wacheechee Basin, the shimmery quality of waterfalls poised at the heads of cliffs, the azure of deep finger lakes, and a classic view of Mokowanis Valley streaming into the hazy distance of endless plains.

The trail starts at the boat dock, passes the ranger station, and retraces the Waterton Valley Trail for 4.9 miles to the junction near Pass Creek.

Trail 122 up Waterton Valley is in heavy timber, cool and lovely in early morning but tending to be hot and very dusty in the afternoon. Before the park was established it was widened as a wagon road over which sawlogs were hauled to the lake for shipment to Canada, but the project never prospered.

In ancient days the trail was used by Stonies and Kutenais (the spelling is that used by Clark Wissler, the celebrated authority on American Indians; the variant, Kootenais, is used for place names officially determined by the U.S. Board on Geographic Names). Stonies came from far north and used Stoney Indian Pass to reach the Belly River country. To avoid encounters with the feared Blackfeet, they kept safe behind the mountain walls, which their plains-loving enemies dreaded. The Kutenais usually crossed Kootenai Pass and Flattop Mt. to reach Lake McDonald and Camas Valley.

Trails 122 and 131 separate just before Pass Creek; trail 131 to Stoney Indian Pass and Cosley Lake turns left to ascend the canyon of Pass Creek by a wearying series of switchbacks.

Leaving the cool forest behind, alder and mountain ash cover the slope up which the trail ascends. Many flowers add to the interest of the climb. The bare crags of Stoney Indian Peaks are on the left, the blocky Wacheechee Mt. (8477) is ahead. This spelling resulted from copy error for "wacheachak," the Cree word for the sandhill crane, which in legends of the Plains Indians transports smaller birds while flying. Wacheechee Mt. is far more imposing viewed from the south. It appears above Stoney Indian Pass like a titanic sarcophagus within which, perhaps, are entombed forever the myriad spirits with which Indian legends peopled the mountains.

Behind, to the northwest, the sawtooth crest of Porcupine Ridge dwindles as one climbs. Two miles above the trail junction, lovely Stoney Indian Lake (6325) fills a rock-rimmed cirque around which the trail winds. The flower-bedecked outlet of the lake is an excellent site to stop for lunch. A small campground is located on a rise above the outlet.

In the old days saddlehorse guides said the lake occupied an abysmal hole over 1500 feet deep at the lower end. When soundings were made the actual depth was established at 34 feet.

STONEY INDIAN PASS (6908) at the top of the switchbacks is in the judgment of many the most beautiful pass in Glacier. The flower-studded amphitheater with a picture lakelet is the headwaters of Mokowanis River. Streams of water tumble from the snowfields and as often as not are caught by uprising air currents as they reach the brink of the cliff to be tossed skyward as inverted waterfalls—capricious, shimmering plumes that are blown back against the mountain. To the right Shepard Glacier cascades over two mammoth shelves on Cathedral Peak. Patches of matted subalpine firs thrive wherever snow disappears earliest in summer.

The wall on the southeast side of the basin culminates in Pyramid Peak (7933). Behind the wall are Natoas Peak (9476), Mt. Merritt (10,004) and Ipasha Peak (9572), all sculptured in fine detail by the storms and frosts of millennia. The trail crosses the flower-strewn floor with idyllic stops for lunch and rest, although some choose to linger in the more sheltered, shrubby sites beside Paiota Falls at the lip of the basin.

Sue Lake (7145) below Mt. Kipp can be easily reached on foot by climbing the slope south of Pyramid Peak. The 400-foot drop of Raven Quiver Falls is the beauty beneath the lip of Sue Lake. It is not difficult to traverse west from Sue Lake to steep-faced Shepard Glacier, exciting because it straddles a cliff over which, in the darkness under the glacier, a tremendous volume of melt water plunges as a roaring waterfall. Chaney Glacier on the far side of the summit ridge of Mt. Kipp is reached by going around the spur southeast of Sue Lake. The headwall of the glacier is low and easily climbed for a view of the mountains around Logan Pass, the Livingston Range and Fifty Mountain. Mountain goats are often seen on the mountains around the basin. Bear have been seen, probably in escape from torment by insects in the valley.

The view of Belly River country from any of the vantage points at the valley head is a picturebook illustration of a trough carved by a glacier: note its U-shaped cross section and gently flowing contours, the long finger lakes impounded by rocky ledges, moraines, or alluvial fans of tributary streams, the cliff glaciers and the series of amphitheaters near the head of the valley each with waterfalls dropping over its edges.

The upper end of Mokowanis Valley is a Cyclopean staircase, a compound cirque carved out by glaciers. Over the lower lip of the broad amphitheater below Stoney Indian Pass the trail plunges between low firs on the north face of Pyramid Peak. Two fine waterfalls tumble over the wall. The nearer is Paiota (pie-oh-tah), the further Atsina (ut-say-nuh), Blackfeet words for Flying Woman and Gut People, meaning the Gros Ventres. At their base Atsina Lake is opalescent with rock flour ground by the scouring action of Shepard Glacier. There are three plank bridges between the pass and Atsina Lake which are pulled during the off-season. The trail swings around the north side of the lake, thence down the north slope above the river. A half-mile below, the dense spruce and fir forest of Upper Mokowanis Valley is reached.

The long cascade, bordered by alders along the trail above the forest, is Mokowanis Cascade. Mokowanis is an alternative Blackfeet name for "Belly Indians," translated by white men as "Gros Ventres." At 4.8 miles from Stoney Indian Pass, Mokowanis Lake Trail (138) branches to White Quiver Falls, beautifully framed by trees with Pyramid Peak as a background. The cascade, called Washboard Falls before 1929, was renamed for the hero in a novel by H. F. Saunders. Trail 138 continues up Pyramid Creek 1.2 miles to Mokowanis Lake (4981) known for good fishing. Upstream, Margaret Lake (5574), a mile away, and Ipasha Lake (5660), three-quarters of a mile beyond, are both gems. Ipasha, Good Spotted Tail, was the Mandan mother of Joe Kipp, frontierman and guide, for whom Mt. Kipp was named.

Stoney Indian Pass Trail (131) follows at a distance the north shore of Glenns Lake (4862), three miles long but very narrow. The water is quite turbid with glacial flour near the inlet of the lake, but is a lovely clear sapphire at the outlet. The arete to the left is Whitecrow Mt. (7824), which is separated from Mt. Cleveland by the deep gorge of Whitecrow Creek. White Crow was a mischievous scamp who appears frequently in Blackfeet myths. Indian friends Dick Sanderville and Bird Rattle told the author, who named the features, that White Crow was the character who hid all the buffalo in a hole in the ground, causing their disappearance from the hunting grounds.

There is a good campground at either end of Glenns Lake, and another near the foot of Cosley Lake (4842), 1.5 miles below Glenns Lake foot. The two lakes are separated by a wide alluvial fan built up by Kaina (kye-nah) Creek. The Kaina are a group of the Blackfeet Confederacy living in southern Alberta. The flat is open but rocky. The big cottonwoods growing along the streams and lakes contrast pleasingly with evergreen forests. Joe Cosley, often pronounced and spelled Crossley and so appearing on older maps and in literature, was a fabulous hunter, trapper, poacher and newspaper correspondent who distinguished himself in World War I. He was one of the first rangers in Glacier National Park and made the Belly River country his life haunt. Joe himself told the author that he was of Chippewa (Ojibway) descent, which is at variance with others who classify him simply as clever and treacherous.

Above Cosley Lake a pleasant open grassy swale is the site of former Crossley (sic) high country camp, justly famous as a fisherman's hangout, for prunes served at every breakfast with verses of praise in Swedish and for the entertainment of tall tales and songs by Dee Wanzer, the Scandinavian manager. The camp was a casualty of the years after World War II. A stunning view of Pyramid Peak, Shepard Glacier and Mt. Cleveland has a foreground including the lake with twisted limber pines lining its shores. The southeast face of Cleveland seen from this site is an imposing precipice, 4500 feet high. From the valley floor Cathedral Peak is to the left of Cleveland. Part of the ice of Whitecrow Glacier resting at the base of the cliff can be seen from the lakeshore. The spur of Cleveland above the glacier is Whitecrow Mt. Looking down the valley, CHIEF MT. (9080) on the right looks like a huge rock resting on a broad shoulder. The larger of the two needles on the ridge conecting Chief and Gable Mts. is called by Indians Ninaki (knee-knocky) which means "the chief's wife." The smaller pinnacle is her papoose, Ninaipokah (knee-nigh-poe-kah).

From the junction of Stoney Indian Pass and Ptarmigan Trails, Cosley Lake Cutoff Trail (142) continues 2.2 miles downstream on the west bank of the valley to Belly River Ranger Station. At 0.2 mile Bear Mt. Overlook Trail (141) climbs 1400 feet in 1.7 miles to the site of a dismantled fire lookout (6280) for a good view of Mokowanis Valley and of Chief Mt. downstream. The prominent shoulder of yellow rock on which the lookout was located is Altyn limestone with greenish Appekunny argillite above. Below a wooded bluff 0.4 mile beyond the foot of the lookout trail, the river takes a foaming plunge over a high overthrust ledge as Gros Ventre Falls.

Trail 142 follows the route of the old logging road mentioned under Chief Mountain International Highway, Canadian Section, mile 16.4. The trail crosses the river over a cable suspension bridge (seasonally dismantled) to the grassy meadows that surround Belly River Ranger Station and campground. This is the meeting place of cutoff trail 151 from Dawn Mist Falls on Ptarmigan Trail, of Gable Pass Trail (149) and of the Belly River Trail (148) from U.S. Customs on Chief Mountain International Highway 6.2 miles.

Cosley Lake to Many Glacier Via Ptarmigan Tunnel

Ptarmigan Trail (152) begins at the outlet of Cosley Lake. During the summer a cable is strung across the creek to serve as a handhold for hikers fording the swift, cold current. Big cottonwoods, willows and creek dogwood grow in the bottomland.

The trail immediately climbs a steep bank by two switchbacks to start its passage over a stony medial moraine covered with alder and buffaloberry bushes.

The first trees are firs, soon replaced by a pure stand of lodgepole pines. The whole lower valley is covered by the weedlike growth of this tree indicating repeated fires. In recent years mountain pine beetles have killed thousands of the lodgepoles. The understory is alder, maple, thimbleberry, menziesia and spirea. Oregon grapes, pipsissewa, spireas and beargrass grow along the edges of the trail. Here and there little islands of spruce break the monotony of pure lodgepoles.

Belly River roars through a yawning chasm below the trail as it cuts around the eastern prow of Cosley Ridge. The strata of Gable Mt. (9262) across the valley ahead show interesting folds. A colony of pikas lives in the bare slide rocks of Altyn limestone.

2.1 miles from Cosley Lake, trail 152 is joined on the left by the Cosley Lake Cutoff Trail (142) coming from the Belly River Ranger Station, 2.2 miles downstream. Continuing 0.3 mile farther a short spur to the left leads to the foot of Dawn Mist Falls (60 feet high) which has the largest volume of water of any high falls in the park. Ptarmigan Trail (152) climbs to its brink for a view from above. Dawn Mist was an Indian maiden beloved by White Quiver for whom the cascade above Glenns Lake was named.

Red raspberries and junipers grow on the ledge above the falls. Here also is seen creeping twinflower or linnea which, though common in McDonald Valley, is unusual east of the mountains. Across an open space along the river, Seward Mountain (8917) in the Red Gap can be seen to the southeast.

Elizabeth Lake (4892) lies 1.5 miles above Dawn Mist Falls. The large campground at the foot of the lake indicates its popularity. Like Belly River below, Elizabeth Lake offers good fishing for rainbow and grayling.

Helen Lake Trail (153), forking to the right from the Ptarmigan Trail, follows the west shore beneath the cliffs of Natoas Peak (9476) for 4.3 miles to Helen Lake.

Ptarmigan Trail fords the foot of Elizabeth Lake on a suspension bridge (dismantled during the off-season) and climbs abruptly the steep slope to the east, covered with a mixed forest. A little higher, the stand is pure lodgepole pine. Trees are frequently swell-butted and distorted or show yawning yellowish cankers, malformations due to the prevalence of a parasitic fungus known as *Cronartium harknessii*. Hikers enjoy the many huckleberry bushes along the trail in fruiting season.

As the trail climbs, increasingly better views of Elizabeth and Helen Lakes open up. The wall of Cosley Ridge across the valley to the west is indented with cirques, the floors of which are beautiful flowery parks.

Sharp-spired Natoas Peak is behind Cosley Ridge; still farther behind are Mt. Merritt (10,004) with Old Sun Glacier. Ahern Peak (8749) and Ahern Pass (7100) are at the head of the valley back of Helen Lake. Trail 152 ahead can easily be followed by eye as it climbs the face of the mountain.

At two miles and 1150 feet above Elizabeth Lake, Red Gap Pass Trail (154) forks to the left and leads over rocky, windswept Red Gap Pass (7600) between an unnamed peak (7814) and Seward Mt. (8917). This is the famous trail to Many Glacier, used more heavily prior to the construction of a trail through Ptarmigan Wall in 1930.

Trail 152 swings to the right on Ptarmigan Wall. A quarter of a mile beyond the Red Gap trail junction two beautiful creeks in a lovely pine forest make an excellent lunch stop. When the trail leaves the forest, it is almost level as it crosses open shale slopes.

In places stunted aspens, affecting the habit of shrubs, grow in the scree and look strangely out of place so high on the bald mountainside. The bladderpod, a curious plant, grows in this environment.

The views here are among the most spectacular in the park. Many fine waterfalls appear near the head of Belly River Valley until late summer. Below Elizabeth Lake the lodgepole forest on the floor of the valley looks like velvet carpet. Beyond these are the plains of Canada.

Above the talus the trail, half-tunneled out of the bright red Grinnell argillite, is blocked with snow past early July. It climbs steadily to a 183-foot tunnel (7200) to the opposite side high above Ptarmigan Lake (6625). Off-season the tunnel doors are locked to prevent winter snows from drifting in. The south portal of the tunnel frames a view of Mts. Wilbur (9321), Grinnell (8851) and Gould (9553). The trail then drops by two long switchbacks over the talus to the lake.

From the lake Ptarmigan Trail descends Ptarmigan Creek along the base of Ptarmigan Wall, upon which mountain goats are frequently seen; bighorns like to graze the slopes on the opposite side. The trail soon enters the forest and 1.6 miles below the lake joins Iceberg Lake Trail (155).

The castellated summit of Mt. Wilbur towers across the valley. The summit on the left is Henkel (8770), with the spire, Crowfeet Mt. (8914), 1.2 miles north. The trail drops down Wilbur Creek permitting good views of Grinnell Point and the Many Glacier country. In late July the burn is ablaze with unbroken bloom of fireweed. Lovely red monkeyflowers and parnassias nod in the streams sparkling beside the way. Two and a half miles below the trail junction (152, 155) a spur descends 0.3 mile to Many Glacier Campground and Swiftcurrent cabins and store, all in plain sight. One may either follow this route and use the road and footpath along Swiftcurrent Lake or continue on the horse trail to Many Glacier Hotel.

Grinnell Lake and Grinnell Glacier

Many Glacier Hotel to Grinnell Lake via trail 167, 180, 171 and 175: 3.2 miles; via 167, 168, 174 and 175: 3.6 miles; via 113, 174 and 175: 3.7 miles.

Many Glacier Hotel to Grinnell Glacier Moraine Overlook via trails 167, 168 and 170: 5.4 miles; via 167, 180, 171, 174 and 170: 6.0 miles; via 113, 174 and 170: 6.2 miles.

Upper dock on Josephine Lake to Grinnell Lake via foot trail 175: 1.1 miles; via horse trail 173: 1.2 miles.

Swiftcurrent Picnic Area to Grinnell Lake via trails 167, 168, 174 and 175: 3.4 miles; via 167, 180, 171 and 175: 3.4 miles.

Swiftcurrent Picnic Area to Grinnell Glacier Moraine Overlook via trails 167, 168 and 170: 5.2 miles. See map on 106 and fold-out map.

Grinnell Lake and Grinnell Glacier are pleasant, popular destinations readily accessible to Many Glacier visitors. An assortment of trails (some reserved for foot use only, others for horse or hiker use) and launch services provide variety and choice, shortening walking distances, while increasing the coverage possible within a comfortable day.

The easy journey to Grinnell Lake (4950) is for the greater part over level ground. The trip to Grinnell Glacier is recommended to those seeking a trail experience in high country.

Various combinations of routes for both destinations involve both east and west shores of Swiftcurrent and Josephine Lakes, which vary greatly, as well as the scheduled daily launch trips on the two lakes. Launch service is taken in two stages, first across Swiftcurrent Lake from Many Glacier Hotel with a 0.2 mile walk on trail 168 to the foot of Josephine Lake, and

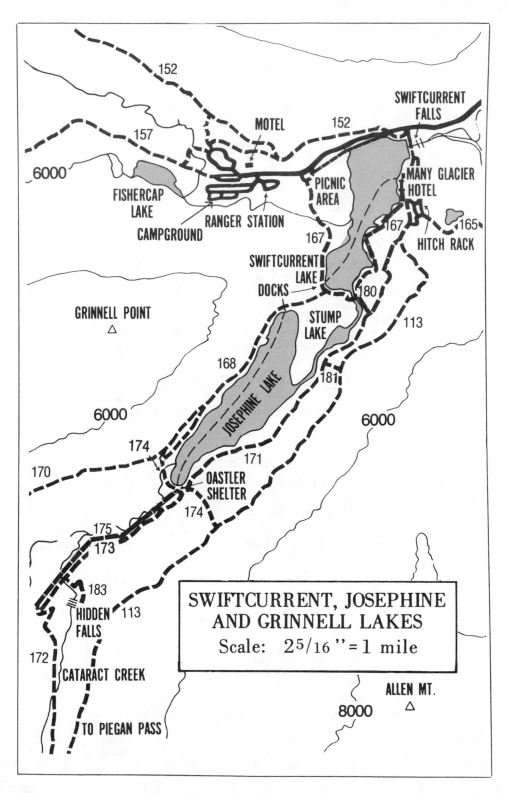

SWIFTCURRENT, JOSEPHINE
AND GRINNELL LAKES
Scale: 2⁵/₁₆ " = 1 mile

then to the upper Josephine dock, where a shelter, a gift of Mrs. Frank Oastler of New York City, is located.

The various trails are best followed by use of the accompanying map and by reference to trail signs at junctions. Trails 167, 168, 170 and 174 between 170 and Oastler Shelter, 175, 180 and 183 are footpaths, not to be used by horses and riders.

Swiftcurrent Lake Trail (167)

Swiftcurrent Lake Trail (167) for foot travel only, around Swiftcurrent Lake; natural features are described elsewhere in this section under "Around Swiftcurrent Lake."

For hikers from Swiftcurrent Motor Inn and Many Glacier Campground bound either for Grinnell Lake or Grinnell Glacier, trail 167 starts at the picnic area, crosses Swiftcurrent Creek and follows the northwest lakeshore under Grinnell Point 0.7 mile to the boat dock at the south (upper) end of the lake. At this point it connects (R) with North Shore Josephine Lake Trail (168). It also continues (L) 0.2 mile to the inlet of Swiftcurrent Lake to connect via trail 180 with trail 171 along the southeast side of Josephine Lake.

Hikers from the hotel area can use Swiftcurrent Lake Trail 167, most easily entered on the lakeshore at the south end of the hotel. From the hotel the head of Swiftcurrent Lake is 0.9 mile for connection with trail 168 and the lower boat dock on Josephine Lake, 0.2 mile farther, at which point trail 168 follows the northwest shore of Josephine Lake.

All saddlehorse trips bound for Josephine or Grinnell lakes start on the Piegan Pass Trail (113) from the corral at the southeast corner of the automobile parking area back of the hotel.

North Shore Josephine Lake Trail (168)

A footpath from Swiftcurrent Lake, above the northwest shore of Josephine Lake, then to Grinnell Lake via trails 174 and 175. The features of these trails are covered elsewhere in this section.

Trail 168 starts at the Swiftcurrent dock 0.9 miles from the hotel, crosses the low hump to Josephine Lake and follows the northwest shore of that lake. At 1.0 mile Grinnell Glacier Trail (170) goes right, joined in 0.3 mile by trail 174, then continues another 3.2 miles to the Grinnell Glacier Moraine Overlook. At 1.4 miles, trail 168 connects with Josephine Walk (174) coming from the upper dock on Josephine Lake, 0.2 mile to the left, and reaching trail 170 0.1 mile to the right.

South Shore Josephine Lake Trail (171)

A foot-horse path on the southeast side of Josephine Lake, from the end of the service road south from Many Glacier Hotel to Oastler Shelter, and to Grinnell Lake via horse trail 173 or foot trail 175. The section to Oastler Shelter is described under "Around Josephine Lake."

Trail 171 can also be entered from Swiftcurrent Lake Trail (167) via trail 180, close to the creek connecting the two lakes. A third connection can be made by starting from the hotel horse corral on Piegan Pass Trail (113). At a junction 2.3 miles from the hotel, the right fork is the start of Josephine Walk (174). Trail 174 drops to the upper dock of Josephine Lake and Trail 171, then goes around the upper end of the lake on a boardwalk to join North Shore Josephine Lake Trail (168) and Grinnell Glacier Trail (170).

Feather Plume Cutoff Trail (172)

Feather Plume Cutoff Trail is an alternate foot trail to Grinnell Lake that branches off

Piegan Pass Trail (113) 4.1 miles from the hotel horse corral. Trail 172 descends 300 feet in 1.2 miles and passes below FEATHER PLUME FALLS enroute to Grinnell Lake. The route is preferred by hikers traveling over Piegan Pass from the St. Mary side who wish to visit the lake and then either avail themselves of the launch service on Josephine and Swiftcurrent Lakes or avoid the sometimes muddy stretches of trail 113 between its junctions with trail 172 and trail 181 near the northeast end of Josephine Lake.

Grinnell Lake, although smaller, has much in common with famed Lake Louise in Canada. Though Grinnell Glacier above is hidden from view, the red argillite of the cirque walls, Grinnell Falls, and the opalescent water provide one of the celebrated pictures in the park.

Grinnell Lake Horse Trail (173)

Leaves trail 174 just above Josephine Lake to follow Grinnell Creek to Grinnell Lake. It is closely paralleled by footpath 175, mentioned previously.

About half a mile from Josephine Lake, the two trails cross Cataract Creek descending from Piegan Pass. Hikers during the offseason may find the suspension bridge dismantled to prevent damage from winter snowpack. On the left, spur trail 183 climbs sharply by switchbacks for 0.2 mile to attractive HIDDEN FALLS, set in a gorge cut in the greenish argillite. Trail 183 is reserved for foot travel only.

Virgin meadows are rare along horse trails. Flowerless, weed-choked or bare plots are a consequence of grazing, trampling stock. To preserve trailside beauty, horses may not be halted, permitted to snack while being ridden or allowed to rove off the trail tread.

Josephine Walk (174)

For hikers connects Oastler Shelter and Grinnell Glacier Trail (170), after a junction with footpath 168. It also provides a link for hikers and horses from the upper end of Josephine Lake to Piegan Pass Trail (113).

Piegan Pass Trail (113)

A major trail between Many Glacier Hotel and several alternative trailheads (Sun Point, Sunrift Gorge, Jackson Glacier Overlook and Siyeh Bend) along Going-to-the-Sun Road on the St. Mary side of Piegan Pass, described later in this chapter.

Grinnell Glacier Trail (170)

Above its junctions with trails 168 and 174 at the upper end of Josephine Lake climbs at a steady grade. Increasingly spectacular views unfold as the forest is left behind and altitude is gained. Red-topped ALLEN MT. (9376) is southeast of the head of Josephine Lake. CATARACT MT. (8180) blocks the head of Cataract Canyon to the south. PIEGAN MT. (9220) behind it, POLLOCK MT. (9190), MT. GOULD (9553) with GEM GLACIER as an epaulet on its left shoulder and the GARDEN WALL flank Cataract Canyon on the right. At higher elevation MT. SIYEH (10,014) and GOING-TO-THE-SUN MT. (9642) loom over the headwall between Allen and Cataract Mts. Much of the trail at higher elevation is hewn out of bright red argillite.

The slopes of Grinnell Mt. are excellent places to see mountain goats, sometimes in groups of one or two score. Black and grizzly bear and bighorn sheep are sometimes seen. Beargrass forms much of the cover and makes these open slopes a paradise in years of bloom.

The trail crosses a pine-fringed park in a rocky pocket north of the glacial moraine. Naturalist-guided parties take a lunch break here. Pit toilets are available. To view the glacier it is necessary to cross the stream through the willows and climb up the moraine trail, marked by man-sized rock piles called cairns. From the top of the moraine, spur trails lead to an overlook of Upper Grinnell Lake, a meltwater lake at the foot of the ice, and to the glacier itself. Travel beyond the moraine is hazardous without an experienced guide.

Grinnell Glacier

During the first decades of the 1900's Grinnell Glacier extended flush against the north moraine as well as against its analog beneath Mt. Gould on the other side of the basin. At that time the glacier reached the edge of the cliff above Grinnell Lake. The upper lobe, The Salamander, on the shelf above was connected at its south end with the ice below by a much-crevassed icefall.

Several outstanding features distinguish this glacier. A big waterfall over the head wall has melted a yawning arcuate pocket in the ice at its foot, which gives an idea of the depth of the glacier. A long fissure in Helena (Siyeh) limestone parallels the face of the cliff below the glacier. It suggests how rock is spalled off cirque walls. A gigantic slab of Helena (Siyeh) limestone rests on the flank of the moraine above the picnic area. This came from the member deposited as the extensive algal reef and now exposed in many parts of the park; it plainly shows the concentric growth of the ancient plants. The side of the boulder in contact with bedrock while being transported is smoothed, striated and polished.

The freshly exposed floor beneath the glacier has been abraded, grooved and polished by rocks held in the viselike grip of ice acting like a flexible rasp as it moves down its bed. Notice the milky color of the water coming from the melting ice. This is technically termed gletscher-milch, or "glacial milk." The opalescence is caused by the suspension of very fine rock flour formed by the grinding action. This can easily be demonstrated by taking a glassful of melt water and letting the suspended matter settle. Many of the rocks and ledges near the glacier are coated with this sediment. Upper Grinnell and Grinnell Lakes owe their opacity to gletscher-milch.

The Garden Wall with Mt. Gould is back of the glacier. Going-to-the-Sun Road and Highline Trail (121) from Logan Pass to Granite Park are on the other side of the Wall. The dark band on the face of the Wall, mentioned frequently in this guide, is composed of igneous rock which, while molten, was squeezed between layers of limestone, bleaching and metamorphosing them. It is often referred to as the diorite intrusion. It is possible to climb the north side of the glacier to the notch above it, but one should have climbing experience and notify park rangers before making an attempt.

Splendid ice caves develop along the edge of the glacier. Dust wells, crevasses, baignoires and other glacial features can be seen.

The gap has been caused by a vertical dike traceable to Granite Park, two miles distant. The notch is more easily reached from the other side of the Garden Wall by foot trail 127 from trail 121 near Granite Park. Tiny GEM GLACIER (above 8000) on the northwest shoulder of Mt. Gould is of great thickness and has changed little while other larger glaciers have shrunk, subdivided and disappeared since the late 1920's.

People not properly shod or inexperienced in glacier travel should not go upon the glacier without a guide. It is hazardous to venture in ignorance into ice caves where the roofs may collapse or upon snow on top of the ice, for a dangerously thin cover can mask a yawning crevasse. In some recent years late season access to the glacier has been entirely cut off by recession of the ice front beyond the outlet stream of Upper Grinnell Lake.

Iceberg and Ptarmigan Lakes

Many Glacier Hotel to Many Glacier Campground and Swiftcurrent Motor Inn via Swiftcurrent Lake shore, 1.3 miles. Many Glacier Campground to Iceberg Lake via trails 152 and 155, 5.0 miles; Many Glacier Hotel to Ptarmigan Lake via trail 152, 5.7 miles; Circuit, Many Glacier Hotel to Iceberg Lake, Ptarmigan Lake and return to the hotel, 15.6 miles. See foldout map.

Iceberg Lake, like Grinnell Glacier, is one of the most popular targets of hikers in Glacier Park. It is an easy, gradual ascent of 1000 feet, a goal attractive beyond description. Ptarmigan Lake is a prime feature between Many Glacier and the Belly River country described earlier under the North Circle. Either lake can be visited in a half-day if time is limited, or both can be included in the itinerary of a single day. Ranger naturalists conduct hikes to one or the other frequently throughout the park season.

The burning of the forest by the 1936 fires along the first few miles of trail 152 has been offset by a profuse growth of wildflowers. No trail seems to offer more splendid flower displays. Each year the burned tract becomes a blaze of fireweed, whose winged seeds fill the air like snowflakes in a snowstorm. Red monkeyflowers and parnassias become the more brilliant growing in a bed of red argillite glistening with trickling waters. The trailside is the haunt of much wildlife: mountain goats clamber along the mountain walls; bighorns graze on the slopes of Mt. Henkel, and pikas scamper over the rock slides.

All four formations composing Glacier's mountains are encountered. Altyn limestone forms the ledge on which the hotel is built; Appekunny argillite imparts greenish tints to the strata of Altyn Peak; Grinnell argillite gives Mt. Henkel a fiery summit and Ptarmigan Creek a purple bed, while Helen (Siyeh) limestone composes the summits of Mt. Wilbur and Ptarmigan Wall with the dark band of igneous rock across their faces.

Trail 152 starts with Trail 167 on the north shore of Swiftcurrent Lake, across the lake outlet from the hotel. In 0.1 mile, it slants across the campground road at grade, then rises gently to traverse an old moraine on the slope of Altyn Peak. A mile from the hotel, Swiftcurrent Pass Trail (157) to Granite Park forks to the left.

At 1.5 miles a steep 0.3 mile spur has risen from the campground and inn as a short cut to both trails 152 and 155. The summit of Mt. Wilbur (9321) called by Indians "Heavy Shield Mt.," rises impressively on the left. Trail 152 is built over deep red argillite as it skips over Ptarmigan Creek by Ptarmigan Falls (5700), 4.0 miles.

At 4.1 miles from the hotel the trail forks, spur 155 to the left, going up Iceberg Creek two miles to Iceberg Lake. Trail 152 to the right ascends 1.6 miles along Ptarmigan Creek to Ptarmigan Lake and to the Belly River country beyond.

Much of trail 155 from the junction to Iceberg Lake is near timberline. The slopes are covered with beargrass which in favorable years puts on a wonderful display. The cliffs on all sides are so-called mountain goat walls; these ungulates are certain to be seen upon them during some time of the day. Deer and other animals also put in appearances. Nearer the lake, surroundings become more alpine in character. Low subalpine fir grow on the lakeshore, and meadows are covered with glacier lilies and showy alpines. During the off-season, a plank bridge across the outlet stream is removed to prevent damage from heavy snowpack and runoff.

Iceberg Lake (6094) completely fills the floor of its cirque; 3000-foot vertical walls enclose three sides of the lake. Sixty years ago a small glacier crowded its upper end, and a wall of ice 75 feet high pushed out into the lake. Large bergs broke off from time to time, giving the lake its name. Snow and ice linger in the pocket today; bergs are still occasionally formed. The lake, which contains no fish, is often frozen until well into July. The rampart of rock along the beach has been pushed up from the lake bottom by ice. As the lake freezes and the weather grows colder, the ice contracts so that water is squeezed along the edges, freezes and encases rocks from the shallow bottom. When the temperature rises again, the ice expands to dump its load of rocks near the shore.

A vertical dike of igneous rock that cuts diagonally across the lake is responsible for the deep notch in Pinnacle Wall to the northwest. It is the cause of the dark streak in the talus southeast of the lake. This dike can be traced across the high bench below Mt. Wilbur, across the face of Grinnell Point, in the lowest notch in the crest of Allen and to the southeast of Canyon Creek. This alignment marks the sites of former mining activity. A prospect hole in the talus above the lake is one of many sunk along the trace of the dike during the heyday of prospecting.

It is 1.6 miles from the junction of trails 152 and 155 to Ptarmigan Lake, at the head of the deep, narrow canyon below Ptarmigan Wall.

From the lake it is only a mile to Ptarmigan Tunnel, whose portal frames a view of Mt. Wilbur and the Garden Wall to make a good photograph. Natoas Peak and Belly River Valley are seen from the north portal, but the view is restricted by the enclosing walls. Those who have come this far are urged to muster enough strength to proceed at least 400 yards beyond the tunnel for a rewarding view of Mt. Merritt with its glistening Old Sun Glacier and many sparkling waterfalls. This mountain is one of the most imposing peaks in the park. A few hundred yards farther, at the start of the talus, the austere cirque back of Helen Lake may be seen.

110

Piegan Pass Trail

Many Glacier Hotel, via trail 113 to Morning Eagle Falls, 5.1 miles; Piegan Pass, 8.3 miles; Preston Park, 10.1 miles; Going-to-the-Sun Road at Siyeh Bend, 12.8 miles; Sun Point via Reynolds Creek, 17.4 miles; Going-to-the-Sun Road at Sunrift Gorge, via Siyeh Pass and trail 117, 17.8. See fold-out map.

The trail between Swiftcurrent and St. Mary valleys over Piegan Pass (7570) gives its patrons many pleasures; superb views of Josephine Lake, Grinnell Lake and Glacier, the Garden Wall, Upper St. Mary Valley and the Blackfoot Glacier country; Morning Eagle and Feather Plume Falls; subalpine larch and limber pine parks; blue columbine, true forget-me-not and alpine fireweed rock gardens; abundant wildlife including high country birds; brightly colored summits; the highest trail pass in the park (Siyeh); side trips to the many cirques on Mt. Allen, to the top of the wall above Cracker Lake and to Sexton Glacier.

Starting from the corral at Many Glacier Hotel parking lot, saddlehorse parties go south, immediately part with Cracker Lake Trail (165) leading to the left, and travel in the forest of giant firs and spruces above Josephine Lake.

Hikers from the hotel may start on trail 167 on Swiftcurrent Lakeshore; from Swiftcurrent picnic area, they may wish to follow trail 167 along the west shore. Crossover to trail 113, 0.3 mile above, is made either between Swiftcurrent and Josephine Lakes via trails 180, 171, and 181 or from the upper Josephine dock via trail 174.

Hikers who wish to avoid the sections of trails 171 and 113 along Josephine Lake's south side that receive heavy horse use can follow foot trail 168 from the head of Swiftcurrent to the head of Josephine Lake, connecting via Josephine Walk (174) with the Grinnell Lake Foot Trail (175). From Grinnell Lake the Feather Plume Cutoff Trail (172) goes 1.2 miles to intersect Trail 113 1.0 mile below Morning Eagle Falls. Trails 168, 174 and 175 are discussed in this section under Grinnell Lake and Grinnell Glacier.

Trail 113 rises above Josephine Lake several hundred feet to leave the forest, providing good views of the hotel, the lakes, picturesque Grinnell Valley, Mt. Pollack and the Garden Wall. Mt. Grinnell (8851) is especially imposing from here. Look for mountain goats upon it!

The meadows above Josephine Lake are gay with larkspurs, gentians, paintbrushes and a host of other flowers. During the off-season two log bridges traversed by trail 113 are removed to prevent damage from snowpack and spring runoff. The trail is built at stream level at Morning Eagle Falls, which lunges over a ledge of red rock. Snowbanks linger at the base of the falls and in several streambeds beyond through July.

The higher, more spectacular FEATHER PLUME FALLS tumbles from a notch below the main summit of MT. GOULD (9553) across the valley. Although it does not have as much volume as Cataract Creek, to which it is tributary, the stream plunges over a cliff, shooting arrows of spray downward, until it is dissipated as mist before it reaches the bottom.

From the base of Morning Eagle Falls, the trail climbs by sharp switchbacks in stunted Hudsonian vegetation. The vertical flank of the Garden Wall across the valley, 3000 to 4000 feet high, is heaven for mountain goats which often congregate in groups of a dozen to fifty. They may look like white flecks on a sheer wall, for the thin ledges on which they move are too distant to be distinguished by the unaided eye.

The bench above the trail and the sloping enclosed basin at the head of the valley appear to be remnants of an earlier valley floor formed during the Ice Age. The large tributary basin to the east is on MT. SIYEH (10,014), but all summits north of the basin are parts of Allen Mt. Cracker Lake and the gorge of Canyon Creek lie on the far side of Allen.

These high mountain basins are exciting fields of discovery for the carefree wanderer; alpine birds and mammals await the patient and unhurried; rare flowers make bright rock gardens of the rocky landscape. Great banks of snow linger long into summer above the Hudsonian life zone. All four principal Algonkian formations of Glacier Park are crossed in the ascent from the hotel which is built on a ledge of Altyn limestone, the oldest formation. Grayish-green argillite forms the bases of Allen Mt., Grinnell Point and Altyn Peak. Their crests are bright red Grinnell argillite, which, when it forms cliffs, is often variegated by golden crustose lichens. The upper reaches of the Garden Wall and Mt. Siyeh are of Helena (Siyeh) limestone. The trail at high elevation is on scree and Helena (Siyeh) limestone. The dark bank of igneous rock, so conspicuous along the face of the Garden Wall, is crossed by the trail below Piegan Pass and again on the summit of the pass itself. The location of many of the passes in the park seems to have been determined by the durability of this hard rock and that of the associated Conophyton, fossil algae, reef. The latter appears above the igneous band and encircles the summits of Matahpi Peak and Going-to-the-Sun Mt.

The trail passes within three life zones. The forest above the hotel is in the Canadian zone. The Hudsonian zone is entered near Morning Eagle Falls at an elevation of 6000 feet, but it drops to a much lower elevation at the base of the cliffs in the shadow of the Garden Wall. It is a narrow strip along the trail as it extends only through some 600 feet of difference in elevation. All higher parts of the trail and all of the mountain summits are in the Alpine-Arctic zone to which most birds, mammals and plants belong that are seen near the base.

In the highest terrain, Clark's nutcrackers, pipits and rosy finches flit here and there. Mountain goats often make an appearance, at times quite close. Marmots are common at Morning Eagle Falls and shuffle on the bare, higher slopes. On rare occasions a weasel may be discovered, like Nemesis, in unrelenting pursuit of an intended victim ground squirrel.

Much of the undershrubby vegetation near the pass appears in uneven lines or windrows, the result of uneven accumulation of soil and seeds on leeward edges of snow banks and loose rock mounds. Among the hardy alpine flowers which stud the bare slopes at random are the rare, memorable blue (Jones) columbine, the true forget-me-not, carpet pink, large-flowered dwarf fireweed, white and purple rock cresses, alpine arnica, alpine asters, sticky Jacob's-ladder, white dryad, purple saxifrage, an alpine poppy reported from very few places in the United States although growing both at Sexton Glacier and on Piegan Pass, the curious bladder-campion and the alpine spring beauty whose roots are so elastic that they stretch if rocks slide over the plant.

The view culminating in Mt. Gould (9553) to the north reveals the remarkable character of the Garden Wall. The balanced pinnacle of rock immediately above the igneous band on Mt. Gould always excites curiosity. Beyond rise the summits of Mts. Grinnell and WILBUR (9321). To the south formidable CITADEL MT. (9030) appears with the white mass of BLACKFOOT GLACIER spread to the right. CATARACT MT. (8180) is nearby, being just slightly northeast of the pass with the bleak summit of Mt. Siyeh behind it. The vertical cliff of the left profile of Siyeh is the top of the awesome wall behind Cracker Lake. The diorite sill outcrops beneath and completely around the summit of Siyeh.

In earlier days, the hotel company mounted big locomotive bells on Piegan and other passes for the amusement of travelers. The bells were removed for their scrap metal in World War II.

From the pass the trail describes a great arc around Siyeh Creek basin with the big road loop prominent below. As the trail drops, wider views open. MT. JACKSON (10,052) shows up first, then the Logan Pass country with the Hanging Gardens. PIEGAN MT. (9220) with the small Piegan glacier is to the west.

The limestone strata of Piegan Mt. dip to the southwest, i.e., into the mountain. Channels are formed in the limestone by solution; their charge of glacial meltwater is carried through the mountain to reappear as giant springs on the opposite flank. These springs are visible from Logan Pass.

PRESTON PARK (7000), an open grove of mixed conifers, is a favorite lunch stop for passing parties. Here Siyeh Pass Trail (117), bound ultimately for Sunrift Gorge, starts its climb up the creek to Siyeh Pass, 1000 feet higher. However, most parties from Many Glacier, weary from the long climb to Piegan Pass, prefer to stay on trail 113, an easier route on gently sloping ledges on the west flank of Going-to-the-Sun Mt.

One mile below Preston Park, Piegan Pass Trail (113) meets trail 115 which once crossed Logan Pass, but now terminates, 1.2 miles from the junction, at Siyeh Bend (5850), the loop on Going-to-the-Sun Road, mile 35.5. Piegan Pass Trail (13) drops 1.3 miles to the roadside exhibit for Jackson Glacier (5284) at road mile 37.3. One and three-tenths miles farther it meets Gunsight Pass Trail (52) near DEADWOOD FALLS (4640) in Reynolds Creek. From the junction, it is 3.2 miles down St. Mary Valley (L) to Sun Point.

Siyeh Pass Trail Alternative

Siyeh Pass Trail (117) from Preston Park over Siyeh Pass is a far more spectacular route to Sun Point, but it is longer and more difficult. Just beyond its junction with trail 113, trail 117 passes near a small grove of graceful subalpine larch. This tree grows only at higher elevations and is deciduous; that is, it drops its needles each fall.

The Siyeh Pass route goes by several unnamed lakelets snuggled under Mt. Siyeh as it traverses grassy meadows with beautiful alpine flowers. Looking back towards Logan Pass, the view dominated by MT. REYNOLDS (9125) is superb. As it reaches the sheer wall at the head of Siyeh Creek, the trail bends right and climbs the rocky north slope of Matahpi Peak where blue alpine columbines blossom later than the plants on Piegan Pass.

The trail reaches the highest point (8150) of any established trail in the park a quarter-mile southeast of Siyeh Pass (7750) proper, a gap blocked by rotten snow through summer. The pass, which is between Matahpi Peak and Cracker Peak (9833) was formed by glaciers, now long disappeared, which eroded the headwall in Boulder and Baring Canyons. From the high point a grand view unfurls down Boulder Canyon to the plains of Canada far northeast. Goat Mt. flares flaming color more brilliant than when viewed from Sun Point.

The view down precipitous Baring Canyon is equally breathtaking. 4000 feet below lie the shimmering waters of St. Mary Lake, one of the world's most beautiful, as exquisitely blue in certain light conditions as Crater Lake in Oregon. A barricade of mountains looms behind the lake. The fretted, cliffy face of Going-to-the-Sun Mt. (9642) with Sexton Glacier tucked on a lofty shelf, appears on the right. At times, a symphony of frenzied winds reverberates in the wild defile.

Siyeh Pass Trail plunges in short switchbacks down the steepest descent of its course. The track is hard to follow when snow-covered. Impressive SEXTON GLACIER lies 0.7 mile off the main trail. Mountain goats are common in this high retreat and sometimes are encountered face to face. The trail descends in the shadow of towering Going-to-the-Sun Mt. down the east incline of an ample, verdant amphitheater called BARING BASIN, in earlier park times a popular excursion goal for visitors at Going-to-the-Sun Chalets.

Just above the big switchback halfway down, a former foot trail branching to the left led by a series of switchbacks to the brilliant red summit of Goat Mt. Baring Creek on the right has cut a deep gorge with fantastic shapes in greenish argillite. This cannot be seen from the trail, but is close to it in the last half-mile above the road. The trail passes quite close to the mouth of Sunrift Gorge before going under the colorful road bridge over Baring Creek at road mile 40.0. It rejoins Piegan Pass Trail, 0.2 mile below, near Baring Falls. It is 0.8 mile from Sunrift Gorge to Sun Point.

Around Swiftcurrent Lake

Circuit on trail 167, 2.7 miles. See fold-out map.

Swiftcurrent Lake never lacks for interesting features: a wide variety of plants from trees to lichens, busy bird and animal life, geological phenomena and noble vistas. Beaver cavort in the lake in the evening and early morning. Columbian ground squirrels scurry here and there. Birds flit in and out of the lush cover and gladden the brushland with cheery warbling. Ducks, mostly goldeneyes and mergansers, feed in weeds in the shallows.

Early photographs show a dense forest crowding the lakeshore and covering slopes which now are bare. The vegetation near the hotel and campground has suffered from heavy use or overuse, and from the severe 1936 fire from which recovery has been slow due to the austere climate.

The gravel footpath (trail 167) around Swiftcurrent Lake starts from either the hotel or Swiftcurrent Picnic Area. It can be strolled leisurely in either direction in two hours or less. Special footwear is unnecessary. The first 1.6 miles, as described here, extending from the lakeshore south of the hotel to the picnic area, is designated as Swiftcurrent Lake Self-Guiding Nature Trail. Leaflets with descriptions of features enroute are dispensed at both ends of the self-guiding section. They may be retained for a small charge or returned without fee.

A half-mile from the hotel, the trail goes by the boathouse used for launch storage in the winter. It then enters a grove of lodgepole pines, firs and spruces. Soon the willows with their gaily singing fox sparrows, warblers, wrens and white-crowned sparrows, are left behind; now one expects chickadees, nuthatches, siskins and juncoes, and perhaps will be thrilled by the appearance of sporadic crossbills or grosbeaks and others. Sharply conical GRINNELL POINT (7716), across the lake, is also known by the Blackfeet name of Fishercap, given to George Bird Grinnell. As editor of "Forest and Stream," Grinnell hunted and fished extensively in the Northwest in the 1880's and 1890's and strongly advocated establishment of Glacier National Park. Many park features were named by him either after hunting episodes or his associates, many of whom never saw the region.

Just before the footbridge at 0.7 mile, foot trail 180 goes 0.1 mile upstream to connect with foot trail 171 above the southeastern shore of Josephine Lake. One crosses the bridge to continue around Swiftcurrent Lake.

Colorful Mt. Henkel (8770) and bear-grassy slopes of Altyn Peak (7947) appear across the lake. Much of the trail on the south end of the lake is in spruce-fir-pine forest in which a wealth of shrubs characteristic of lower east-side valleys thrive. Dominant menziesia is mixed with Utah and red twinberries, mountain ash, blackbead elderberry, thinleaf alder, willows, red ozier dogwood, spirea, serviceberry, huckleberries, thimbleberry and others. The ground cover has many strawberries with small but delicious fruit, kinnikinnick, which Indians mixed with tobacco, and low huckleberries with small, tart fruit relished by bears. Many dainty wildflowers appear in favorable locations. False hellebore, cow parsnip and beargrass are among the coarser herbs.

At the upper dock for the Swiftcurrent launch, Trail 168, to the left, climbs over the mound to the dock on Josephine Lake, 0.2 mile away. Trail 167 turns right and continues along the lakeshore below Grinnell Point. The lodgepoles here are reproductions from the forest which burned in 1926. Farther on young conifers are making headway reclothing the region denuded by the 1936 fire. Across the lake Altyn, Appekunny (9068) and Allen (9376) Mts. sweep impressively upward.

A half-mile beyond the dock, trail 167 comes to the end of talus and swings northwesterly to avoid wetlands at the mouth of Swiftcurrent Creek. The willowy tangle entered is homeland for a host of accomplished songsters that make the mountain walls reverberate with rich, cheerful melody in early season. The wet, brushy bottomland is probably the reason fishing appears to be best at the mouth of the stream and why beaver like to frolic offshore. Marshy sites such as this are precious, especially so near visitor concentrations.

The trail crosses Swiftcurrent Creek by a wooden bridge and reaches the turnout for the picnic area 1.6 miles from its start. The campground and cabins are to the left. To reach the hotel, one mile distant, follow the road across the picnic area, then the trail along the lakeshore.

Around Josephine Lake

Shortest distance, 3.5 miles. See map on page 106.

A walk around Josephine Lake is a pleasing recreation for visitors at Many Glacier. It is conveniently close to both Many Glacier Hotel and Many Glacier Campground and Motor Inn. There are many excellent views from Josephine Lake, the one south and west from the outlet being especially rewarding. On quiet, cooler days "too-perfect" reflection scenes of the lake surface make striking photographs. Fishermen are drawn to the lake by its kokanee and brook trout.

To plan your route in this locality, consult the map of the Many Glacier area on page 106. Beginning at the south end of the hotel, Swiftcurrent Lake Trail 167 follows the lakeshore to the southern inlet, 0.7 mile; trail 180 then goes up the creek to connect with the South Shore Josephine Lake Trail (171). Besides birds mentioned in the description of the trail around Swiftcurrent Lake, one usually sees sandpipers on teetering legs making short dashes on the gravelly bank. Listen for the loud, clear whistle of the olive-sided flycatcher calling, "What Cheer!" or "Free Beer!" and look for the bird perched upright, flycatcher fashion, on the very top of a bare snag. River ducks, including the bizarre harlequin, kingfishers and dippers are attracted by the stream. Water-loving plants, ferns, mosses and liverworts are abundant and the tread is springy underfoot.

Midway between the lakes, the creek widens to a pool. At the shore of Josephine Lake, the Garden Wall, Grinnell Glacier and the ramparts of Grinnell Point are displayed across the turquoise waters. A bright streak made by fresh, green argillite tailings from a copper mineshaft may be detected near the top of the talus beneath the profile of Grinnell Point. Trail 171 continues past the vista at the outlet of Josephine Lake into dense woods a short distance from the lakeshore. Trail 181 goes 0.1 mile up the mountainside to join the Piegan Pass Trail (113).

Near the head of the lake, 2.5 miles from the hotel, Trail 174 on the left connects the lakeshore trail 171 with Piegan Pass Trail (113). The upper boat dock and Oastler Shelter are on the beach. A prospect hole, the last to be worked in the park in the '40s and finally abandoned in the early '60's, is marked by its brightly colored tailings so that it can easily be seen from Oastler Shelter. It is near the top of the talus to the left of the prow of Grinnell Point. Continue 1.1 miles on foot trail 175 up the left side of the creek to Grinnell Lake to add that feature to the outing.

The foot trail around Josephine Lake, now 174, crosses the inlet over a footbridge, and continues as a plank trail through a willow swamp. There are good views both up and down the valley. North Shore Josephine Lake Trail (168) is met, 0.2 mile from the dock; it links Swiftcurrent and Grinnell Lakes via the northwest shore of Josephine Lake.

It is a mile from the junction of 174 and 168 to the lower boat landing on Josephine Lake, and 0.2 mile farther to the upper dock on Swiftcurrent Lake and Swiftcurrent Lake Trail (167). It is 0.7 mile from the dock at the head of Swiftcurrent Lake to Swiftcurrent Picnic Area; it is 0.9 mile from the dock to the hotel via the south shore, 1.7 miles via the north shore of Swiftcurrent Lake.

The total distance from the hotel around both Swiftcurrent and Josephine Lakes is a little over four miles. The distance is about the same from the picnic area using trail 167 on the northwest shore of Swiftcurrent Lake.

Horses are not allowed on trails 167, 168 and 175, making them preferable for hikers, especially in wet weather. Launch services on the two lakes can be combined with the use of either route around Josephine Lake.

Around Swiftcurrent Falls

Distance, 0.6 mile.

In the days when the park was young, roads few and wretched, autos breezy and troublesome, radios and TV beyond wildest imagination, people were composed and sought simple delights and pleasures always present and close at hand. These same unassuming sources of durable satisfaction persist to be "discovered" today by the patient and observant. Many footpaths in the Many Glacier area wind to a secluded waterfall or mossy woodland bower; ascend a rocky knob for sunset or the invigorating freshness of the winds; lead to the doorstep of wildfolk busy with their own particular world. The little area around Swiftcurrent Falls, heeded by very few, is a modest lure popular before the Motor Age, before man forgot that the purpose of legs is for walking.

The route starts across the road from the water-gauging station near the foot of the grade from the parking lot. The path follows down the beautiful little gorge cut in yellow Altyn limestone. Since the strata dip to the southwest, the lake occupies a basin scooped out by a glacier which simply moved up the bedding planes.

In the cave below the upper falls is a typical home of a spritely pack rat often seen here. Apparently pack rats have occupied this site for generations, for they have gathered a tremendous pile of trash. The family which occupied this place 60 years ago is described in "Wild Animals of Glacier Park," by Vernon and Florence Merriam Bailey. Another resident of the gorge, also described in this entertaining work, is the gray dipper or water ouzel whose nest of moss is built in a crevice close to the upper falls. The dippers constantly curtsy on the banks, fly up or down close to the foaming torrent, or dash madly into its spray to walk on the bottom of the creek.

Cracker Lake

Many Glacier Hotel to foot of Cracker Lake, 5.6 miles. See fold-out map.

At the height of mining excitement at Many Glacier before Glacier Park was established, a wagon road to Cracker Lake was built at great expense, and a costly crusher was installed there. The venture died because it did not pay, but a trail remains for those in quest of nature's richer beauty. The old road and superimposed trail were largely obliterated by spring floods in 1935 and 1964 and required extensive reconstruction. Cracker Lake was a popular destination in earlier saddlehorse days, but is often overlooked today in favor of other places. The trip can be made on foot or on horseback in a long half-day if time is at a premium.

Cracker Lake Trail (165) begins south of the hotel parking lot. It immediately parts from Piegan Pass Trail (113) and turns left under the shadow of Allen Mt. It crosses the Altyn limestone ledge on which the hotel is built and which forms the outer rim of the bowl holding Swiftcurrent Lake. It passes through a gap, 0.3 mile, made long ago when the lake was much bigger and deeper than it is today and presumably had an outlet at this place. It passes shallow, muddy Governor Pond in the stream bed of that earlier outlet and the head of Sherburne Lake which becomes an ugly mud flat in mid-season due to drawdown of the reservoir.

Allen Creek is reached 1.8 miles from the hotel. It drains two beautiful lakelets, Falling Leaf and Snow Moon, tucked snugly in a niche on Allen Mt. The names are Indian for September and October and were given by the author on an autumn visit while fall colors still flared at the lower lake, but somber, silvery hues of winter were already stealing upon the upper basin. Allen Creek flows northeast in a tight canyon with numerous waterfalls, until it reaches the big alluvial fan built by Canyon Creek which bends it forcedly west. The fan, called Cracker Flats, was the site of the boomtown of Altyn in the late 1890's, but is now a lush flower meadow, a short walk from the hotel or campground. The Cracker Flats Horse Trail (277) loops 0.9 mile past the old townsite before rejoining trail 165.

Turning up Allen Creek and leaving Swiftcurrent Canyon, Cracker Lake Trail (165) enters a heavy forest in a deep canyon to climb over a bold ridge into the canyon of Canyon Creek. The trees gradually decline in vigor as the trail ascends until only patches of crushed subalpine fir with storm-bitten leaders cover the cobbly slopes. Dippers and seldom-seen water shrews make their homes along the creek. The wall of Allen Mt. is a good place for mountain goats.

Like other trails in the vicinity, trail 165 encounters the four principal rock formations in the park. The diorite sill appears plainly on the face of Mt. Siyeh. Though mostly covered by out-wash, the base rock at the mouth of Canyon Creek is Cretaceous and contains fossil clamshells. Geologists interested in climbing Mt. Wynn (8404) can reach the sharp line of contact between Cretaceous and overthrust Algonkian rocks by following the base of the north face above the talus.

Canyon Creek is boulder-strewn, with stretches of foaming white water between deep pools. Since it has no falls, fish can swim upstream. But food seems to be scarce, so the valley has gained little acclaim for fishing. The lower forest of spruce, fir and pine is gradually displaced by low-growing subalpine fir. The display of wildflowers is generous, especially at the lake—gentians, monkeyflowers, harebells, penstemons, yellow columbines, paintbrushes, asters and many others.

Turquoise Cracker Lake (5910) extends from the top of a moraine to the profound north wall of Mt. Siyeh (10,014). The abandoned shaft of the Cracker Mine, the tailings and the remains of a big ore-crusher are on the east side of the lake not far above the outlet. For safety reasons entry into the mine shaft is discouraged. A small campground is nearby. It is possible to walk around the lake or explore the ravine penetrating Allen Mt. northwest from the lake head. Siyeh Glacier rests in a pocket above the lake.

Appekunny Falls

Many Glacier Road to Appekunny Falls, 1.0 mile. No horses allowed.

The oft-photographed, vertical, deeply notched face of Appekunny Mt. (9068), intriguing to the visitor in Swiftcurrent Valley and a dominant feature of the drive to Many Glacier, is the scarp of the Lewis Thrust Fault. Rocks composing the cliffs are ancient Algonkian limestones and argillites resting on soft Cretaceous shales which make up the gentle slopes to the valley floor. Tough Altyn limestone strata appear as a plumb wall. Because soft underlying beds weather and erode more easily, great slabs break off along cleavage planes of the hard rock when support is removed. The rocks slide down chimneys to create the big cones of talus, larger blocks concentrating at the bottom. This is termed mass wasting, a process controlled by gravity.

Appekunny Creek Trail (166) follows the east bank of Appekunny Creek above the road at the bridge, 1.2 miles from the hotel. The lower section in lodgepole pine forest may be confusing due to old, random horse paths, but the notch with Appekunny Falls, a mile from the road, is always in sight ahead to serve as a target. For experienced hikers, above and to the right of the falls, an old trail, no longer maintained and partially blocked by rockslides, is etched in the limestone cliff. Snow adds problems in early season.

As the scene widens above the falls, passage is easier, for the trail remains 100 feet or more above the bouldery floor. Bases of surrounding walls are of green argillite with brilliant red strata above them.

The trail quickly fades in the lower basin, but the country is open and the narrow exit is exposed, so that no one is likely to become lost. A second, higher basin to the west can be reached by climbing from ledge to ledge a few hundred yards north of the waterfall. Lovely Natahki Lake (6575) lies in the shadow of Mt. Henkel. All climbers should register out and in at the ranger station.

The saddle (7360) on the left between Mt. Henkel (8770) and Altyn Peak may be cautiously scaled, and the ridge followed to the summit of either peak. Once on top, Ptarmigan Trail (152) can be reached for return to Swiftcurrent or Many Glacier Hotel by slanting southwest and zigzagging down the beargrass slope.

It is also possible to zigzag gentler slopes north from Natahki Lake to the gap (8080) a half-mile northeast of the summit of Mt. Henkel. A magnificent view of Kennedy Lake (6800) below, Crowfeet Mt. (8914) above Ptarmigan Lake and the Red Gap country is revealed. The ridge northeast of the saddle leads to the summit of Appekunny Mt., two miles away.

Red Gap Pass Trail

Many Glacier Road to Swiftcurrent Ridge Lake, 3.8 miles; to Poia Lake, 6.1 miles; to Red Gap Pass, 11.7 miles; to Ptarmigan Trail (152) Junction, 14.3 miles; to Cosley Lake, 20.0 miles.

Before completion of Ptarmigan Tunnel in 1931, the direct trail connection between Many Glacier and Belly River was over Red Gap Pass (7600). Red Gap Pass Trail (154) is still used as an alternative route to Belly River. Sherburne Cutoff Trail (159) is a very steep, one-mile short cut from Sherburne Ranger Station, cutting off 2.4 miles of the distance to SWIFTCUR-RENT RIDGE LAKE (6092). The trail junction is 0.4 mile south of the lake.

Trail 154 leaves the Many Glacier Road near Appekunny Creek, 1.2 miles below the hotel and over two miles from Many Glacier Campground and Swiftcurrent Motor Inn. It climbs diagonally across slopes of talus and glacial detritus below APPEKUNNY MT. (9068) in old burns overgrown today mainly by lodgepole pines.

The trail is easy to follow beyond the nose of Appekunny Mt. 1200 feet above Sherburne Lake. Swiftcurrent Ridge Lake lies near the very top of the ridge.

Crossing the ridge, the trail drops 700 feet through an old burn to Kennedy Creek. YELLOW MT. (8966) with a fine waterfall is across the valley. Trail 154 continues left to POIA LAKE and a campground at the foot. Like that in Swiftcurrent Lake, the water in Poia Lake is impounded at the thrust fault line by Altyn limestone strata dipping southwest. A waterfall analogous to Swiftcurrent Falls drops over the lip of the basin.

Above Poia Lake valleys broaden and are especially beautiful. After three miles, the trail leaves the valley floor and climbs a series of short switchbacks. To the southeast, Kennedy Lake (6800) lies in a beautiful cirque with a sheer wall on Mt. Henkel (8770) towering 2000 feet above it. Red Gap is named for the bright color of the adjacent slopes. A solitary red pillar detached from the mountain mass to the west resembles a potbellied Hindu idol and bears the nickname, "Ruggles of Red Gap." The name is derived from the delightfully humorous novel by Harry L. Wilson, published in 1915 and popularized by Charles Laughton's acting in Paramounts's 1935 movie. Breath-taking views of MT. MERRITT (10,004), OLD SUN GLACIER and the Belly River country greet the hiker on crossing the pass. After more switchbacks 2.6 miles to the north and west, trail 154 joins Ptarmigan Trail (152) to Elizabeth Lake (4892) and to Cosley Lake (4842), 5.7 miles from the junction.

Trails from Goat Haunt

Bowman Lake Trail

Goat Haunt to Brown Pass, 8.6 miles; to the head of Bowman Lake, 15.3 miles; to the foot of Bowman Lake, 22.4 miles. See map on page 123.

This description assumes a start at Goat Haunt. The route for the first 8.6 miles coincides with that described in the next section on the trail to Kintla Lake, as far as Brown Pass (6255) where trail 6 turns right on its way to Hole-in-the-Wall, Boulder Pass and the Kintla area.

Trail 15, the left fork at this junction, goes past Brown Pass Campground to Bowman Lake by descending a glaciated canyon.

The cirque at the head of Bowman Creek is compound, its west wall being most spectacular. Above lies Hole-in-the-Wall Basin. The trail down the valley floor is through dense forests.

Near Pocket Creek, one gets glimpses of Weasel Collar Glacier in a steep restricted channel in Mt. Carter (9843), which rises 5900 feet above the valley floor. Note the milky color of the creek draining the glacier. Picturesque Rainbow Peak (9891) behind is beautifully sculptured. Rainbow Glacier, which can be seen from Going-to-the-Sun Road below Logan Pass, is on the other side of the ridge between these two mountains.

Bowman Lake, 256 feet deep, washes abutting Cerulean Ridge, a cockscomb spine with Rainbow Peak and Mt. Carter as its climax and deep Quartz Lake on the other side. The floor of upper Bowman Valley is an old lake bed, now swampy and covered with brush. It is prime wildlife country. The bugling of elk reverberates from the mountain walls in early autumn chill. Tracks of caribou have been reported from time to time in the past. This is remotely possible, for the animals are great wanderers and inhabit similar territory in British Columbia and the Idaho panhandle. Cougars, bobcats, wolverines, fishers, a rare wolf, and much more frequently, martens, minks and weasels are also observed. Grizzlies are often seen, possibly lured by the presence of the elk.

The route follows close to the lakeshore for several miles at the base of long, timbered Numa Ridge. Numa is Kutenahan for "thunder." There is a fire lookout on top of the ridge, two miles southwest of the summit of Numa Peak (9003), reached by trail 14 which branches off from trail 15, 6.4 miles from Upper Bowman Lake Campground, or 0.7 mile above the campground at the foot of the lake.

Many ups and downs characterize the lower half of the distance of 7.1 miles down the lake. The last mile was constructed by Eagle Scouts, selected on merit and brought from all parts of the United States. They camped annually for two weeks in the park. Under guidance and instruction by park foremen, they spent a half of each week day on actual trail construction. Other trails to which their efforts were devoted are the trail to Two Medicine Pass and the trail along the south shore of St. Mary Lake.

There is an auto campground at the foot of Bowman Lake. This is connected by a spur road to the Inside North Fork Road, six miles down the valley.

Kintla Lakes

Goat Haunt to Lake Janet, 3.5 miles; to Lake Frances, 6.3 miles; to Brown Pass, 8.6 miles; to Hole-in-

the-Wall, 10.6 miles; to Boulder Pass, 13.7 miles; to Kintla Lake, upper end, 24.8 miles; to Kintla Lake Campground at the lake's lower end, 31.4 miles. See map on page 123.

In logical treatment of trails in Glacier National Park the last one, and one of the best, falls naturally to the Boulder Pass Trail (6). Much of the course is above timberline; chasms and prominences are profoundly precipitous, vistas awesome and varied; wildlife and vegetation is befittingly intriguing and has been little disturbed by man's intrusion. The trail itself is invitingly narrow and primitive, lacking in broad refinements which impart a feeling of superhighway construction. It is comforting that one trail has so far escaped the slashing and disfiguration of unimaginative engineers. It is regarded by many people as the most spectacular in the park. Certainly parts vie with anything the park has to offer, despite a few tedious segments. In additon to ruggedness and great elevation, most of its charm rises from the feeling of remoteness, splendid solitude, and the close kinship with unspoiled, unexploited nature. There are no chalets or tent camps; one must limit oneself to a return trip of a single day or else camp out overnight.

From Goat Haunt Ranger Station at the head of Waterton Lake, the route to Kintla Lakes starts with Waterton Lake Trail (135) for a half-mile. It bears southwest as it crosses Cleveland Creek and passes the junction of Rainbow Falls Trail (196) which goes 0.5 mile upstream to the waterfalls in Waterton River. Trail 135 crosses the river on a seasonally dismantled suspension bridge where a spur to the right leads to an attractive campground in a large grassy park among venerable cottonwoods. Beaver work on the lakeshore and the many birds which frequent hawthorn and willow shrubs fill this spot with interest.

On the northern edge of the campground Waterton Lake Trail (135) continues down the willowy shore 3.2 miles to the International Boundary and North Boundary Trail (137), and eight miles to Waterton Townsite. See page 123. Boulder Pass Trail (6) breaks off to the left and begins a steep climb by switchbacks in a forest which includes a few western larches, apparently the only ones in this valley.

After 800 feet of climb in two miles up the side of Olson Mt. (7913), LAKE JANET (4950) is reached. This was once a most beautiful sheet of water, dammed by an avalanche of huge blocks among which large trees now grow. Increase in the rate of drainage has lowered the lake level to create extensive mud flats in the summer which invite study of the plant succession despite their unattractiveness.

The mountains on the south side of the valley are massive and monumental. CITADEL PEAKS, the sharp spires on the end of the knife-edge to the south, terminate and give the name to long PORCUPINE RIDGE (9128).

Above the lake the trail passes a campground beside the creek, then goes alternatively through spruce-fir forest and across open meadows with thickets of brush. The small bushes, which grow in patches on these warm open places and bear yellow-green leaves and black, bitter, berry-like fruits, are buckthorns, close relatives of the coffeeberry which furnishes cascara. Just above the trail is a band of igneous rock which rises to the west and appears 100 feet above Brown Pass.

LAKE FRANCES (5255) is 2.8 miles beyond Lake Janet. The glowering cliffs 3500 feet high enclosing the lake overhang in places. The great rock on the south overlooking Lake Frances is THE SENTINEL (8835); DIXON GLACIER is cupped in a narrow cirque carved from its face with a thousand-foot waterfall plunging over the lip into the lake. The great slab of rock which has split off of the sheer mountain wall creating a great recessed frame is dubbed "The Guardhouse Door." Lake Frances Campground lies about two-thirds of the way up the lake down a short spur to the left. Hawksbill Campground is located about half a mile beyond the lake, just off the main trail. Forests thin into brushland as one passes dainty THUNDER-BIRD POND, a mile above Frances.

The slope upward is beautified by wildflowers in the ascent of broad, open BROWN PASS (6255), 8.6 miles from Goat Haunt. The trails down Bowman Valley (15) and to Kintla Lake (6) part on the pass. Looking back one can see the overhang on the south wall known as "The Hawk's Bill," the spires of Porcupine Ridge below and the broad crest of Mt. Cleveland. Brown Pass, carpeted by beargrass, makes a delightful stop for lunch. A campground lies a short distance ahead on trail 15 to Bowman Valley.

The imposing mass of THUNDERBIRD MT. (8790), with Thunderbird Glacier and Falls, rises in imposing majesty to the south, while CHAPMAN PEAK (9406) stands as guardian on the north. It is easy to go to the glacier directly from the pass, while an ascent of Thunderbird Mt. is feasible by keeping to the right of the long ridge extending northerly from the summit. Snow banks can make climbing hazardous early in the season. Mt. Chapman presents no difficulties, as a climber can zigzag over the open scree slopes with no particular hazards. Below Thunderbird Glacier is the band of igneous rock, also appearing 100 feet above the trail on the ridge to the north. Bowman Lake cannot be seen from Brown Pass, but becomes visible from a short distance below it on trail 15 down Bowman Valley. It can also be seen from trail 6 above the pass.

The view expands with altitude as trail 6 to the Kintla country climbs on Mt. Chapman after leaving Brown Pass. Within a mile, all of the Bowman country is seen with the long curved lake resting in a heavily wooded setting. Not only Thunderbird Mt. with its glacier, but also MT. CARTER (9843) and jagged MT. PEABODY (9216) are in full view.

WEASEL COLLAR GLACIER is the long body of ice squeezed tightly between high walls on Mt. Carter. It is an example of a cascading glacier, tumbling down 1200 feet in its narrow chasm.

The trail grows narrow and exhilarating, chiseled out of a sheer rock wall from which one peers down several thousands of feet into Bowman Creek. Horses should be walked along the ledge, especially if one is understandably gripped by fear of high places which may cause giddiness and panic.

1.7 miles from Brown Pass, a short spur (L) drops quickly to the floor of the delightful cirque with its scattered clumps of trees and crystal-clear flowing water. This is HOLE-IN-THE-WALL, a pleasant place to camp, although no wood fires are permitted in this fragile area. The name is derived from the small stream which seeps into the limestone, then drops from a crevice in the cliff into the lower basin.

Some of the best mountain goat country in the world is on both sides of BOULDER PASS, now just ahead. Great numbers of mule deer, wholly unafraid, constantly invade one's privacy. Campers have awakened at night to discover a mule deer standing over them and staring them in the face. This should be warning enough to place shoes, food, saddles and other chewables beyond the reach of these as well as other animals, notably porcupines and bears.

The serrate Continental Divide on MT. CUSTER (8883), to the north, is easily climbed for a breath-taking view of North Lakes, the trough of Boundary Creek and the cluster of peaks in the Carthew Lakes country of Waterton Lakes Park.

As the trail ascends steadily in a wide arc around the basin wall, it reaches a bed of Purcell lava which was poured out under water, leaving characteristics as distinct as those at Granite Park. The ledges are scored with stria and are highly polished and smoothly rounded by glacial action. The well-rounded polished bosses of bed rocks, elongate with a steeper side toward the glacier, are called roches moutonnees, "mutton rocks," since they resemble sheep.

On reaching the top of the flow, a barren rock bench stretches ahead with all evidence of fresh glaciation. BOULDER GLACIER to the left has shrunk to a little patch of ice huddled close to Boulder Peak (8528). A long moraine 30 to 35 feet high extends along the north side of the pocket to the gap in the mountain wall. Only two score of years ago, the glacier completely filled the basin to the moraine; when the trail was constructed, the only feasible route around it was on top of the moraine.

The route to BOULDER PASS (7470) follows directly up the flat rock pavement of the cirque floor. Its course is marked by stone cairns, small columnar piles of flat rocks. On its way, it passes by a number of tiny glacial ponds. It is an easy matter to walk from the pass to the top of BOULDER PEAK (8528) and see lovely POCKET LAKE (6613) tucked 2000 feet beneath the summit. On the west side of the Divide, an unusual flat-bottomed valley stretching to the north has only recently been free of ice. It is floored with lava and dotted with little lakes. Along the trail are mossy, resilient bits of turf and fine displays of alpine plants. A campground lies half a mile west of the pass.

A high bench fashioned from the lava beds is covered with park-like stands of that most beautiful of trees, the subalpine larch. Wildflowers are in abundance, especially nodding onions, paintbrushes and asters. KINNERLY (9944) and KINTLA (10,101) PEAKS with AGASSIZ GLACIER behind them are to the southwest. The BOUNDARY MTS. are on the north with Long Knife Peak (9784) topping their serrate crest.

Agassiz Glacier, once one of the largest in the park, has all but vanished through rapid recession. A long, thin, much-crevassed tongue extended as late as the 40's a quarter-mile down the valley from the broad field of ice. The limestone strata dip with the glacier and have had big bites taken out of them by the glacier. AGASSIZ FALLS, lofty and beautiful, plunges over one of the ledges. Besides mule deer, elk are sometimes seen. Porcupines appear to be especially numerous.

As the trail drops by long switchbacks over slopes covered with brush and groups of trees, the towering pyramid of Kinnerly Peak, turquoise Upper Kintla Lake and sharp-spired Long Knife Peak are features appearing along the route. The trail zigzags back and forth as it plunges from one bench to another down the south face of GARDNER POINT (7405).

Firs and spruces grow to their maximum dimensions for this region, but the lower forest has only spindling trees, dense growing, full of windfalls and almost barren underneath so that it is comparatively monotonous.

After crossing Kintla Creek, the trail reaches UPPER KINTLA LAKE (4371) with a campground on the shore a half-mile below the shallow inlet. Cutting of trees by beavers is in great evidence; here, young Douglas firs seem to be preferred. Before reaching the foot of the lake, one can see a series of craggy spires which constitute an imposing reentrant in the west face of Kintla Peak. The once-great KINTLA GLACIER spread as an expansive sheet several miles wide so that it covered all of the benches above the valley. It has now faded to a few scattered scallops.

From the foot of Upper Kintla Lake the classical view of Kinnerly Peak is at this site and much photographic film is expended to perpetuate the traveler's experience. PARKE PEAK (9038) looms to the south. The trail downstream plunges into a dense mature forest which dissolves as a bow-shaped KINTLA LAKE (4008) comes into view. The lake extends six miles down the valley. A patrol cabin stands on the northeast shore.

Trail 6 follows along the north shore down the lake to a campground a quarter-mile below the cabin. An oil seep and relics of Butte Oil Well are near the waterline. Piles of cordwood cut for its operation remain nearby in a state of decay. Sinking of the well was attempted in 1901 and 1902, predating the park. The heavier equipment was hauled from the foot of the lake over ice in wintertime. Much of the forest along the north bank (Starvation Ridge) is Douglas fir which is attractively open. The trail travels up and down throughout its length of over eight miles, making a very tiring journey. At the lower end of the lake is an auto campground and the Kintla terminus of the Inside North Fork Road.

Trails from Other Points in Glacier Park

A number of trails in Glacier National Park have not been described in this chapter. Glacier has 750 miles of trails, but those not given detailed descriptions are of lesser public interest and receive insufficient maintenance. Some trails serve as access for National Park Service rangers making periodic inspection trips. Some are trails at relatively low elevations, of interest to those not wishing strictly alpine adventures. Among the trails not described in this chapter are those mentioned in the chapter on Highways and Roads. In particular, there are many relatively unfrequented trails in the southern and the extreme western and northwestern parts of the park with termini at or close to a road or highway. References to these are included in the Logs of U.S. Highway 2, Camas Road, Inside North Fork Road, and Chief Mountain International Highway.

Trails in Waterton Lakes Park

Hell Roaring Creek and Crypt Lake

Crypt Landing to Crypt Lake, 5.5 miles; Bosporus to Crypt Lake, 8.0 miles. See map on page 123.

The Crypt Lake Trail is the most challenging of popular trails in Waterton-Glacier Park. Swimming horses across the Bosporus, a crawl through a natural, albeit enlarged, tunnel; the mystery of the subterannean outlet of Crypt Lake and the cringing path around the cirque wall stamp a Crypt Lake experience as adventure with distinction. The lower trail is for horse travel, wide and easy, but the half-mile ledge above the kitchen shelter, for foot travel only—narrow, sloping, precarious—is not for the timid. The climb up a steel ladder and the crawl through a constricted tunnel for access to the lake in the lofty basin may change the walker's mind so that he will be satisfied with a look from the kitchen shelter rather than be embarrassed by facing a warden who has had to rescue him because of failing courage.

The traveler has several options. The most direct and easy approach is by launch from Emerald Bay to Crypt Landing. Arrangements must be made in advance with boat operators at the townsite dock. Horseback parties must swim mounts across the Bosporus except at a time of very low water. A third approach, from Chief Mountain International Highway, mile 6.4, at Maskinonge Lake, is too long to be practical.

Starting on the south bank of the Bosporus, the trail climbs 300 feet in a half-mile up a jutting peninsula. The trail to Stoney Flats and Vimy Peak departs to the left. The right member circles a low ridge and proceeds through a mixed forest high above the lakeshore to Crypt Landing, two miles distant. Good views are plentiful of the lake and its surroundings, including the outwash delta of Cameron River where the town is located. Boat passengers arriving at Crypt Landing should make previous arrangements with the launch operator to be picked up later.

The route climbs quickly up a diagonal horse trail which heads directly, except for two short switchbacks, southeast to the Hell Roaring Creek Canyon. The route passes through heavy spruce-fir forest with an understory of many shrubs: menziesia, snowberry, spirea, huckleberry, thimbleberry, rose, alder, Oregon grape, mountain lover and ribes, beneath which are Solomon's seals and saxifrages.

Two switchbacks ascend around the southwest ridge of Vimy Peak to the 5000-foot contour before dropping several hundred feet on an unforested slope to a level above graceful Twin Falls. The trail assumes an easy grade for a mile over a barren slope of southern exposure. The box canyon on the right is called Burnt Rock because of the black lichens that cover the perpendicular walls.

At the head of the basin, Burnt Rock Falls drops over a thick block of Waterton Formation dolomitic limestone which rests on much sheared and broken younger Grinnell argillite, from which it is separated by the Mt. Crandell thrust. The shattered material erodes into a gully with sloping convex slopes; the limestone forms the vertical cliffs above the fault line. The dark brown rocks add to the illusion of a fire-scorched kiln.

Having climbed to 6000 feet and now heading southeast, the trail begins a final effort to climb another 500 feet by a dozen sharp switchbacks. The compound cirque at the head of Hell Roaring Creek unfolds to the south. Its two levels are separated by an 800-foot wall of Altyn limestone, over which a slim waterfall plunges into a placid pond in a verdant meadow. The narrow trail above the waterfall and upper cirque floor can be seen as it feels a way around the cirque wall and threads through a tunnel bored in a rib of rock. Elk and deer spoor, grizzly tracks and claw marks on the bark of trees, and other signs of the presence of wildlife are abundant at many places along the trail.

A kitchen shelter, fireplaces, tables and simple camp facilities are located by a small waterfall in a timberline grove in a feeder valley to the east. Horses must be tethered at the hitch rack, for the remainder of the journey of half a mile can only be made on foot.

Leaving the campsite, the foot trail cautiously climbs the rocky wall to the tunnel at 6700 feet. It is a natural tunnel through a vertical slab of limestone that has been slightly enlarged to

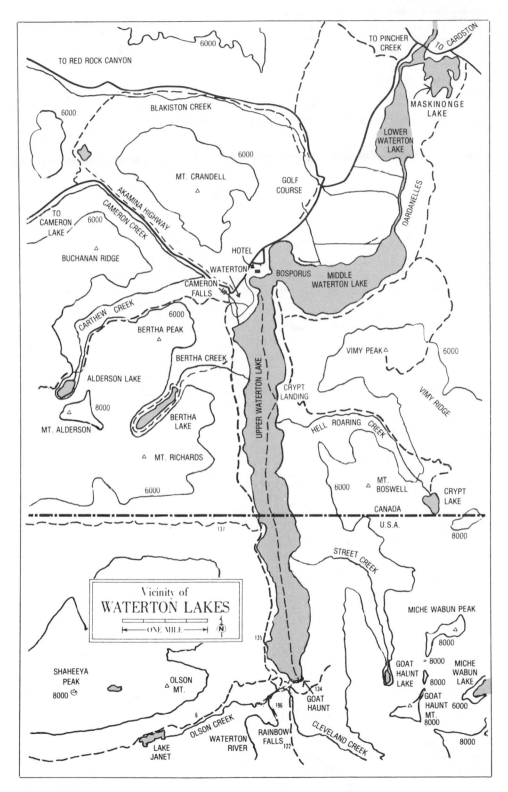

TO PINCHER
CREEK

TO CARDSTON

TO RED ROCK CANYON

6000

6000

BLAKISTON CREEK

MASKINONGE
LAKE

LOWER
WATERTON
LAKE

6000

MT. CRANDELL

6000

GOLF
COURSE

DARDANELLES

AKAMINA HIGHWAY

CAMERON CREEK

TO
CAMERON
LAKE

6000

HOTEL

WATERTON

BOSPORUS

MIDDLE
WATERTON LAKE

BUCHANAN RIDGE

CAMERON
FALLS

CARTHEW CREEK

6000

BERTHA PEAK

VIMY PEAK

6000

BERTHA CREEK

UPPER WATERTON LAKE

VIMY RIDGE

ALDERSON LAKE

CRYPT
LANDING

8000

HELL ROARING CREEK

BERTHA
LAKE

MT. ALDERSON

MT. RICHARDS

6000

MT.
BOSWELL

CRYPT
LAKE

6000

CANADA

137

U.S.A.

8000

STREET CREEK

Vicinity of
WATERTON LAKES

ONE MILE

N

MICHE WABUN PEAK

135

8000

8000

SHAHEEYA
PEAK

8000

OLSON
MT.

GOAT
HAUNT
LAKE

8000

MICHE
WABUN
LAKE

134

8000

196

GOAT
HAUNT

GOAT
HAUNT
MT.
8000

6000

6

OLSON CREEK

RAINBOW
FALLS

CLEVELAND CREEK

8000

LAKE
JANET

WATERTON
RIVER

122

123

enable a person to crawl on hands and knees for a few dozen feet. At the near end of the trail tunnel an 8-foot steel ladder has been anchored to give hikers access to the tunnel mouth.

Clear, blue Crypt Lake (6400) half fills the basin in the Wilson Range (8579) straddling the International Border. It is tightly enclosed on three sides by high walls; its southern tip barely touches the U.S. line. The snow and ice of previous winters lingers long into summer within this bowl in the shadow of high cliffs on the east, south and west. Many mountain goats may be seen on the surrounding rock ledges. The floor of the basin below the lake is bestrewn with blocks of talus and clad with a timberline forest of whitebark pine, fir, spruce and subalpine larches, the latter adding splashes of gold on the palette of autumn colors of shrubs and herbs. The lake outlet seeps underground in rock seams and bouldery detritus, but reappears in a 600-foot leap.

Carthew Trail

Cameron Falls to Alderson Lake, 4.5 miles; Carthew Lakes, 6.0 miles; Cameron Lake to Summit Lake, 2.6 miles; Carthew Pass, 5.7 miles; Cameron Falls, 12.0 miles.. See map on page 123.

A great part of the Carthew Trail between Cameron Falls and Cameron Lake is above timberline. The pass, crossing the ridge at 7900 feet, is the highest elevation traversed by a Waterton trail. Views of peaks at the head of Waterton Lake, of the Kintla region and of British Columbia mountains are superb. The lakes are stocked with cutthroat and are provided with delightful though simple campsites. A trip may be started from either end of the trail, but the start from Cameron Lake is easier, since it avoids 1250 feet of climbing. At the east end of the trail, a service road on the left of Cameron Falls leads 100 yards to the foot of the trail.

From the terminus of Akamina Highway at the foot of Cameron Lake (5445), the trail turns east and immediately climbs 1000 feet by long switchbacks in a spruce-fir forest. At first only FORUM PEAK (7922) across the lake is prominent, but soon MTS. ROWE (8043) and LINEHAM (8900) come into view to the north. After crossing a broad, sparsely vegetated flat ridge, tiny SUMMIT LAKE (6350) is reached on a broad bench. Here the Boundary Trail (see description below) continues ahead along the lakeshore while the Carthew Trail turns left to follow the southwest ridge of Mt. Carthew.

As it climbs with long switchbacks, it is soon above timber and affords stunning views. CAMPBELL MT. (8245) with its deeply seamed north face is to the southeast. Imposing CHAPMAN PEAK (9406), with WURDEMAN LAKE (5265) under its summit, and MT. CUSTER (8883), with HERBST and HUDSON GLACIERS and LAKE NOONEY (5599) tucked in a pocket beneath its eastern wall, are to the west of Mt. Campbell across the deep valley of Boundary Creek. The ice fields of MT. CARTER (9843) and RAINBOW PEAK (9891) are behind Mt. Custer.

The bulky massif of KINTLA PEAK (10,101) with the sharp spire of KINNERLY PEAK (9944) and BOUNDARY MTS. ridge, dominated by LONG KNIFE PEAK (9784), are on the right. Long Knife in many Algonkian tongues is the term for "white man," its use reaching all the way back to Powhatan's Confederacy in the Virginia Colony of the earliest Seventeenth Century. These mountains, all south of the border, appear a rugged jumble whose highest reaches are daubed bright red and yellow by argillites of the Missoula group.

The forests yield to bright red scree as one climbs with two bold arcs in a broad bowl on Mt. Carthew. Little rock rims, pushed up by snow, shelter lines of subalpine fir krummholz on this windy, exposed climb. There is no drinking water on the long route. To avoid crossing persistent snow, the trail climbs to 7900 feet on the warm, south-facing slope, high above the pass (7500) between MT. ALDERSON (8833) and MT. CARTHEW (8600), which lies a half-mile east and 500 feet below the transit of the trail over the summit. The connecting ridge between the two mountains is strikingly barren.

From the top of the ridge, Carthew Lakes are seen on the floor of the subalpine cirque 800 feet below. Snow lasts through summer in this protected pocket.

The second lake, whose outlet expands into a pond, lies 100 feet below the upper one. Mats of subalpine fir on the lakeshore afford some shelter, but small stands of vigorous subalpine larches appear on rock ledges to the south.

124

An 800-foot rim below these lakes is descended by short switchbacks to ALDERSON LAKE (6000), of deepest blue, shaded by a sinister 2500-crescentic precipice. A good kitchen shelter and campsite is in the shrubby growth at the outlet, 300 feet off Carthew Trail.

The trail proceeds for several miles almost on contour as it bends around BERTHA PEAK (7613) until it is 1000 feet above Carthew Creek, which drains the lakes. The frowning precipice of BUCHANAN RIDGE (8499), barren, sheer and wild, is in the northwest. The trail hugs the 6000-foot contour in a gradually deepening spruce-fir forest with some Douglas firs.

As the trail starts to descend, Akamina Highway comes into view across the valley of Cameron Creek on the left. Switchbacks help make the descent rapid to Cameron Falls and the townsite.

Stoney Flats and Vimy Peak Summit

Bosporus to Stoney Flats, 3.1 miles; to summit, 6.8 miles. See map on page 123.

The Palliser Expedition of 1868 named the mountain Observaton Peak. At the height of World War I emotionalism, enthusiasts renamed it Vimy Peak (7825). It commands attention even as it commands the Waterton country which it oversees. The climber's route ascends from Stoney Flats, which probably were created from a lake that included the present Middle and Lower Waterton, and Maskinonge Lakes, now separated from each other by glacio-fluvial detritus.

The foot of the trail to the summit is on the Bosporus Trail at the south end of Stoney Flats and the southeastern tip of Middle Waterton Lake. Several approaches are possible: (1) from the Bosporus as described under Hell Roaring Creek and Crypt Lake; (2) from Chief Mountain International Highway, mile 2.7, by crossing Pass Creek Flats, passing Marquis Hole Picnic Site, fording the Dardanelles and a half-mile farther, turning right on the Bosporus Trail coming from Lower Waterton and Maskinonge Lakes; (3) from the highway, mile 6.4, passing Maskinonge Lake.

From its junction with the Bosporus Trail at the foot of Middle Waterton Lake (4192), Vimy Peak Trail ascends as a faint lane with gentle rise southward through aspens and cottonwoods. The tree cover is delightful as it shifts from broadleafs to lodgepoles, with an understory of menziesias, alders and gooseberries, finally grading into spruce-fir. There is a dearth of drinking water in mid-summer.

Curving westward, a pleasant waterfall appears in a forested setting ahead, but the trail does not pass close to it. The trail enters grasslands behind an assertive yellow crag towering over the trees. It starts to climb in earnest a rounded acclivity scarred by an ancient fire, leaving charred snags of giant whitebark pines protruding through a healthy growth of young subalpine larch.

The trail ascends a col happy with asters, parnassias and monkeyflowers. The crest of VIMY RIDGE, the thin rocky wall ahead, yields a magnificent view of Hell Roaring Creek Canyon, Crypt Lake and Mt. Cleveland's pointed spire, eight miles to the south. The trail bends right for an abrupt rise between prostrate firs on a crumbly rock slope. From the sharp summit is a panorama of Waterton Lake, the townsite, Cameron Valley, the north and east parts of Waterton Lakes Park, the Great Plains and the trail on which climbers panted and sweated.

Bertha Lake, Goat Haunt and Boundary Creek Trails

Cameron Falls to Bertha Lake, 3.5 miles; International Boundary, 5.0 miles; Goat Haunt, 8.7 miles. Cameron Lake to Waterton Lake Trail (135), 12.3 miles. See map on page 123.

Bertha Lake Trail is popular with Waterton visitors because it is short and close at hand. The Waterton Lake Trail above the west shore of Waterton Lake is the only practical trail link between the two national parks. All other links depend upon automobile or launch connections. The trail is not heavily used because of its unevenness and because launch service is so handy. The long Boundary Creek Trail is relatively outside the mainstream of trail travel.

Bertha Lake Trail

Starting at Cameron Falls, the trail south climbs 700 feet in 1.9 miles of heavy forest. It crosses Bertha Creek on a hair pin curve. The left hand member is the Waterton Lake Trail.

The branch on the right to Bertha Lake rises rapidly 1000 feet by short switchbacks, then enters a long, glacier-scoured basin between Mt. Richards (7800) and Bertha Peak (7613). The narrow trough is conspicuous along Chief Mountain International Highway approaching Waterton Townsite from the Entrance Station. A long cascade pours from the lip of Bertha Basin which is almost filled by Bertha Lake, a mile long, but scarcely 200 yards across at greatest width. It is tightly hemmed on three sides by cliffs of Grinnell argillite. A two-mile trail goes all the way around the lake. A kitchen camp is at the lower end of the lake which is stocked with rainbows.

The outcrops on Waterton lakeshore for a mile on each side of Bertha Creek are Waterton Formation which is present in two thick strata or slices piled one over the other. Several overthrust members and faults are apparent on the ascent of Bertha Creek. All dip to the southwest, away from the lake.

Complex overthrusting like this is also well exhibited on Vimy Peak and Yellow Mt. north of Kennedy Creek, where it is easy to see that older slices have been shoved over younger. The low but prominent bald ledge which juts above the forest near the lakeshore and through which Bertha Creek has cut a channel is the result of the dip and overthrusting. The basin of Waterton Lake, like that of Swiftcurrent Lake at Many Glacier, results from the dip of strata towards the head of the glacier which carved it out of the mountain. The tilted ledge below the foot of the lake is the dam which restrains the water.

Waterton Lake Trail

The Waterton lakeshore trail south of Bertha Creek descends gradually for three miles until it reaches an International Boundary marker (4213) and warden patrol cabin. One tenth-mile farther it crosses West Boundary Creek. Glacier's North Boundary Trail (137) joins from the west, 0.4 mile from the International Boundary. A half dozen streamlets tumble down the east slope of MT. OLSON (7913) creating fatiguing climbs and descents at trail crossings.

From a broad cottonwood meadow on Olson Creek, Boulder Pass Trail (6) starts its long "dream trip" westward over Brown and Boulder Passes. This trail is described elsewhere in this chapter (page 119). Facilities at Goat Haunt are described under Trails from Many Glacier, North Circle Trail.

Boundary Creek Trail

Starting at Cameron Lake on the Carthew Trail and parting from it at tiny Summit Lake, 2.6 miles, the Boundary Creek Trail drops 1350 feet by six long switchbacks on a shrubby declivity with remarkable views of Wurdeman and Nooney Lakes in steep-walled cirques, Herbst and Hudson Glaciers and the terrific wall connecting Mt. Custer, Chapman Peak and Mt. Campbell. Upon crossing the International Boundary, the trail becomes North Boundary Trail (137) which descends West Boundary Creek in heavy timber to Waterton Lake Trail (135), 5.8 miles distant. From the junction, it is 3.5 miles to Goat Haunt where the launch may be boarded for Waterton Townsite.

For other Canadian trails see chapter on Highways and Roads.

Short Walks and Half-day Hikes

For visitors with limited time the following short or half-day hikes are suggested. Refer to the index for descriptions.

From Lake McDonald Lodge

Short walks to the Sacred Dancing Cascade Circuit (including Paradise Canyon, McDonald Falls, Sacred Dancing Cascade and Johns Lake), the big cedars from mile 14.5 on Going-to-the-Sun Road. Longer jaunt: Fish Lake via the Gunsight Pass and Snyder Ridge Trails.

From Avalanche Campground

Short walks to Avalanche Gorge, Trail of the Cedars. Longer jaunts: Avalanche Lake, Lake McDonald Lodge.

From Logan Pass

Short hike to Hidden Lake Overlook. Longer jaunt: Haystack Butte.

From Sun Point and Vicinity

Short walks to Sunrift Gorge, Baring Falls, St. Mary Falls, along St. Mary Lake above Sun Point. Longer jaunts: Virginia Falls, Florence Falls, Baring Basin.

From Two Medicine

Short walks to Running Eagle Falls, Appistoki Falls, Paradise Point, Twin Falls and Upper Two Medicine Lake, using the boat service.

From Many Glacier

Short walks around Swiftcurrent Falls, around Swiftcurrent Lake, around Josephine Lake, Appekunny Falls. Longer jaunts: Grinnell Lake and Hidden Falls, Ptarmigan Falls and Red Rock Falls. Boat service is available on Swiftcurrent and Josephine Lakes.

From Granite Park

Short hikes to Swiftcurrent Lookout and Grinnell Glacier Overlook. Longer jaunt: Ahern Pass and notch above Iceberg Lake.

From Goat Haunt

Short walks to Rainbow Falls and Goat Haunt Overlook. Longer jaunts: Lake Frances and Kootenai Lakes.

From Waterton Townsite

Short walks to Bear's Hump and the Centennial Trail around Lake Linnet. Longer jaunt: Bertha Lake.

Camping and Fishing in Glacier Park

Because use of national park facilities has grown enormously in recent years, camping at designated sites, camping in backcountry sites and picnicking in designated areas are carefully and diligently regulated. These rules are enforced so that natural features may be preserved for future visitors. There is no space in this guide for detailing all these regulations, so you are strongly urged to secure a copy of the regulations prior to your visit. Do not make the mistake of driving many miles only to find that sites are occupied to their capacity—or that facilities you require are not available.

Campground	No. of camp sites	Boat Access**	Flush Toilets	Cafe/ Store	Recommended Maximum Trailer Length	Piped Water
Apgar	196	Yes	Yes	Yes	26'	Yes
*Avalanche	87	No	Yes	5 mi.	26'	Yes
Bowman Creek	6	No	No	2 mi.	22'	No
Bowman Lake	48	Yes	No	7 mi.	22'	Yes
Cut Bank	19	No	No	17 mi.	22'	Yes
Fish Creek	180	No	Yes	2 mi.	26'	Yes
Kintla Lake	19	Yes	No	18 mi.	18'	Yes
Logging Creek	8	No	No	8 mi.	18'	Yes
*Many Glacier	117	Yes	Yes	Yes	26'	Yes
Quartz Creek	7	No	No	6 mi.	18'	Pump
Rising Sun	83	Yes	Yes	Yes	26'	Yes
River North River	7	No	No	6 mi.	18'	No
Sprague Creek	25	No	Yes	1 mi.	0	Yes
St. Mary Lake	156	No	Yes	1 mi.	26'	Yes
Two Medicine	99	Yes	Yes	12 mi.	26'	Yes

*Restricted to Hard-sided Camping Units Only (No tents or sleeping on the ground).
**On Bowman, Kintla and Two Medicine Lakes, motor boats are limited to 10 horsepower or less.

Trailers permitted at all campgrounds except Sprague Creek. Camping limit: 7 days. Season varies: many are open during the first week in June and closed September 30 or somewhat earlier depending on weather and staffing availability. Make inquiry as to seasons and fees at specific campgrounds. Each campsite has a table and firegrate. Campsites cannot be reserved; they are on a "first-come, first-served" basis. Sanitary dump facilities are located at Apgar, Avalanche, Fish Creek, Many Glacier, Rising Sun, St. Mary and Two Medicine campgrounds. Half of the park campgrounds are reached by improved road, the others by unimproved road. There are no water or electrical hookups at any site.

Fishing in Glacier requires a non-fee permit, available at ranger stations and visitor centers. Also obtain a copy of current regulations, with information on season, catch and possession limits, equipment and bait and restricted waters. Some park waters are barren of fish.

If you plan to do any hiking or backpacking during your visit, you should obtain a back-country brochure prior to your arrival. This folder includes a map indicating backcountry campgrounds, distances between each, specific restrictions on use (such as no wood fires in some areas or limits on size of groups and length of stay), general regulations and advice on weather, clothing, equipment, etc. All backcountry travelers who intend to have a fire or camp overnight must obtain a backcountry use permit. These permits are not issued previous to the day before you start your backcountry trip. Six (6) days is the maximum length of trip that can be reserved at a time. Pets, including packdogs, firearms and vehicles of any kind are not permitted in the backcountry. Campers may use authorized sites only, except in the wilderness camping zone of the Nyack and Coal Creek drainages, where special guidelines apply. (Note: Camping, fishing, and hiking regulations in Waterton Park vary somewhat from those in Glacier. Consult Canadian officials before beginning trip. Identification is required by all parties entering Waterton by trail from Glacier.)

Upon arrival in the park, each backcountry user should check at a ranger station or visitor center for current information on trail and weather conditions. Special hazards may include (but are not limited to): high water or flooding; avalanches; steep, icy or undercut snowbanks; hypothermia ("exposure"); wildlife (especially bears); wood ticks; and giardiasis (gee-ar-DYE-a-sis), an intestinal disease obtained by drinking untreated "natural" water. Study available literature on recognizing and avoiding the above hazards. Proper preparation, common sense and good judgement help assure a safe, enjoyable backcountry experience. Remember, your safety is your own responsibility.

Naturalist Interpretive Program

Enjoyment of nature is enhanced through personal understanding. To this end both Waterton Lakes and Glacier National Parks maintain scheduled programs at key locations during the park season. Services include guided trips afield, exhibits, popular talks and powwows at visitor centers, amphitheaters, campgrounds and lodges. Special features are designed for children. There is no charge for the services of a naturalist. Interested visitors should check for details at entrance, information and ranger stations, and at hotels, lodges and stores as the program is modified from time to time.

The Glacier Institute

For those visitors who have several days at a time to concentrate on outdoor learning, the Glacier Institute offers an opportunity to participate in field-oriented college-level classes. The Glacier Institute is a non-profit organization, established in 1983, that "examines Glacier's cultural and natural resources while increasing public awareness of management policies, resource issues, and research efforts...and contributes to the public's appreciation of Glacier's aesthetic qualities through the creative arts." For further information, write The Glacier Institute, Number One First Street East, Kalispell, Montana 59901.

Advice in Regard to Wild Animals

Bears, both black and grizzly, are potentially dangerous; they definitely should not be considered the gentle playmates of man that are sometimes portrayed in films and on television. On the other hand, excessive media attention to bear maulings—a few fatal—may give the public an exaggerated impression of the risk involved. Such risk is statistically slim; many more park injuries and deaths result from water and automobile accidents, falls and hypothermia. Exercising a few simple precautions and keeping reasonably alert will greatly reduce dangers from the bears of Waterton-Glacier.

Free brochures available in each park describe basic bear behavior, distinction between black and grizzly bears, and specific suggestions for improving your safety in bear country. Learning the facts about bears is your best defense, but nothing will provide an absolute guarantee against an unpleasant encounter. Camping guidelines center around maintaining a clean camp, with proper food storage and garbage disposal. Standard trail procedures include being alert for signs of bear activity, making noise to avoid surprising a bear at close range, and not hiking alone, at night, off-trail or with your dog.

Both Waterton and Glacier Parks have procedures for posting warning signs on trails where bears have been recently observed and for temporarily closing areas where concentrated bear activity may pose a higher risk for visitors. For the safety of other visitors, never collect such warning signs for souvenirs! Observe all trail closures! Report all bear sightings to park staff.

TRYING TO FEED, ENTICE, PHOTOGRAPH AT CLOSE RANGE OR TOUCH wild animals is a common cause of accidents and injuries. Even lovable, tame-acting deer have razor-sharp hoofs with which they might unexpectedly strike if impetuous or frightened. Behaviorally, elk, deer, moose, mountain goats, bighorn sheep, bison and bear may show warning signs of disturbance by tail flicking, sniffing the air, foot stomping or pawing the ground, grinding teeth and snorting. At other times animals may react swiftly, without the above warning signs of their annoyance. Birds may display with head bobbing, feather ruffling, circling overhead, dive bombing, pretending an injury such as a broken wing, with increased vocalization.

Viewing the wildlife can be one of the greatest thrills of a national park experience. The following suggestions are ways of channeling the enthusiasm of wildlife viewers to minimize unintentional disturbances:

—Avoid crowding an animal for a close look or a photograph. Use binoculars for viewing and a telephoto lens for photographs. Winter and spring are especially stressful times for many mountain dwellers, when vital energy reserves may be depleted by unwarranted disturbances. Remember, if an animal changes its behavior because of you, you're too close!

—Interference during mating and rearing young may result in desertion or inadvertent separation of mates or of adults from their young. Restrict your activities around breeding areas, including bird nests, and avoid approaching too closely animals with young.

—Feeding wild animals is dangerous and may drastically alter natural feeding habits, with unhealthy or even fatal results for the animal. It is unlawful in Waterton-Glacier to feed, entice or molest any wild animal, even those which appear tame or approach to beg. One of the great privileges of a national park visit is the opportunity to observe wildlife in their natural habitats. Make it a project during your stay to sharpen your powers of observation; note the behavior of the animals and their selection of natural foods without disruption from humans.

Crime Prevention in our National Parks

Leave valuables and unnecessary equipment at home. Keep purses and wallets with you at all times. Take time to put your name and address on each of your photographic items. Keep gear out of sight, especially at night, during interpretive programs and while you're away from camp.

It is illegal to have an open container of alcohol in a vehicle on roads or in parking areas in Glacier Park, or in picnic areas in Waterton.

Since hunting by man is illegal in most parks, wildlife therein may eventually lose its wariness and become especially vulnerable to unscrupulous people. Unfortunately, it is a fact of life that national parks worldwide are attractive centers of operation for illegal activities of poachers, some of whom act singly, others as members of extensive, sophisticated rings. Alert visitors can assist park law enforcement personnel in discouraging such exploitative practices by promptly notifying authorities of any suspicious activity. NEVER PLACE YOURSELF IN JEOPARDY by interfering directly, but take careful note of time, place, number and description of individuals and vehicles involved. In recent years several park poachers have been successfully prosecuted with the assistance of cooperating witnesses.

Glacier National Park is a member of the Crimestoppers Program. Should you have any information relating to a crime that occurred in the park, call 257-TIPS collect. You will not need to identify yourself. In Waterton, call 859-2244.

Rare and endangered plants (orchids, ferns, cacti, even trees), fossils, prehistoric cultural relics, eagle feathers and claws, animal heads, skins, claws and antlers and live specimens such as falcons are items for trade on the international black market. Help discourage such trade by learning applicable laws, refusing to purchase any protected plant or animal or its parts, and supporting the prosecution of unethical and illegal hunters, hunting guides and taxidermists and the blackmarket dealers whom they supply. Our international natural heritage should not be abused!

Salmon and Eagles

Each fall beginning in October with numbers generally peaking in November, bald eagles concentrate along Glacier's lower McDonald Creek to feed on spawning kokanee salmon. After spawning, the salmon gradually die off, providing a ready food source for hundreds of southward migrating bald eagles. To avoid disturbance of feeding eagles and an occasional grizzly bear, public access to lower McDonald Creek is seasonally restricted. However, visitors can readily observe both salmon and eagles from the viewing site at Apgar Bridge over the creek downstream from the foot of Lake McDonald (see Lower McDonald Creek, page 25). Readers desiring information about Glacier's salmon-eagle rendevous can contact park headquarters (address and telephone number on page 132). Also, several publications on the topic are available through the Glacier Natural History Association (see Additional Reading).

Glacier Park Concessioner Services:

Belton Chalets, Inc., Southside U.S. 2, East, West Glacier, MT 59936 (406)888-5511.
 Reservations for food and lodging at Sperry and Granite Park Chalets (accessible only by trail). Season: July 1 through Labor Day.

Glacier Park Boat Company, 444 Woodland Ave., Kalispell, MT 59901
 Winter Phone: (406)257-1046 Summer Phone: (403)859-2455
 Scenic cruises on St. Mary Lake; cruises and small rental boats available at Lake McDonald, Many Glacier and Two Medicine.
 Season: approximately mid-June through Labor Day.

Glacier Park, Inc. Mid September to Mid May: Greyhound Tower, Station 5510, Phoenix, AZ 85077 Reservations: (602)248-6000
 Mid May to Mid September: East Glacier Park, MT 59434 Reservations:
 (406) 226-5551 Montana In-State Watts: 800-332-9351
 Accommodations at lodges and motor inns; general store and coffee shop facilities; scenic bus tours. Season: approximately June 1 through Labor Day.

Glacier Wilderness Guides, Box 535, West Glacier, MT 59936 (406) 888-5333
 Guided backpacking trips, backpacking equipment rentals and combination hiking/rafting trips. Office at Apgar Village. Season: May 1 through September 30.

Lake McDonald Boat Company, Inc. (406)888-5227
Boat, canoe and buoy rentals and fishing tackle sales at Apgar Village on Lake
McDonald.

Rocky Mountain Outfitters, 55 Aimley Lane, Kalispell, MT 59901 (406)257-0972
Guided saddle horse trail rides from corrals at Many Glacier, Lake McDonald
and Apgar.
Season: approximately June 10 through Labor Day.

Waterton Inter-Nation Shoreline Cruises, Box 126, Waterton Lakes,
Alberta TOK 2 MO (403)859-2362
Scenic boat tours from Waterton Townsite, Canada, to Goat Haunt, Glacier
National Park, on Waterton Lakes.

For Additional Information, call or write:

Headquarters
Glacier National Park
West Glacier, MT 59936
(406)888-5441

Information Bureau
Waterton Lakes National Park
Waterton Park, AB TOK 2MO
(403)859-2445

Further Reading

Much of the fun of travel is learning about the human and natural history of one's
goal. Reading is preliminary as well as sequent to a meaningful trip. Waterton-
Glacier is rich in descriptive and scientific literature although many of the citations
below are available only in larger libraries. The following are recommended:
*The Glacier Natural History Association, Inc., West Glacier, Montana 59936, is a
non-profit organization, cooperating with the National Park Service in the interpretive program of Glacier National Park and promoting the broad public understanding of the geology, plant and animal life, history, Indians and related subjects on
the park. Items starred below are currently carried in its line of books, pamphlets and
maps for sale at information stations and shops or by mail order.
A similar organization in Waterton offers additional items. Write the Waterton
Natural History Association, Box 145, Waterton Park, Alberta, TOK 2MO or call
(403)859-2624.

GENERAL
* Beaumont, Greg: Many-Storied Mountains—The Life of Glacier National
     Park, 1978
* Buchholtz, Curt: Man in Glacier, 1976
  Dightman, R.A.: Climate of Glacier National Park, 1967
* Edwards, J. Gordon: A Climber's Guide to Glacier National Park, 1976, Rev. 1984
  Everhardt, William C.: The National Park Service, 1972
  Ferber, Peggy: The Freedom of the Hills, 1982
  Hardy, W.G.: Alberta, a Natural History, 1967
* Holterman, John: Places Names of Glacier and Waterton National Parks, 1985
* Houk, Rose: Going-to-the-Sun—The Story of the Highway Across Glacier National Park,
     1984

* Larson, Rolf: Mountain Hazards, 1984
* McClintock, Walter: The Old North Trail—Life, Legend and Religion of the Blackfeet Indians, 1968. First published in 1910
* On, Danny and Sumner, David: Along the Trail, A Photographic Essay of Glacier National Park and the Northern Rocky Mountains, 1979
* Rinehart, Mary Roberts: Through Glacier Park in 1915, 1983. First published in 1916
* Siebel, Roberta: Motorist's Guide to Glacier National Park, 1979
  Tilden, Freeman: The National Parks, 1968
  Udall, Stewart L.: The Quiet Crisis, 1963
  Waterton Natural History Association: Waterton and Northern Glacier Trails for Hikers and Riders, 1984
  Wirth, Conrad L.: Parks, Politics, and the People, 1980

Animals

Bailey, Vernon and Bailey, F.M.: Wild Animals of Glacier National Park, 1918
Borror, Donald J. and White, Richard E.: A Field Guide to the Insects of America North of Mexico, 1970
* Chadwick, Douglas H.: A Beast the Color of Winter—The Mountain Goat Observed, 1983
Geist, Valerius: Mountain Sheep: A Study in Behavior and Evolution, 1971
* Gildart, Robert C.: Meet the Mammals of Waterton-Glacier International Peace Park, 1975
* Herrero, Stephen: Bear Attacks — Their Causes and Avoidance, 1985
Lechleitner, R.R.: Mammals of Glacier National Park, 1955
* McNamee, Thomas: The Grizzly Bear, 1982, 1984
Murie, Olaus J.: A Field Guide to Animal Tracks, 1974
* Patent, Dorothy H.: Where the Bald Eagles Gather, 1984
Peterson, Roger Tory: Field Guide to Western Birds, 1961
* Robbins, C.S., Bruun, B., and Zim, H.S.: Birds of North America, 1983
Salt, W.R. and Salt, J.R.: The Birds of Alberta, 1976
* Shea, David S.: Animal Tracks of Glacier National Park, 1969
* Ulrich, Tom: Birds of the Northern Rockies, 1984

Plants

Brockman, C. Frank: Trees of North America, 1968
Craighead, John J., Craighead, Frank C., Jr., and Davis, Ray J.: A Field Guide to Rocky Mountain Wildflowers, 1963
* Hart, Jeff, illustrated by Moore, Jacqueline: Native Plants and Early Peoples, 1976
Kuijt, Job: A Flora of Waterton Lakes National Park, 1982
* Nelson, Alan: Wildflowers of Glacier National Park, 1970
Robinson, Donald H: Trees and Forests of Glacier National Park, 1961
* Shaw, Richard J. and On, Danny: Plants of Waterton-Glacier National Parks, 1979
Standley, Paul C.: Flora of Glacier National Park (Contributions from the U.S. National Herbarium, 22, part V.), 1921. Plants of Glacier National Park, 1926

Geology

Alden, W.C.: Physiography and Glacier Geology of Eastern Montana, 1932
* Alt, D.D. and Hyndman, D.W.: Rocks, Ice and Water—The Geology of Waterton-Glacier Park, 1973
Campbell, M.R.: The Glacier National Park; A Popular Guide to its Geology and Scenery; U.S. Geological Survey Bulletin 600, 1914
Carrara, P.E. and McGimsey, R.G.: The Late-Neoglacial Histories of the Agassiz and Jackson Glaciers, Glacier National Park, Montana; Arctic and Alpine Research, v. 13, 1981
Fenton, C.L. and Fenton, M.A.: Algae and Algal Beds in the Belt Series of Glacier National Park; Journal of Geology, v. 39, 1931

Harrison, J.E.: Precambrian Belt Basin of Northwestern United States—Its Geometry, Sedimentation and Copper Occurrences; Geological Society of America Bulletin, v. 83, 1972

* Johnson, Arthur: Grinnell and Sperry Glaciers, Glacier National Park, Montana—A Record of Vanishing Ice; U.S. Geological Survey Professional Paper 1180, 1980

Mudge, M.R.: General Geology of Glacier National Park and Adjacent Areas, Montana; Canadian Society Petroleum Geologists, v. 25, no. 4, 1977

* Raup, Omer B., Earhart, Robert L., Whipple, James W. and Carrara, Paul E.: Geology Along Going-to-the-Sun Road, Glacier National Park, Montana, 1983

Rezak, Richard: Stromatolites of the Belt Series in Glacier National Park and Vicinity, Montana; U.S. Geological Survey Professional Paper, 294-D, 1957

Ross, C.P.: Geology of Glacier National Park and the Flathead Region, Northwestern Montana; U.S. Geological Survey Professional Paper, 296, 1959

Ross, C.P. and Rezak, Richard: The Rocks and Fossils of Glacier National Park—The Story of their Origin and History; U.S. Geological Survey Professional Paper 296, 1959

Willis, Bailey: Stratigraphy and Structure, Lewis and Livingston Ranges, Montana; Geological Society of America Bulletin, v. 13, 1902

Index

Page numbers in italics indicate illustrations

139

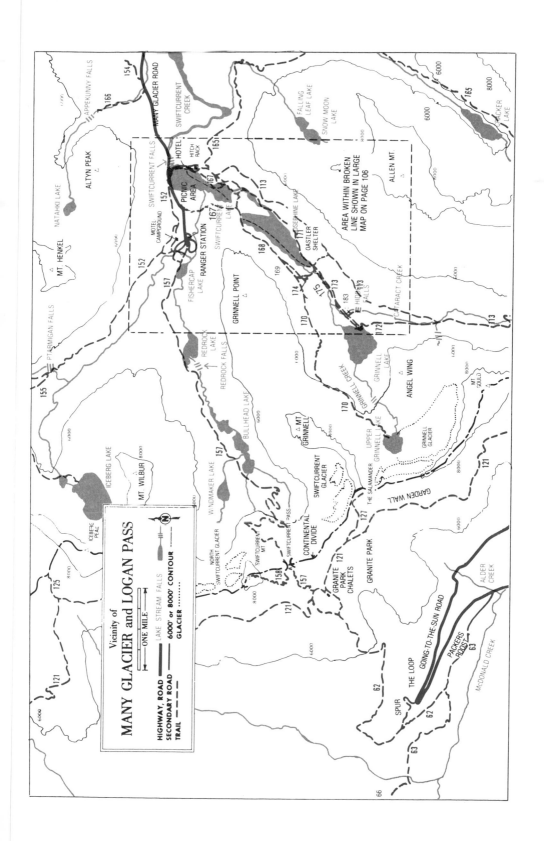

Vicinity of
MANY GLACIER and LOGAN PASS

⊢——— ONE MILE ———⊣

HIGHWAY, ROAD ▬▬▬
SECONDARY ROAD ━━━━
TRAIL ━ ━ ━ ━

LAKE STREAM FALLS ▬▬▬
6000' or 8000' CONTOUR ━━━━
GLACIER ⋯⋯⋯⋯⋯

AREA WITHIN BROKEN
LINE SHOWN IN LARGE
MAP ON PAGE 106

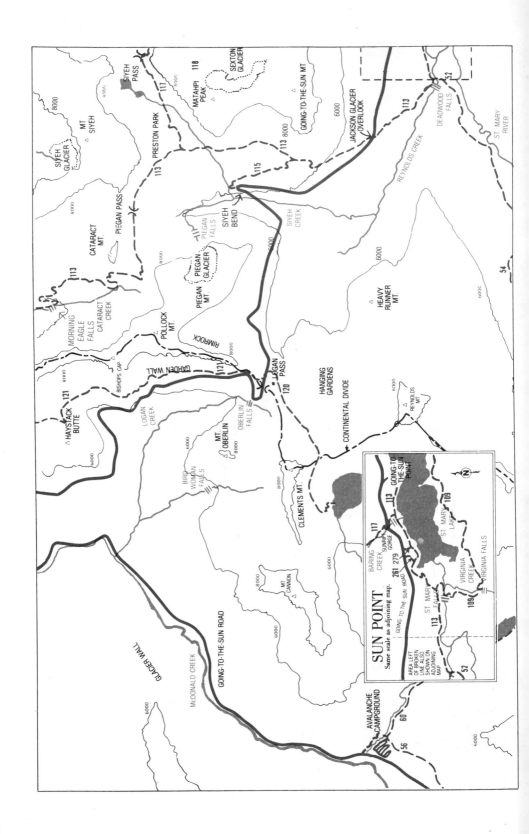

SIYEH PASS

SIYEH GLACIER

8000

MT SIYEH

PRESTON PARK

117

MATAHPI PEAK 118

SEXTON GLACIER

GOING-TO-THE-SUN MT

6000

113

113 8000

115

JACKSON GLACIER OVERLOOK

113

DEADWOOD FALLS

52

ST. MARY RIVER

REYNOLDS CREEK

PIEGAN PASS

CATARACT MT.

113

MORNING EAGLE FALLS

CATARACT CREEK

POLLOCK MT.

PIEGAN FALLS

SIYEH BEND

PIEGAN GLACIER

PIEGAN MT.

RIMROCK

GARDEN WALL

SIYEH CREEK

6000

6000

HEAVY RUNNER MT.

54

BISHOPS CAP

121

LOGAN PASS

120

HAYSTACK BUTTE

121

LOGAN CREEK

6000

HANGING GARDENS

CONTINENTAL DIVIDE

REYNOLDS MT.

MT OBERLIN

8000

OBERLIN FALLS

BIRD WOMAN FALLS

CLEMENTS MT.

6000

MT CANNON

8000

6000

GLACIER WALL

McDONALD CREEK

GOING-TO-THE-SUN ROAD

6000

SUN POINT
Same scale as adjoining map.

N

GOING-TO-THE-SUN POINT

BARING CREEK

117

113

SUNRIFT GORGE

261 279

GOING-TO-THE-SUN ROAD

ST. MARY LAKE

109

VIRGINIA CREEK

VIRGINIA FALLS

109

ST. MARY FALLS

113

52

AREA LEFT OF BROKEN LINE ALSO SHOWN ON ADJOINING MAP

AVALANCHE CAMPGROUND

60

56

6000